Acknowledgements

I want to show thanks to my family for giving me the support needed by any individual living abroad for an extended period of time. Thanks also go to Song Wei, Jiang Jin, Cheng Yue, Liu Dansong, Fu Zhong, David Van Menderbrook, Andy Kuo, Gary Chen, Rocky Dean, Nima Yousefian, Sean Blacksmith, France Houdard, Parlc Su Young, Zhang Youjun, Song Yinong, Teng Yun, Wen Fangtang, Dr. Dennis Donham, and Professors Thomas McKechnie and Anthony Giunta for helping me deepen my understanding of the Chinese culture and language and for being there when I needed advice. To Li Tingting of LeesDesign for designing such a wonderful cover. To Wang Biao, Guo Rong and the rest of the BLCU Press staff for making *Urban Chinese* a reality. Finally, special thanks go to Zhao Yunfeng, for having the confidence in me to take on this project.

Gerald Scott Klayman

About the Authors

Gerald Scott Klayman came to Beijing in the summer of 1998 to do an internship for an international consulting firm. Through his work he realized that China's economy was full of potential, but that he needed to learn Chinese, as well as possess a deep understanding of the Chinese culture in order to efficiently operate in China's business environment. As a result he embarked on a sojourn that he thought would take six months, but lasted two and a half years. During this time he immersed himself into the Chinese culture, living and working with Chinese. Gerald also conducted research into the social, economic and political issues facing Beijing cabdrivers that became the basis for his Honors thesis. In 2001 Gerald graduated Magna Cum Laude from the University of Pittsburgh with an Honors Political Science degree. He now works for Baoying Fund Management in Shenzhen. He is one of the first foreigners to work in China's fund management industry.

Michael Zhao Yunfeng, came to know jerry in front of the library in college and they have since become good friends and language exchange partners. A regular tutor of Jerry, Michael had been impressed by his friend's startlingly fast progress in his language studies and persistency in note-taking. These notes turned out to be the basis upon which the two invested a great deal of time and energy to publish a very handy Chinese learning material.

Following graduation, Michael served the Bureau of International Cooperation at the China Academy of Sciences. He currently works at The New York Times Beijing Bureau.

Introduction

Regardless of how you break it down, studying Chinese is an overly daunting task. When people invest their time to study, they want to know that the material that they are struggling to learn is used in public discourse. Over the past two and a half years, I have had access to a cross section of Chinese life. I have lived with two young Chinese professionals; had Chinese classmates, tutors and friends with whom I spent time on both formal and informal occasions; worked in an all-Chinese professional services firm; taught English to students aged 6-50; and conversed with my older generation neighbors on a regular basis. Due to this complete immersion, I have been able to capture the contemporary nuances of urban Chinese. *Urban Chinese: Mandarin in 21st Century China* is a compilation of my notes which will give the reader the vocabulary, and more saliently the usage necessary to effectively operate in 21st Century China.

I started studying Chinese in the fall of 1998. At that time, like most foreigners, the characters, tones, pronunciation, etc. overwhelmed me. What I did to overcome these obstacles was subconsciously develop word association techniques that facilitated my learning process, utilizing Chinese strong logic, based on my native language English. After all, when studying a foreign language, one cannot help but use their mother tongue as a base, at least in the beginning stage. By breaking down the meaning of each individual character, words became easier to learn, as I was not memorizing a word, but an idea. These mnemonics also proved helpful when learning grammar.

Throughout the course of my studies, I have been a very diligent note taker. If I heard a new word, I would write it down and the next time I met with my tutor, we would go over how I could apply it into my everyday vocabulary. Indeed, these techniques have made it possible for me to attain a high level of proficiency, something that I thought would never happen when I commenced my studies. In fact, a Chinese language teacher at Tsinghua University learned of my experience and invited me to lecture on the very techniques introduced here.

I began working on this project after a few of my classmates expressed their dissatisfaction with their Chinese learning materials, and suggested that I explore the options of publishing my notes. My sincere hope and belief is that *Urban Chinese* will satisfy their and your demands.

Gerald Scott Klayman
Beijing, 2001

Structure

Urban Chinese is broken down into five sections. The first section, *Pinyin and Tones* provides the reader training wheels for learning Chinese. Based upon standard American English, the *pinyin* component will present similarities to which speakers of English can relate. The tones section will outline and explain the tones of Chinese, providing tips and practice exercises.

Section Two, *Radicals*, reveals the logic and meanings of the most commonly used radicals, the components that are mixed and matched like puzzle pieces to form Chinese characters.

The third section, *Category Usage Dictionary*, provides the most frequently used words on topics such as the body, business, cabs and directions, colors, countries and country leaders, education, electronics, emotions and feelings, foods and restaurants, hobbies, holidays, language study, telling time, vehicles, weather and Chinese zodiac signs.

Learning the stories behind Chinese idioms is a great way of deepening your understanding of the Chinese culture while also expanding your vocabulary. In Section Four, *Idioms*, the background stories of 25 idioms are told along with an example sentence that will enable the student to use the idiom in public discourse.

Section Five, *Slang*, will provide the student with the "real" language that is not printed in textbooks, but is said as much as, if not more than, the material that is. Each entry has undergone a usage test. Only if a majority of the people questioned use the word, was it selected. Examples with the "Chinglish" formula are used to guarantee the student complete understanding and usage.

Lastly, throughout the book, there are backgrounds and words of some of China's most commonly referenced personages including Lei Feng, Da Shan, Norman Bethune, etc., which will give the reader a basic understanding of why these persons are brought up today.

Table of Contents

Chapter I

PINYIN

拼音

The Pinyin Romanization System

English has a phonetic alphabet, which enables the reader to pronounce with rather certainty a never-seen-before word even if he/she does not know the meaning. Chinese, on the other hand, is an ideographic language, meaning that if the reader has not studied the character, he/she probably will not be able to read it. In order to facilitate the learning process for Chinese and foreign students of Chinese alike, an official international transcription system was introduced by the Chinese government in the 1950s. This system, called *pinyin*, which in Chinese means *pin* — spell and *yin* — sound, constitutes your training wheels for Chinese.

FINALS

1. Simple vowels

a   like 'a' in 'father'
e   like 'ur' in 'fur'
i   like 'i' in 'bin'
o   like 'o' in 'or'
u   like 'u' in 'flute'
ü   place your lips as if you were going to whistle and pronounce 'ee', like 'u' in 'lune' (French pronunciation)
er   like 'ar' in 'are'

2. Compound vowels

ai   like 'y' in 'fly'
ao   like 'ow' in 'cow'
ei   like 'ay' in 'say'
ia   like 'ya' in 'yard'
ie   like 'ye' in 'yesterday'
iu   like 'yo' in 'yolk'
iao   like 'i' in 'bin' plus 'ow' in 'cow'
ou   like 'ow' in 'blow'
ua   pronounced like **wah**
ui   like 'way' in 'sway'

uo	like the word '**war**'
uai	like the word '**why**'
üe	like 'u' in '**lu**ne' (French pronunciation) plus 'e' in '**ye**sterday'

3. Nasal finals

an	like 'an' in '**an**d'
ang	like 'a' in 'f**a**ther' plus 'ng' in 'lo**ng**'
en	like 'en' in 'stol**en**'
eng	like 'en' in 'stol**en**' plus 'ng' in 'lo**ng**'
ong	like 'o' in 'w**o**rn' plus 'ng' in 'lo**ng**'
in	like 'in' in 'b**in**'
ing	like 'ing' in 'sitt**ing**'
ian	like the word '**yen**'
iang	like the word '**young**'
iong	like 'i' in 'b**i**n' plus 'o' in 'w**o**rn' plus 'ng' in 'lo**ng**'
uan	like 'wan' in 's**wan**'
uang	like 'u' in 'fl**u**te' plus 'a' in 'f**a**ther' plus 'ng' in 'lo**ng**'
un	like 'u' in 'fl**u**te' plus 'en' in 'stol**en**'
ueng	like 'u' in 'fl**u**te' plus 'ng' in 'lo**ng**'
üan	after j, q, and x, like 'u' in 'l**u**ne' (French pronunciation) plus 'an' in '**an**d'
ün	like 'un' in 'l**un**e' (French pronunciation)

INITIALS

b	like 'p' in 's**p**eak'
p	like 'p' in '**p**eak'
m	like 'm' in '**m**e'
f	like 'f' in '**f**ast'
d	like 't' in 's**t**ate'
t	like 't' in '**t**ea'
n	like 'n' in '**n**eed'
l	like 'l' in '**l**et'
g	like 'g' in '**g**ame'
k	like 'k' in '**k**eep'
h	like 'h' in '**h**e'
j	like 'j' in '**j**eep'
q	like 'ch' in '**ch**eck'
x	like 'sh' in '**sh**irt'
z	like the 'ds' in 'fa**ds**'
c	like 'ts' in 'nu**ts**'

s	like 's' in 'sir'
zh	like 'j' in 'jeep'
ch	like 'ch' in '**ch**eese'
sh	like 'sh' in '**sh**y'
r	like 'r' in '**r**aise'

When pronouncing 'zh', 'ch', 'sh' and 'r', curl the tongue over and press it onto the roof of the mouth to create retroflex sounds.

When 'i' appears after retroflexed consonants 'zh', 'ch', 'sh' and 'r', it is always pronounced like 'r'.

When 'i' appears after 'z', 'c' and 's', it is always pronounced like 'z'.

Tones

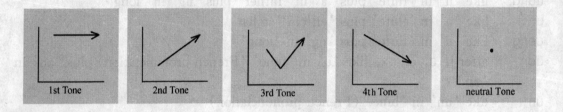

Chinese is a tonal language, which means that the tone of your voice changes the meaning of the word. For instance, if you say mɑi in the third tone, it means to buy, but in the fourth tone means to sell. Tones are by far the biggest obstacle confronted by foreigners when studying Chinese. Getting your tones down early in your studies will pave the way for future success. And, not placing enough importance on your tones will lead to frustration. Chinese ears are very sensitive to tones. So if your tones are not accurate, more often than not, they will not understand you. As time goes on, the tones will become more and more natural.

If asked, most Chinese will say that there are only four tones in Mandarin Chinese, but actually there are five. The first tone is flat and high-pitched and is conveyed by a ¯ .

The second tone is the rising tone and is conveyed by a ´ . Your voice starts out low and rises, kind of like the intonation of your voice when you are asking a question. Notice the difference in your voice when you say these two sentences: "He is coming here." and "He is coming here?" Another hint is to make your voice explode upwards.

The third tone starts at a low pitch and then rises. It is conveyed by a ˇ . The secret to the third tone is to make a dip or pause in the voice. The second and third tones are the hardest for foreigners to conquer, as they are the most similar. If your voice does not go directly up when pronouncing the second tone, it very likely will be mistaken for the third tone.

The fourth tone starts out high and then sharply declines, similar to the situation when you are speaking in a shrewd manner. Shut up! It is conveyed by a ` .

The tone that Chinese often forget is the silent tone, or neutral tone. The neutral tone, which has no tone mark, is the easiest to pronounce, as the speaker just needs to speak in his normal voice inflection.

Tonal Changes

There are a few words in Chinese whose tones are dependent upon the tone of the character by which it is followed. The most common four are yī(one), qī(seven), bā(eight) and bù(no). If the word following these words has a first, second or third tone, the bù and yī are pronounced in the fourth tone. If the following word carries a fourth tone, the bù or the yī is pronounced as a second tone. The following are the examples of yī and bù:

bù			
bù hē	won't drink	bù xíng	not alright
bù gǎn	not dare	bú qù	won't go

yī			
yì tiān	one day	yì píng	one bottle
yì tǒng	one pitcher	yí guàn	one can (of soda)

When there are consecutive third tones, the tone of the first character automatically becomes a second tone while the tone of the second character stays a third tone. In theory this sounds rather difficult, actually as you will see, this is the natural shape that your voice will take when pronouncing consecutive third tones.

mǐngǎn becomes míngǎn	(sensitive)
zhǐyǒu becomes zhíyǒu	(only)
miǎnqiǎng becomes miánqiǎng	(reluctant)

Tonal Exercises

First Tone

fēijī (airplane)	jīhū (almost)	bōxuē (exploit)
gōngmín (citizen)	gōngrén (worker)	yāoqiú (request)
zībǔ (nutritious)	shēntǐ (body)	yōngjǐ (crowded)
yālì (stress)	yōuhuì (discount)	gāngà (awkward)
qīzi (wife)	tāmen (they)	yīfu (clothes)

Second Tone

tígōng (provide)	tígāng (outline)	báichī (idiot)
hégé (qualified)	shímáo (fashionable)	méiménr (no way)
niúnǎi (milk)	píngguǒ (apple)	huáxuě (ski)
tóupiào (vote)	dúlì (independent)	quánlì (power)
péngyou (friend)	zhémo (torture)	máfan (hassle)

Third Tone

zǔzhī (organization)	xiǎo māo (kitten)	měi tiān (everyday)
jiǎohuá (cunning)	hǎowánr (fun)	Měiguó (America)
huǒtuǐ (ham)	jiǎngpǐn (prize)	lǎobǎn (boss)
lǐlùn (theory)	dǎjià (fight)	kěxiào (funny)
qǐzi (opener)	dǐzi (base)	yǐzi (chair)

Fourth Tone

càidān (menu)	sàichē (race car)	fùdān (burden)
quèshí (indeed)	nèiróng (content)	zìrán (natural)
yàodiǎn (key point)	bùguǎn (regardless)	tèdiǎn (feature)
huòbì (currency)	tèsè (special)	chìzì (deficit)
kuàizi (chopsticks)	hùshi (nurse)	rènao (lively)

Chapter II

RADICALS

部首

There are around 200 separate components or radicals, as they are referred, that are mixed and matched to form new characters. The characters are, however, penetrable if you can break down the meaning of each radical. Below are the meanings of the most commonly seen radicals and examples containing them. Please note that Chinese characters have been utilized for over four thousand years and the meanings of many Chinese radicals have their roots in ancient China.

1) 宀   宝盖头 bǎogàitóu   roof (protection)
完   wán   whole, intact   宪   xiàn   constitution
安   ān   safe   家   jiā   home

2) 贝   贝字旁 bèizìpáng   money
贫   pín   poor   贪   tān   to covet
货   huò   goods   贸   mào   trade

3) 疒   病字旁 bìngzìpáng   illness
癌   ái   cancer   痛   tòng   ache, pain
病   bìng   illness   症   zhèng disease

4) 艹   草字头 cǎozìtóu   grass
苹   píng   apple   葡萄 pútáo grapes
花   huā   flower   茶   chá   tea

5) 车   车字旁 chēzìpáng   vehicle
轮   lún   wheel   辆   liàng MW* for vehicles
轨   guǐ   track (RR)   轴   zhóu   axle

6) 虫   虫字旁 chóngzìpáng   insects
蟑螂 zhānláng cockroach   蜘蛛 zhīzhū spider
蚂蚁 mǎyǐ   ant   蝴蝶 húdié   butterfly

---

* MW for Measureword

7)	刂	立刀旁 lìdāopáng	cutting tool			
刑	xíng	punishment		剃	tì	to cut
剑	jiàn	sword		削	xiāo	to peel (apple)

8)	鬼	鬼字旁 guǐzìpáng	ghosts			
魂	hún	soul		魔	mó	devil
魇	yǎn	nightmare		魄	pò	spirit

9)	禾	禾字旁 hézìpáng	grain or crops			
秋	qiū	fall		秧	yāng	seedling
种	zhòng	to plant		稼	jià	crops

10)	户	户字旁 hùzìpáng	door			
房子	fángzi	house		所	suǒ	MW for buildings
启	qǐ	to initiate		扉页	fēiyè	title page

11)	戈	戈字旁 gēzìpáng	weapon			
战	zhàn	war		威	wēi	might
戮	lù	to kill, to slay		戎	róng	military

12)	火	火字旁 huǒzìpáng	fire			
烤	kǎo	to bake		烟	yān	smoke
炮	pào	cannon, firecracker		烫	tàng	hot

13)	灬	四点底 sìdiǎndǐ	fire			
煮	zhǔ	to boil		蒸	zhēng	to evaporate
熟	shú	well-done		焦	jiāo	burnt, charred

14)	钅	金字旁 jīnzìpáng	metal			
钢	gāng	steel		铁	tiě	iron
钱	qián	money		银	yín	silver

15)	斤	斤字旁	jīnzìpáng	axe
斧	fǔ	axe	斩	zhǎn	to chop

16)	巾	巾字旁	jīnzìpáng	cloth
帆	fān	canvas	纱布	shābù	gauze
旗帜	qízhì	banner	帽	mào	hat

17)	口	口字旁	kǒuzìpáng	mouth
吃	chī	to eat	吸	xī	to suck
告诉	gàosu	to tell	吻	wěn	to kiss

18)	冫	两点水	liǎngdiǎnshuǐ	ice
冰	bīng	ice	冻	dòng	to freeze
冷	lěng	cold	凉	liáng	cool

19)	力	力字旁	lìzìpáng	strength
功	gōng	achievement	动	dòng	to move
劳	láo	labor	勇	yǒng	brave

20)	马	马字旁	mǎzìpáng	horse
驴	lǘ	donkey	腾	téng	to gallop
驼	tuó	camel	马	mǎ	horse

21)	米	米字旁	mǐzìpáng	rice
粥	zhōu	porridge	糕	gāo	cake
粉	fěn	flour	粒	lì	grain; MW for grains

22)	木	木字旁	mùzìpáng	tree or wood
床	chuáng	bed	材料	cáiliào	materials
桥	qiáo	bridge	柴	chái	firewood

23)	目	目字旁	mùzìpáng	eye			
	眼	yǎn	eye		睹	dǔ	to witness
	泪	lèi	tears		睡	shuì	to sleep

24)	鸟	鸟字旁	niǎozìpáng	bird			
	鸣	míng	to chirp		鸡	jī	chicken
	鸭	yā	duck		鹰	yīng	eagle

25)	牛	牛字旁	niúzìpáng	cattle			
	牛	niú	cow		牢	láo	enclosure for animals
	牯	gǔ	bull		犀牛	xīniú	rhinoceros

26)	女	女字旁	nǚzìpáng	woman			
	奸	jiān	to rape		妒	dù	envy
	娇	jiāo	lovely, tender		婚	hūn	to marry

27)	青	青字旁	qīngzìpáng	blue or green			
	青	qīng	blue or green		静	jìng	quiet

28)	犭	反犬旁	fǎnquǎnpáng	animal with claws			
	狗	gǒu	dog		狮子	shīzi	lion
	猫	māo	cat		猴子	hóuzi	monkey

29)	日	日字旁	rìzìpáng	sun			
	晚	wǎn	night		早	zǎo	morning
	明	míng	bright		晴	qíng	sunny

30)	礻	示字旁	shìzìpáng	rites			
	福	fú	happiness		礼	lǐ	rite, ceremony
	祷	dǎo	to pray		祸	huò	misfortune

31) 氵 三点水 sāndiǎnshuǐ   water

| 江 | jiāng | river | 洋 | yáng | ocean |
| 海 | hǎi | sea | 湖 | hú | lake |

32) 石 石字旁 shízìpáng   stone

| 砖 | zhuān | brick | 矿 | kuàng | mine |
| 硬 | yìng | hard | 磨 | mò | millstone |

33) 饣 食字旁 shízìpáng   food

| 饮 | yǐn | drink | 饿 | è | to be hungry |
| 饭 | fàn | meal | 饱 | bǎo | to be full |

34) 纟 绞丝旁 jiǎosīpáng   silk or thread

| 缝 | féng | to sew | 绸 | chóu | silk |
| 绢 | juàn | thin rough silk | 绳 | shéng | rope |

35) 扌 提手旁 tíshǒupáng   hand(usually a verb)

| 拉 | lā | to pull | 推 | tuī | to push |
| 打 | dǎ | to hit, to play, etc. | 扔 | rēng | to throw |

36) 田 田字旁 tiánzìpáng   field

| 富 | fù | rich (wealth from crops) | 界 | jiè | boundary |
| 亩 | mǔ | acre (Chinese unit) | 男 | nán | man, male |

37) 土 土字旁 tǔzìpáng   ground

| 址 | zhǐ | address | 埋 | mái | to bury |
| 壤 | rǎng | soil | 尘 | chén | dust |

38) 王 王字旁 wángzìpáng   king or jade

| 皇 | huáng | emperor | 珍 | zhēn | treasure |
| 望 | wàng | look for ahead | 珠 | zhū | pearl |

39)	心	心字底	xīnzìdǐ	heart			
志	zhì	ambition		忍	rěn	to bear	
忠	zhōng	faithful		恩	ēn	benefit	

40)	忄	竖心旁	shùxīnpáng	heart			
忆	yì	to recall		怕	pà	to be afraid	
悦	yuè	to be happy		憾	hàn	to regret	

41)	讠	言字旁	yánzìpáng	words			
说	shuō	to speak		诗	shī	poem	
词	cí	words		讲	jiǎng	to speak	

42)	页	页字旁	yèzìpáng	head			
颈	jǐng	neck		顶	dǐng	apex, acme	
颊	jiá	cheek		额	é	forehead	

43)	衤	衣字旁	yīzìpáng	clothing			
裤	kù	pants		裙	qún	skirt	
袜	wà	socks		衫	shān	garment	

44)	阝	右耳刀	yòu'ěrdāo	town, geography			
郊	jiāo	suburbs		邦	bāng	nation	
都	dū	capital		部	bù	department	

45)	鱼	鱼字旁	yúzìpáng	fish			
鳄	è	crocodile		鳞	lín	scales	
鲨	shā	shark		鳃	sāi	fish gills	

46)	雨	雨字头	yǔzìtóu	rain			
雪	xuě	snow		雾	wù	fog	
雷	léi	thunder		雹	báo	hail	

47)	月	肉月旁	ròuyuèpáng	body			
腿	tuǐ	leg		脑	nǎo	brain
脸	liǎn	face		肺	fèi	lungs

48)	⺮	竹字头	zhúzìtóu	bamboo			
筷子	kuàizi	chopsticks		竿	gān	pole
笔	bǐ	pen (ancient times)		箱	xiāng	box

49)	孑	子字旁	zǐzìpáng	son			
孙	sūn	grandchild		孩	hái	child
孕	yùn	pregnant		孝	xiào	filial piety

50)	辶	走之底	zǒuzhīdǐ	walking motion			
逃	táo	to escape		追	zhuī	to follow, to pursue
送	sòng	to send off, to deliver		过	guò	to pass by (walking)

51)	𧾷	足字旁	zúzìpáng	foot			
跑	pǎo	to run		跳	tiào	to jump
踩	cǎi	to step on		跪	guì	to kneel

Chapter III

MEASURE WORDS

量词

把	bǎ		something with a handle
把伞	sǎn bǎ sǎn		[for] umbrella
两把刀/剪刀	liǎng bǎ dāo /jiǎndāo		two knives/pair of scissors
两把钥匙/锁	liǎng bǎ yàoshi /suǒ		two keys/locks
包	bāo		pack or package
六包烟	liù bāo yān		six packs of cigarettes
两包饼干	liǎng bāo bǐnggān		two packs of cookies
杯	bēi		drinks measured in cups
两杯咖啡/茶	liǎng bēi kāfēi /chá		two cups of coffee/tea

Measure words, or noun classifiers, are one of the biggest problems facing English native speakers when studying Chinese. The reason is simple. The number of English classifiers is relatively small and the classifiers that do exist are not thought of in the same way as they are in Chinese. As a result, the concept of giving every noun a classifier takes some time to digest.

In the English sentence, "I have 3 <u>bottles</u> of beer", the word *bottle* classifies beer. In the corresponding Chinese sentence, 我有三瓶啤酒(Wǒ yǒu sān <u>píng</u> píjiǔ), the word 瓶(*píng*) also classifies beer.

However, if you want to say "I have three books" in Chinese, you must add a measure word for books, 我有三本书(wǒ yǒu sān <u>běn</u> shū), 本(*běn*) being the classifier for books.

Below are the meanings of the most commonly used measure words and some of the words that they classify.

把	bǎ	something with a handle
三把伞	sān bǎ sǎn	three umbrellas
两把刀/剪刀	liǎng bǎ dāo/jiǎndāo	two knives/pairs of scissors
两把钥匙/锁	liǎng bǎ yàoshi/suǒ	two keys/locks

包	bāo	pack or package
六包烟	liù bāo yān	six packs of cigarettes
两包饼干	liǎng bāo bǐnggān	two packs of cookies

杯	bēi	drinks already in cups
两杯可乐/茶	liǎng bēi kělè/chá	two cups of coke/tea

本	běn	books, magazines, dictionaries, but not newspapers
六本词典/书	liù běn cídiǎn/shū	six dictionaries/books
四本小说/杂志	sì běn xiǎoshuō/zázhì	four novels/magazines

笔	bǐ	sums of money, pieces of business
一笔钱/收入	yì bǐ qián/shōurù	a certain amount of money/income
一笔生意	yì bǐ shēngyi	a business deal

部	bù	movies, telephones
两部电话/电影	liǎng bù diànhuà/diànyǐng	two telephones/movies

场	chǎng	recreational events, downfall
一场雨/雪	yì chǎng yǔ/xuě	one rainfall/snowfall
一场比赛/电影	yì chǎng bǐsài/diànyǐng	one game/movie

层	céng	floor of a building
六层楼	liù céng lóu	a 6-story building
一层灰	yì céng huī	one layer of dust

袋	dài	bags
六袋米/面粉	liù dài mǐ/miànfěn	six bags/sacks of rice/flour
两袋苹果	liǎng dài píngguǒ	two bags of apples

滴	dī	drops of a liquid
一滴汗/水	yì dī hàn/shuǐ	one drop of sweat/water

顶	dǐng	caps or hats
两顶帽子	liǎng dǐng màozi	two hats

段	duàn	length of time or distance
一段路	yí duàn lù	a segment of road
一段时间	yí duàn shíjiān	a period of time
一段话	yí duàn huà	a few words

堆	duī	articles in pile, sometimes presumably messy
一堆垃圾	yì duī lājī	a pile of rubbish
一堆作业	yì duī zuòyè	a pile (ton) of homework

顿	dùn	meals
一顿饭	yí dùn fàn	one meal

份	fèn	jobs, different types of magazines and newspapers
两份工作	liǎng fèn gōngzuò	two jobs
三份杂志/报纸	sān fèn zázhì/bàozhǐ	three types of magazines/newspapers

封	fēng	written messages sealed in an envelope
两封信/电报	liǎng fēng xìn/diànbào	two letters/telegraphs

幅	fú	painting, clothing, silk
三幅画	sān fú huà	three paintings

副	fù	pair, things that are complimentary to each other
一副眼镜/扑克牌	yí fù yǎnjìng/pūkèpái	one pair of glasses/deck of cards

个	gè	The scope of *gè* is the widest of all measure words. In fact, it can pretty much be used and understood for every noun. However, the more measure words you know, the better your Chinese will be.
六个人	liù ge rén	six persons
三个苹果	sān ge píngguǒ	three apples
两个小时	liǎng ge xiǎoshí	two hours
一个故事	yí ge gùshi	one story

根	gēn	stick-shaped items, such as the pencil, single matches, lollipops
六根火柴	liù gēn huǒchái	six matches
三根/支铅笔	sān gēn/zhī qiānbǐ	three pencils
五根棒棒糖	wǔ gēn bàngbàngtáng	five lollipops

次/回/趟	cì/huí/tàng	used to refer to the number of times one does something
去了六回	qùle liù huí	have (has) been there for 6 times

家	jiā	the people of the family, stores, companies, banks, etc.
一家人	yì jiā rén	an entire family
三家商店/公司	sān jiā shāngdiàn/gōngsī	three stores/companies

架	jià		aircraft
一架飞机	yí jià fēijī		an airplane
一架直升机	yí jià zhíshēngjī		a helicopter

间	jiān		room
一间房间	yì jiān fángjiān		a room
一间办公室	yì jiān bàngōngshì		an office

件	jiàn		article, piece
一件衣服/礼物	yí jiàn yīfu/lǐwù		one piece of clothing/gift
一件事	yí jiàn shì		one piece of business

句	jù		sentences
两句话	liǎng jù huà		two sentences

卷	juǎn		roll
一卷胶卷	yì juǎn jiāojuǎn		a roll of film
一卷手纸	yì juǎn shǒuzhǐ		a roll of toilet paper

棵	kē		trees, head of vegetables
四棵树	sì kē shù		four trees
一棵大白菜	yì kē dàbáicài		one head of cabbage

颗	kē		round-shaped items
六颗星星	liù kē xīngxing		six stars
三颗花生	sān kē huāshēng		three peanuts
两颗牙	liǎng kē yá		two teeth

刻	kè	15-minute unit of time	
三刻钟	sān kè zhōng	forty-five minutes	

口	kǒu	number of people in a family	
我家三口人。	Wǒ jiā sān kǒu rén.	There are three people in my family.	

块	kuài	piece, lump, chunk, also a colloquial term for RMB yuan	
四块玻璃	sì kuài bōli	four pieces of glass	
十块砖	shí kuài zhuān	ten bricks	
三块巧克力	sān kuài qiǎokèlì	three pieces of chocolates	
一块手表	yí kuài shǒubiǎo	one wrist watch	
两块钱	liǎng kuài qián	¥2.00 (two pieces of money)	

摞	luò	a neatly ordered stack or pile	
一摞书	yí luò shū	a pile of books	

面	miàn	flat, sheet-like items	
两面镜子	liǎng miàn jìngzi	two mirrors	
三面国旗	sān miàn guóqí	three national flags	

枚	méi	small, delicate articles	
两枚戒指	liǎng méi jièzhi	two rings	
四枚勋章	sì méi xūnzhāng	four badges	
一枚硬币	yì méi yìngbì	one coin	

名	míng	respectful term for people
四名大学生	sì míng dàxuéshēng	three university students

盘	pán	cassettes or disc
两盘磁带	liǎng pán cídài	two cassette tapes

盆	pén	things held in a basin or a container
三盆水	sān pén shuǐ	three basins of water
两盆花	liǎng pén huā	two pots of flowers

桶	tǒng	barrel that holds liquids
两桶葡萄酒/汽油	liǎng tǒng pútáojiǔ/qìyóu	two barrels of wine/gas

篇	piān	papers, articles or reports
三篇文章/报告	sān piān wénzhāng/bàogào	three articles/reports

片	piàn	area
一片森林/草地	yí piàn sēnlín/cǎodì	a forest, grassland

瓶	píng	bottles
两瓶酒/汽水	liǎng píng jiǔ/qìshuǐ	two bottles of alcohol/soda

起	qǐ	for negative occurrences
一起车祸	yì qǐ chēhuò	a car accident

首	shǒu	songs
一首歌	yì shǒu gē	a song

双	shuāng	pair
一双手/眼睛	yì shuāng shǒu/yǎnjing	a pair of hands/eyes
一双鞋/袜子	yì shuāng xié/wàzi	a pair of shoes/socks

艘	sōu	boats or ships
一艘船	yì sōu chuán	a ship

套	tào	set, apartment
一套西服	yí tào xīfú	a suit
一套公寓	yí tào gōngyù	an apartment

台	tái	electronic appliances
两台电脑/打印机	liǎng tái diànnǎo/dǎyìnjī	two computers/printers

条	tiáo	long and narrow things
三条街/路	sān tiáo jiē/lù	three streets/roads
两条鱼/蛇	liǎng tiáo yú/shé	two fish/snakes
四条裤子	sì tiáo kùzi	four pairs of pants
一条命/尾巴	yì tiáo mìng/wěiba	one life/tail

头	tóu	certain animals
三头猪/牛	sān tóu zhū/niú	three pigs/cows
两头骆驼	liǎng tóu luòtuo	two camels

位	wèi	people (showing politeness)
三位科学家	sān wèi kēxuéjiā	three scientists
四位教授	sì wèi jiàoshòu	four professors
六位工程师	liù wèi gōngchéngshī	six engineers

页	yè	pages of paper
三页课本	sān yè kèběn	three pages of text

张	zhāng	flat objects
三张纸/照片	sān zhāng zhǐ/zhàopiàn	three sheets of papers/pictures
四张桌子	sì zhāng zhuōzi	four tables
一张脸	yì zhāng liǎn	a face

只	zhī	some farm animals
两只鸡/鸭/羊	liǎng zhī jī/yā/yáng	two chickens/ducks/sheep

支	zhī	long straight things
四支铅笔/钢笔	sì zhī qiānbǐ/gāngbǐ	four pencils/pens
三支玫瑰	sān zhī méigui	three roses

座	zuò	large structure
一座桥/山	yí zuò qiáo/shān	a bridge/mountain
一座城市	yí zuò chéngshì	a city
一座纪念碑	yí zuò jìniànbēi	a monument

Chapter IV

"Chinglish" Key

Chinese words are composed of one, two or more characters. In order to emphasize the meaning of each individual character, we have separated each word by marking the characters that make up the word with a specialized Song typeface. Because there is no space between Chinese words, without doing so, one would not be able to determine when one word ends and when a new word begins. For instance one would not be able to differentiate between 我(wǒ), 我是(wǒ shì), 我是美(wǒ shì měi), etc. By this, we know that 我 by itself is a word composed of only one character. Because 是 is only one character and is not marked specially, we know that 是 by itself is a word. Because 美国人 is marked specially, we know that it is one word composed of three characters.

(I, am, American)	
我是**美国人**。	I am an American.
Wǒ shì Měiguórén.	

For instance, if asked the first word that comes to mind after hearing the three words, "changing", "color", "dragon", most would say the word "chameleon", which is in fact a changing color dragon. In Chinese, biàn = change, sè = color, and lóng = dragon, when put together forms the word biànsèlóng, or chameleon. While the word chameleon is not often used, the logic behind it makes it difficult for the student to forget. How about "electric" + "brain" = computer, "basket" + "ball" = basketball, "suck" + "pipe" = straw, "rent" + "vehicle" = cab?

While this formula does not work for every word, it works for enough words to make it worthwhile for the student to learn. For those words where the "Chinglish" formula did not work perfectly, or did not work at all, obviously nothing was provided.

This formula is also effective in learning grammatical structures as the student can use their mother tongue to compare, and then in their mind translate into Chinese.

English   音译词(yīnyìcí)、外来词(wàiláicí)
Words derived from English or other languages, loan words.

QW   吗 ma(疑问词 yíwèncí)   (Question Word)
Used to make a yes-or-no question.   这是你的书吗？   Is this your book?

MW   量词(liàngcí)   (Measure Word)
Please refer to Chapter III *Measure Words* for explanation.

PT   过去时(guòqùshí)   (Past Tense)

PT 了 le   Indicating the completion of an action. Placed after the verb.

我已经吃饭了。   I have already eaten.
（Wǒ yǐjing chī fàn le.）

我已经吃了饭。   I have already eaten.
（Wǒ yǐjing chīle fàn.）

PT 的 de   Indicating the completion of an action. Placed after the verb.

他什么时候来的？   When did he come?
（Tā shénme shíhou lái de?）

她怎么学汉语的？   How did he study Chinese?
（Tā zěnme xué Hànyǔ de?）

他去年来中国的。   He came to China last year.
（Tā qùnián lái Zhōngguó de.）

的（de）and 了（le）both indicate the completion of an action but, their usages are not the
same. 的（de）is used to stress the method or time by which an action was completed, while
了（le）is used to stress the fact that the action has been completed.

PT 过 guo   Indicating that the person has had the experience. Placed after the
               verb.

他去过长城吗？   Has he had the experience of going to the Great Wall?
（Tā qùguo Chángchéng ma?）   (Has he been to the Great Wall?)

我没见过毛泽东。   I have never met Mao Zedong.
（Wǒ méi jiànguo Máo Zédōng.）

10 把 bǎ   (Introduce Object)

Used to introduce an object in a sentence. There must be something done to this object, therefore the object must be followed by a verb. "把" sentences have following characteristics: (1) the verb is usually transitive; (2) the object of "把" is specific; and (3) the verb in a "把" sentence cannot exist alone, it is either reduplicated itself or takes a supplementary component which either describes the handling of the object of "把" or the influence on it. There is no English equivalent.

把我的书拿过来。   Bring my book here.
(Bǎ wǒ de shū ná guòlai.)

把窗户打开。   Open the window.
(Bǎ chuānghu dǎkāi.)

把房间整理整理。   Clean your room.
(Bǎ fángjiān zhěnglǐ zhěnglǐ.)

一下 yíxià

When preceded by a verb, it expresses that the action from start to completion will not consume a large amount of time. The usage of *yíxià* is subjective, based upon the speaker's perception of how long a short time is.

我可以看一下你的书吗？   Can I have a look at your book?
(Wǒ kěyǐ kàn yíxià nǐ de shū ma?)
* The speaker uses *yíxià* here to let the person know that he only wants to have a look, not take the book for a long time.

我想说一下。   I'd like to say something.
(Wǒ xiǎng shuō yíxià.)
* The speaker uses *yíxià* to comfort the listeners that he will not be speaking for a long time, thus boring them or consuming their time.

Only verbs dealing with physical action can be modified by *yíxià*. For instance, ONE CANNOT SAY:

我喜欢她一下。   I like her for a little bit.
(Wǒ xǐhuan tā yíxià.)

一点儿 yìdiǎnr

A bit, a little more than the adjective that precedes it

我现在有一点儿时间。   I have a little time.
(Wǒ xiànzài yǒu yìdiǎnr shíjiān.)

| 一点儿 + 也/都 + 没/不 |
(yìdiǎnr + yě/dōu + méi/bù)   Not at all, not even a little.

我一点儿也不知道。   I didn't even know a little, I didn't know at all.
(Wǒ yìdiǎnr yě bù zhīdào.)

| 形容词 + 一点儿 |
(adj. + yìdiǎnr)

请你快一点儿。   Please move faster than your current pace.
(Qǐng nǐ kuài yìdiǎnr.)

了 le

了 (le) indicates that a change has taken place.

天气热了。   It has gotten warm. (Before, it was not warm.)
(Tiānqì rè le.)

他会汉语了。   He now speaks Chinese. (Before he could not.)
(Tā huì Hànyǔ le.)

了 (le) is used to soften the tone of words.

别去了。(Bié qù le.)   Please don't go.

Don't do something is a command; adding le softens the command tone. If le is not used, the tone of bié is rather strong. Le can be used to show concern and caring for a person.

呢 ne

呢 (ne) is used in the same fashion as "What about _____?"

我想吃比萨饼, 你呢?   I want to eat pizza, how about you?
(Wǒ xiǎng chī bǐsàbǐng, nǐ ne?)   (What do you feel like eating pizza?)

呢 (ne) is used to express that the action is still in progress.

他在学习呢, 别打扰他。   He is studying, don't disturb him.
(Tā zài xuéxí ne, bié dǎrǎo tā.)

吧 ba

Used as a suggestion or a solid guess, rather informal.

咱们一起吃饭吧。   Let's grab a bite to eat!
(Zánmen yìqǐ chī fàn ba.)

你是中国人吧?   Are you Chinese?
(Nǐ shì Zhōngguórén ba?)   (Conversation is in China and the person appears to
                                   be Chinese.)

就 + 动词
(jiù + verb)

Used to stress the verb.

你等一会儿,我就来。   Wait a second; I'll be there. (Soon)
(Nǐ děng yíhuìr, wǒ jiù lái.)

那就是我想要的。   That is exactly what I want.
(Nà jiù shì wǒ xiǎng yào de.)

就 + 动词   earlier or better than expected
(jiù + verb)

他三岁就会写汉字。   He could write Chinese when he was three.
(Tā sān suì jiù huì xiě Hànzì.)   (Most people start when they are six.)

才 + 动词   later than expected
(cái + verb)

小王七岁才上幼儿园。   Xiao Wang didn't start kindergarten until
                                   he was seven.
(Xiǎo Wáng qī suì cái shàng yòu'éryuán.) (Most people start when they are three
                                   or four.)

的 de

Used to show possession.

我的书 (wǒ de shū)	my book
他的女朋友 (tā de nǔpéngyou)	his girlfriend
你们的错误 (nǐmen de cuòwu)	your mistake

If the noun is omitted, the 的 (de) implies the noun.

Q) 这本书是谁的？
(Zhè běn shū shì shéi de?)   Whose book is this?

A) 是他的（书）。
(Shì tā de [shū].)   It is his (book).

得 de

Without actual meaning. It is used when describing how something performs, and is often put behind a verb or an adjective.

Q) 他的汉语说得怎么样？
(Tā de Hànyǔ shuō de zěnmeyàng?)   How is his spoken Chinese?

A) 他的汉语说得很流利。
(Tā de Hànyǔ shuō de hěn liúlì.)   He speaks Chinese fluently.

小刘笑得很开心。
(Xiǎo Liú xiào de hěn kāixīn.)   Xiao Liu laughed very happily.

他跑得很快。
(Tā pǎo de hěn kuài.)   He runs really fast.

天气热得很。
(Tiānqì rè de hěn.)   It is terribly hot.

地 de

Used when describing an action. (adverb)

你们一定要认真地做作业。   You have to do your homework carefully.
(Nǐmen yídìng yào rènzhēn de zuò zuòyè.)

她耐心地听我的意见。   She patiently listens to my suggestions.
(Tā nàixīn de tīng wǒ de yìjiàn.)

着 zhe

着 (zhe), used to express that at the time of speaking, the action has already taken place and there is no reason to believe that it will end in the very near future. Obviously, the very near future is determined by the speaker.

墙上挂着国旗。   The flag is hanging on the wall.
(Qiáng shang guàzhe guóqí.)

别站着,坐下来吧。   Don't stand, have a seat.
(Bié zhànzhe, zuò xiàlai ba.)
* At the time of speaking, it is obvious that the person standing has no intention of sitting down.

着 (zhe), used to describe two verbs occurring at the same time. The second verb is more important.

他关着门学习。   He studies with the door closed.
(Tā guānzhe mén xuéxí.)

我们走着去吧。   Let's walk there.
(Wǒmen zǒuzhe qù ba.)

Below is a list of words that are commonly used together and their structures.

太 + 形容词 + 了   very, too
(tài + adjective + le)

她太漂亮了。   She is very pretty.
(Tā tài piàoliang le.)

他太骄傲了。   He is too cocky.
(Tā tài jiāo'ào le.)

挺 + 形容词 + 的   fairly
（tǐng + adjective + de）

他人挺好的。   He is a very good person.
（Tā rén tǐng hǎo de.）

你的衣服挺好看的。   Your clothes are very pretty.
（Nǐ de yīfu tǐng hǎokàn de.）

好像……似的   as if…
（hǎoxiàng……shìde）

他的态度不好，好像他是老板似的。   His attitude is like that of a boss.
（Tā de tàidù bù hǎo, hǎoxiàng tā shì lǎobǎn shìde.）

他很高兴，好像孩子似的。   He is so happy, just like a kid.
（Tā hěn gāoxìng, hǎoxiàng háizi shìde.）

（不）会……的
（[bú] huì……de）

Used to stress that something will or will not occur.

你的书我会还给你的。   I will definitely return your book to you.
（Nǐ de shū wǒ huì huán gěi nǐ de.）

他今天不会来的。   He is definitely not coming today.
（Tā jīntiān bú huì lái de.）

是……的
（shì……de）

Used to stress time or place.

我是刚从美国来的。   I just came from US.
（Wǒ shì gāng cóng Měiguó lái de.）

一……就

(yī……jiù)

Once one action takes place, another action will follow. The 一(yī) can be omitted and the meaning remains the same.

我一回家就给你打电话。   I'll call you as soon as I get home.
(Wǒ yì huí jiā jiù gěi nǐ dǎ diànhuà.)

我妈妈一听到消息就去了医院。   After hearing the news, my mother
(Wǒ māma yì tīng dào xiāoxi jiù qù le yīyuàn.)   went to the hospital
                                                    immediately.

快……了

(kuài……le)

Used to express that the action will take place soon.

我快要出去了。   I am going to leave soon.
(Wǒ kuài yào chūqu le.)

Q) 你什么时候考试?   When is your test?
   (Nǐ shénme shíhou kǎoshì?)
A) 快了。   Soon!
   (Kuài le.)

Chapter V

CATEGORY DICTIONARY

分类词典

Hobbies

爱 好

(you, have, what, hobbies) **Q**) 你有什么爱好？ Nǐ yǒu shénme àihào?	What are your hobbies?
(I, like, _____) **A**) 我喜欢_____。 Wǒ xǐhuan _____.	I like _____.

泡吧	pàobā	bar hopping, clubbing
(they, every, MW, weekend, all, bar hop) 他们每个周末都泡吧。 Tāmen měi ge zhōumò dōu pàobā.		They go bar hopping every weekend.

烹饪	pēngrèn	cooking
(she, very, excel at, cooking) 她很擅长烹饪。 Tā hěn shàncháng pēngrèn.		She is a very good cook.

(jump, disco)		
蹦的	bèngdī	disco dancing

(release, kite)		
放风筝	fàng fēngzheng	flying kites

(garden, art)		
园艺	yuányì	gardening

卡拉 OK	kǎlā OK	karaoke
(very, many, Chinese, young people, like, sing, karaoke) 很多中国的年轻人喜欢唱卡拉 OK。 Hěn duō Zhōngguó de niánqīngrén xǐhuan chàng kǎlā OK.		A lot of Chinese youth love going karaoke.

(listen, ____ music)		
听_____音乐	tīng yīnyuè	listening to music
(*English*)		
布鲁斯	bùlǔsī	blues
古典	gǔdiǎn	classical
乡村	xiāngcūn	country
爵士	juéshì	jazz
流行	liúxíng	pop
说唱	shuōchàng	rap
摇滚	yáogǔn	rock and roll

(raise, pets)		
养宠物	yǎng chǒngwù	pet raising

(play, bridge, cards)		
打桥牌	dǎ qiáopái	playing Bridge
(play, Chinese chess)		
下象棋	xià xiàngqí	playing Chinese chess
(play, mahjong)		
打麻将	dǎ májiàng	playing mahjong

(play, *English*, cards)		
打扑克牌	dǎ pūkèpái	playing Poker
(play, encirclement, chess)		
下围棋	xià wéiqí	playing (Chinese) *weiqi*

(music, instrument)		
乐器	yuèqì	musical instrument
(pluck, piano)		
弹钢琴	tán gāngqín	playing the piano
(blow, sax)		
吹萨克斯	chuī sàkèsī	playing the sax
(draw, violin)		
拉小提琴	lā xiǎotíqín	playing the violin

(play, game)		
玩游戏	wán yóuxì	play games (board, video)

(shoot, image)		
摄影	shèyǐng	photography

(read, novel / magazine)		
看小说 / 杂志	kàn xiǎoshuō / zázhì	reading novels / magazines

(sports)		
运动	yùndòng	sports
(health, beauty, exercise)		
健美操	jiànměicāo	aerobics
(fist, strike)		
拳击	quánjī	boxing

(*English*)		
蹦极	bèngjí	bungee jumping
(jump, water)		
跳水	tiàoshuǐ	diving
(slip, ice)		
滑冰	huábīng	ice skating
(fight, technique)		
武术	wǔshù	(Chinese) martial arts
(climb, mountain)		
爬山	pá shān	mountain climbing
(race, run)		
赛跑	sàipǎo	race
(roll, axle)		
滚轴	gǔnzhóu	roller-skating
(run, pace)		
跑步	pǎobù	run
(slip, board)		
滑板	huábǎn	skateboarding
(slip, snow)		
滑雪	huáxuě	skiing
(swim, swim)		
游泳	yóuyǒng	swimming
(health, body)		
健身	jiànshēn	working out
(throw, fall)		
摔跤	shuāijiāo	wrestling

(I, especially, like, playing, ____-ball)	I like very much playing ____-ball.
我特别喜欢打____球。	
wǒ tèbié xǐhuan dǎ ____ qiú.	

(play, feather, ball)		
打羽毛球	dǎ yǔmáoqiú	playing badminton

(play, stick, ball)		
打棒球	dǎ bàngqiú	playing baseball

(play, basket, ball)		
打篮球	dǎ lánqiú	playing basketball

(play, *English*, ball)		
打保龄球	dǎ bǎolíngqiú	going bowling

(play, *English*, ball)		
打高尔夫球	dǎ gāo'ěrfūqiú	playing golf

(play, ice, ball)		
打冰球	dǎ bīngqiú	playing hockey

(play, ping-pong, ball)		
打乒乓球	dǎ pīngpāngqiú	playing ping-pong

(play, platform, ball)		
打台球	dǎ táiqiú	playing pool / billiards

(kick, foot, ball)		
踢足球	tī zúqiú	playing soccer

(play, wall, ball)		
打壁球	dǎ bìqiú	playing squash

(play, net, ball)		
打网球	dǎ wǎngqiú	playing tennis

(play, set, ball)		
打排球	dǎ páiqiú	playing volleyball

(collect, stamp)		
集邮	jíyóu	stamp collecting

(on, Net)		
上网	shàngwǎng	surfing the Internet
(on, Net, talk about, the Heaven)		
上网聊天	shàngwǎng liáotiān	to log onto a chat room

(Taiji, fist)		
太极拳	tàijíquán	Taiji, shadow boxing
(park, in, every, day, morning, all, have, old people, play, Taiji)	Every morning in parks, there are many old people doing Taiji.	
公园里每天早晨都有老人打太极拳。		
Gōngyuán li měi tiān zǎochén dōu yǒu lǎorén dǎ tàijíquán.		

旅游	lǚyóu	traveling

(play, game)		
玩游戏	wán yóuxì	playing video games
(watch, movie)		
看电影	kàn diànyǐng	watching movies
(watch, TV set)		
看电视	kàn diànshì	watching TV

(stroll, street / stroll, mall)		
逛街 / 逛商场	guàng jiē / guàng shāngchǎng	window-shopping

The way that people spend their free time can tell a lot about a country. Below is a list of the most commonly practiced hobbies in modern China.

Children

flying kites

hacky sack

hide and seek

jumping rope

watching television and movies

collecting Pokeman cards

Teenagers and Adults

Chinese chess

Disco

flying kites

karaoke

mahjong, Chinese board game

playing cards

shopping (mainly women)

sports: badminton, basketball, bowling, pingpong, pool, soccer, swimming, etc.

traveling

watching television and movies

Older Persons

The same as teenagers and adults providing their health permits

Taiji, shadow boxing

Walking in the morning with their birdcage in hand (Sounds strange, but it is true, especially in the north!)

Numbers

数　字

零	líng	0
一	yī / yāo*	1

* When reading a telephone number, one is preferably read as yāo instead of yī. This rule also applies to room and bus numbers that have over three digits.

二/两	èr / liǎng*	2

* When 2 appears in the zero or tens place, it should be read èr. 2 èr, 12 shí'èr, 22 èrshí'èr.

In the hundreds place, both èr and liǎng can be read. 200 èr / liǎng bǎi, 2,222 liǎngqiān èr / liǎngbǎi èrshí'èr.

In the thousands place and above, liǎng should be read. 22,222 liǎngwàn liǎngqiān èr / liǎngbǎi èrshí'èr.

In front of a measure word, 2 should be read liǎng, except before 两 (liǎng), when it is read èr.

两辆车 liǎng liàng chē, 二两米饭 èr liǎng mǐfàn

三	sān	3	七	qī	7
四	sì	4	八	bā	8
五	wǔ	5	九	jiǔ	9
六	liù	6	十	shí	10

(ten, one)		
十一	shíyī	11
(ten, two)		
十二	shí'èr	12

(ten, three)		
十三	shísān	13
(two, ten)		
二十	èrshí	20
(two, ten, one)		
二十一	èrshíyī	21
(three, ten)		
三十	sānshí	30
(one, hundred)		
一百	yìbǎi	100
(one, hundred, zero, one)		
一百零一	yìbǎi líng yī	101
(one, hundred, one, ten)		
一百一十	yìbǎi yīshí	110
(one, hundred, one, ten, one)		
一百一十一	yìbǎi yīshíyī	111
(one, hundred, two, ten)		
一百二十	yìbǎi èrshí	120
(nine, hundred, nine, ten, nine)		
九百九十九	jiǔbǎi jiǔshíjiǔ	999

(one, thousand)		
一千	yìqiān	1,000
(one, thousand, zero, two, ten)		
一千零二十	yìqiān líng èrshí	1,020

(one, thousand, three, [hundred])		
一千三(百)	yìqiān sān (bǎi)	1,300

(nine, thousand, nine, hundred, nine, ten, nine)		
九千九百九十九	jiǔqiān jiǔbǎi jiǔshíjiǔ	9,999

In Chinese, the comma is placed after the fourth number as opposed to the third number in English. Regardless of how many zeros there are before a number, only one zero is read (except to the right of a decimal point).

(one, ten thousand)		
一万	yíwàn	1,0000 (English 10,000)

(one, ten thousand, zero, three, hundred)		
一万零三百	yíwàn líng sānbǎi	1,0300 (10,300)

(two, ten thousand, seven, [thousand])		
两万七(千)	liǎngwàn qī (qiān)	2,7000 (27,000)

(three, ten thousand, zero, three)		
三万零三	sānwàn líng sān	3,0003 (30,003)

(four, ten, ten thousand)		
四十万	sìshí wàn	40,0000 (400,000)

(one hundred, ten thousand)		
一百万	yìbǎi wàn	100,0000 (1,000,000)

(three, hundred million)		
三亿	sānyì	3,0000,0000 (300,000,000)

第四	dì sì	**four**th

To make an ordinal number, add *dì* in front of a number.

(zero, decimal point, seven)		
零点七	líng diǎn qī	0.7

(zero, decimal point, zero, zero, four)		
零点零零四	líng diǎn líng líng sì	0.004
(three, division, of, one)		
三分之一	sān fēn zhī yī	1 / 3
(hundred, division, of, five, ten)		
百分之五十	bǎi fēn zhī wǔshí	50 %
(three, and, four, division, of, one)		
三又四分之一	sān yòu sì fēn zhī yī	3¼

(ten, eight, and, nine, division, of, seven)		
十八又九分之七	shíbā yòu jiǔ fēn zhī qī	18⅞
(nine, is, three, three, times)		
九是三的三倍。	Jiǔ shì sān de sān bèi.	9 is three times 3.
三加四等于七	sān jiā sì děngyú qī	$3 + 4 = 7$
十减六等于四	shí jiǎn liù děngyú sì	$10 - 6 = 4$
五乘六等于三十	wǔ chéng liù děngyú sānshí	$5 \times 6 = 30$
一百除以二十等于五	yìbǎi chúyǐ èrshí děngyú wǔ	$100 \div 20 = 5$

(you, this year, how many, year / how old)	How old are you? (jǐ suì is used when asking children their age, while duō dà is used when asking teenagers and up.)
Q) 你今年几岁 / 多大？	
Nǐ jīnnián jǐ suì / duō dà?	

(I, this year, 6 years old / 18)	I am six years old / 18.
A) 我今年六岁 / 十八。	
Wǒ jīnnián liù suì / shíbā.	

(you [polite], this year, how, big, age)	How old are you? (Duō dà niánjì is used when asking elderly persons their age.
Q) 您今年多大年纪?	
Nín jīnnián duō dà niánjì?	

(I, this year, 65)	I am 65.
A) 我今年六十五了。	
Wǒ jīnnián liùshíwǔ le.	

(you, how, tall)	What's your height?
Q) 你多高?	
Nǐ duō gāo?	
(I, one, meter, eight, three)	I'm 1.83 meters. (5 ft = 1.52m, 6 ft = 1.83m, 1 inch = 2.54cm)
A) 我一米八三。	
Wǒ yì mǐ bā sān.	

(you, how, heavy)	What do you weigh?
Q) 你多重?	
Nǐ duō zhòng?	
(I, 150, half-kilo)	I weigh 150 jin. (1 jin = 1.1 pounds)
A) 我 150 斤。	
Wǒ yìbǎi wǔshí jīn.	

Lucky Numbers

Chinese are very superstitious people, especialy when it comes to numbers. Below is a list of superstitious numbers and their origins.

6-Six or liù, is a very good number because its ancient Chinese pronunciation is very similar to Shùn, which means all the best.

8-Eight or bā, is a very good number because its pronunciation is very similar to that of fā, which means becoming rich.

9-Nine or jiŭ, is a very good number because its pronunciation is identical to that of jiŭ, which means forever.

4-Four or sì pronounced in the fourth tone, is a very bad number because its pronunciation is very similar to that of sĭ, pronounced in the third tone, which means death.

When planning weddings, business openings, funerals, or traveling, dates that have a four in them are avoided at all costs, for instance the 4th, 14th or 24th of any given month and especially April 4th. Dates that have a six, eight, or nine in them are considered auspicious, for instance the 6th, 8th, 9th, 16th, 18th, 19th, 26th, 28th, 29th of any given month and especially in the months of June, August, and September.

Time and Calendar

时间和日期

(now, how many, hour) 现在几点？ Xiànzài jǐ diǎn?	What time is it?

(I, forget, wear, watch, PT, can, look, a little, time, QW) 我忘带表了，能看一下时间吗？ Wǒ wàng dài biǎo le, néng kàn yíxià shíjiān ma?	I forgot to take my watch. Could you tell me the time?

(now, one, hour) 现在一点。 Xiànzài yì diǎn.	It's one o'clock.

(one, hour, fragment, five, minute) 一点零五分 yì diǎn líng wǔ fēn	1:05

(one, hour, one, quarter) 一点一刻 yì diǎn yí kè	1:15

(one, hour, fifteen) 一点十五 yì diǎn shíwǔ	1:15

(three, hour, half)	3:30
三点半	
sān diǎn bàn	

(six, hour, forty)	6:40
六点四十	
liù diǎn sìshí	

(seven, hour, short, twenty)	6:40
七点差二十	
qī diǎn chà èrshí	

(now, soon, three, hour)	It's almost 3:00.
现在快三点了。	
Xiànzài kuài sān diǎn le.	

(now, eleven, hour, sharp)	It's 11:00 sharp.
现在十一点整。	
Xiànzài shíyī diǎn zhěng.	

秒 / 秒钟	miǎo / miǎozhōng	second
分 / 分钟	fēn / fēnzhōng	minute
(small, time) / (bell, head)		
小时 / 钟头	xiǎoshí / zhōngtóu	hour

(she, 10, minute / MW, hour, before, leave, PT)	She left ten minutes / hours ago.
她十分钟 / 个钟头之前走的。	
Tā shí fēnzhōng / ge zhōngtóu zhīqián zǒu de.	

(I, pass, 2, minute / MW, hour, give, you, make, phone call)	I'll give you a call in two minutes / hours.
我过两分钟 / 个钟头给你打电话。	
Wǒ guò liǎng fēnzhōng / ge zhōngtóu gěi nǐ dǎ diànhuà.	

礼拜 (star, period)	lǐbài	week (most colloquial)
星期	xīngqī	week
周	zhōu	week (more formal)
(previous, MW, week)		
上个礼拜/星期, 上周	shàng ge lǐbài / xīngqī, shàng zhōu	last week
(this, MW, week)		
这个礼拜/星期, 这周	zhè ge lǐbài / xīngqī, zhè zhōu	this week
(next, MW, week)		
下个礼拜/星期, 下周	xià ge lǐbài / xīngqī, xià zhōu	next week
礼拜 / 星期 / 周一	lǐbài / xīngqī / zhōu yī	Monday
礼拜 / 星期 / 周二	lǐbài / xīngqī / zhōu èr	Tuesday
礼拜 / 星期 / 周三	lǐbài / xīngqī / zhōu sān	Wednesday
礼拜 / 星期 / 周四	lǐbài / xīngqī / zhōu sì	Thursday
礼拜 / 星期 / 周五	lǐbài / xīngqī / zhōu wǔ	Friday
礼拜 / 星期 / 周六	lǐbài / xīngqī / zhōu liù	Saturday
礼拜 / 星期 / 天/日	lǐbài / xīngqī tiān / rì	Sunday
周 日	zhōu rì	

(today, week, how many) **Q)** 今天星期几? Jīntiān xīngqī jǐ?	What day is today?
(today, week, one) **A)** 今天星期一。 Jīntiān xīngqīyī.	Today is Monday.

前天	qiántiān	two days ago
昨天	zuótiān	yesterday
今天	jīntiān	today
明天	míngtiān	tomorrow
后天	hòutiān	the day after tomorrow

(I, the day before yesterday, go, PT, Tian'anmen)	I went to the Tian'anmen Square the day before yesterday.
我前天去了天安门。	
Wǒ qiántiān qùle Tiān'ānmén.	

(he, tomorrow, will, go, Great Wall)	He is going to go to the Great Wall tomorrow.
他明天要去长城。	
Tā míngtiān yào qù Chángchéng.	

(moon)		
月	yuè	month (colloquial)
(moon, share)		
月份	yuèfèn	month (formal)
(previous, MW, month)		
上个月	shàng ge yuè	last month
(this, MW, month)		
这个月	zhè ge yuè	this month
(next, MW, month)		
下个月	xià ge yuè	next month
一　月 / 月份	yī　yuè / yuèfèn	January
二　月 / 月份	èr　yuè / yuèfèn	February
三　月 / 月份	sān　yuè / yuèfèn	March
四　月 / 月份	sì　yuè / yuèfèn	April
五　月 / 月份	wǔ　yuè / yuèfèn	May
六　月 / 月份	liù　yuè / yuèfèn	June
七　月 / 月份	qī　yuè / yuèfèn	July
八　月 / 月份	bā　yuè / yuèfèn	August
九　月 / 月份	jiǔ　yuè / yuèfèn	September
十　月 / 月份	shí　yuè / yuèfèn	October
十一　月 / 月份	shíyī　yuè / yuèfèn	November
十二　月 / 月份	shí'èr　yuè / yuèfèn	December

(today, how many, date)	What's the date today?
Q) 今天几号？	
Jīntiān jǐ hào?	
(today, September, 12, date)	Today is September 12.
A) 今天九月十二号。	
Jīntiān jiǔ yuè shí'èr hào.	

年	nián	year
前年	qiánnián	the year before last
去年	qùnián	last year
今年	jīnnián	this year
明年	míngnián	next year
后年	hòunián	the year after next
闰年	rùnnián	leap year

(today, is, 2002, year, 1, month, 16, date)	Today is January 16, 2002.
今天是 2002 年 1 月 16 号。	
Jīntiān shì èr líng líng èr nián yī yuè shíliù hào.	
(he, the year before last, go, PT, USA)	He went to the US the year before last.
他前年去了美国。	
Tā qiánnián qùle Měiguó.	
(I, next year, will, go, N. Korea)	I am going to go to North Korea next year.
我明年要去朝鲜。	
Wǒ míngnián yào qù Cháoxiǎn.	

(ten, year)		
十年	shí niàn	decade
(in, past, decade) 在过去的十年…… zài guòqù de shí niàn…		In the past decade...

(year, generation)		
年代	niándài	decade
(in, 80, decade, beginning / middle, period / end) 在八十年代初 / 中期 / 末…… zài bāshí niándài chū / zhōngqī / mò…		In the beginning of / middle of / late 80s...

世纪	shìjì	century
(in, 20, century, first / latter, half, part of a historical period) 在二十世纪上 / 下半叶…… zài èrshí shìjì shàng / xià bàn yè…		During the first / second half of the 20th century...
(in, 19, century, beginning / middle, period / end) 在十九世纪初 / 中期 / 末…… zài shíjiǔ shìjì chū / zhōngqī / mò…		In the beginning of / middle of / late 19th century...

(thousand, year)		
千年	qiān nián	millennium
(next, MW, millennium, mankind, have to, face, very, many, challenge) 下个千年人类得面临很多挑战。 Xià ge qiān nián rénlèi děi miànlín hěn duō tiǎozhàn.		There are a lot of challenges facing mankind in the next millennium.

Weather
天 气

(today's, weather, how is it) **Q)** 今天的**天气**怎么样? Jīntiān de tiānqì zěnmeyàng?	What' the weather like today?
(today, weather, very, **good**) **A)** 今天**天气**很**好**。 Jīntiān tiānqì hěn **hǎo**.	It's **nice** today.

糟	zāo	bad
冷	lěng	cold
凉快	liángkuai	cool
干燥	gānzào	dry
热	rè	hot
闷热	mēnrè	humid
不错	búcuò	pretty nice
凑合	còuhe	so-so
暖和	nuǎnhuo	warm

(clear, sky) 晴天	qíngtiān	clear
(today, is, MW, clear day) 今天是个晴天。 Jīntiān shì ge qíngtiān.		It's clear today.

(many, cloud)		
多云	duōyún	cloudy

(today, cloudy)		It's cloudy today.
今天多云。		
Jīntiān duōyún.		

(today, cloudy, turn, clear)		Today is cloudy but will turn sunny.
今天多云转晴。		
Jīntiān duōyún zhuǎn qíng.		

(cold, wave)		
寒潮	háncháo	cold wave
(tomorrow, cold wave, will, come, more, put on, a little, clothing)		You'd better bundle up. A cold wave is coming tomorrow.
明天寒潮要来,多穿点儿衣服。		
Míngtiān háncháo yào lái, duō chuān diǎnr yīfu.		

度	dù	degree
(Celsius, degree)		
摄氏度	shèshìdù	Celsius degree
(Fahrenheit, degree)		
华氏度	huáshìdù	Fahrenheit degree
Formula: $°F \approx 2(°C + 15)$; $°C \approx 1/2°F - 15$		
(air, temperature)		
气温	qìwēn	temperature

(today, how many, degree) **Q) 今天多少度？** Jīntiān duōshao dù?	What's the temperature today?
(today, 30, degree) **A) 今天 30 度。** Jīntiān sānshí dù.	It's 30 degrees today.
(today, zero, below, 5, degree) **A) 今天零下 5 度。** Jīntiān líng xià wǔ dù.	It's 5 below today.

雾	wù	fog
(today, morning, fall, PT, fog) 今天早上下了雾。 Jīntiān zǎoshang xiàle wù.		It was foggy this morning.

(evaporate, cage)		
蒸笼	zhēnglóng	food steamer
(Bejing's, summer, truly, hot, exactly like, MW, food steamer) 北京的夏天真热, 好像个蒸笼似的。 Běijīng de xiàtiān zhēn rè, hǎoxiàng ge zhēnglóng shìde.		The summer in Beijing is like a food steamer. (Ridiculously hot)

(frost, freeze)		
霜冻	shuāngdòng	frost
(yesterday, night, launch, PT, frost) 昨天晚上起了霜冻。 Zuótiān wǎnshang qǐle shuāngdòng.		There was frost last night.

冰雹	bīngbáo	hail
(tomorrow, has, hail) 明天有冻雹。 Míngtiān yǒu bīngbáo.		It will hail tomorrow.

(flash, electricity)		
闪电	shǎndiàn	lightning
(thundering, when, usually, accompany, has, lightning) 打雷的时候，通常伴有闪电。 Dǎléi de shíhou, tōngcháng bànyǒu shǎndiàn.		When there is thundering, there usually is lightning.

阴天	yīntiān	overcast
(today, is, MW, overcast) 今天是个阴天。 Jīntiān shì ge yīntiān.		It's overcast today.

雨	yǔ	rain
(fall, rain)		
下雨	xiàyǔ	to rain
(today, will, fall, rain) 今天会下雨。 Jīntiān huì xiàyǔ.		It will rain today.

(flurry, rain / small, rain)		
毛毛雨 / 小雨	máomáoyǔ / xiǎoyǔ	drizzle
(today, has, drizzle) 今天有毛毛雨 / 小雨。 Jīntiān yǒu máomáoyǔ / xiǎoyǔ.		It will drizzle today.

(fierce, rain)		
暴雨	bàoyǔ	heavy rain
(today, has, heavy rain)	There will be some heavy rain today.	
今天**有**暴雨。		
Jīntiān yǒu bàoyǔ.		
(short period, rain)		
阵雨	zhènyǔ	off-and-on rain
(today, has, off-and-on rain)	It will rain off and on today.	
今天**有**阵雨。		
Jīntiān yǒu zhènyǔ.		
(thunder, rain)		
雷雨	léiyǔ	thundershowers
(today, has, thundershowers)	There will be thundershowers today.	
今天**有**雷雨。		
Jīntiān yǒu léiyǔ.		

雪	xuě	snow
(this year, very, little, fall, snow)	It snowed very little this year.	
今年很少**下**雪。		
Jīnnián hěn shǎo xiàxuě.		
(today's, snow, unusually, big)	It was a blizzard today.	
今天的雪非常**大**。		
Jīntiān de xuě fēicháng dà.		
(goose, fur, big, snow)		
鹅毛大雪	émáo dàxuě	heavy snow

(sky, on, floating, heavy snow)		It is really coming down out there. (snow)
天上飘着鹅毛大雪。		
Tiānshang piāozhe émáo dàxuě.		

打雷	dǎléi	to thunder
(yesterday, night, thunder)		It thundered last night.
昨天**晚上**打雷了。		
Zuótián wǎnshang dǎléi le.		

(dragon, curl, wind)		
龙卷风	lóngjuǎnfēng	tornado
(tornado, yesterday, attack, PT, USA, west, sea, coast)		A tornado hit America's west coast yesterday.
龙卷风**昨天**袭击了美国西海岸。		
Lóngjuǎnfēng zuótián xíjīle Měiguó xī hǎi'àn.		

(English)		
台风	táifēng	typhoon
(Hong Kong, summer, always, blow, typhoon)		There are always typhoons in Hong Kong during the summer.
香港夏天总是**刮**台风。		
Xiānggǎng xiàtiān zǒngshì guā táifēng.		

风	fēng	wind
(today, will, blow, big, wind)		It will be very windy today.
今天会刮**大**风。		
Jīntiān huì guā dà fēng.		

(weather, forecast)

| 天气预报 | tiānqì yùbào | weather forecast |

(today, is, 9, month, 12, date)

今天是 9 月 12 号。

Jīntiān shì jiǔyuè shí'èr hào.

Today is September 12.

(today, daytime, cloudy, turn, clear)

今天白天多云转晴。

Jīntiān báitiān duōyún zhuǎn qíng.

It will be cloudy during the daytime, clearing up later.

(fall, water, probability, 30％)

降水概率百分之三十。

Jiàngshuǐ gàilǜ bǎi fēn zhī sānshí.

30％ chance of rain.

(north, turn, south, wind)

北转南风。

Běi zhuǎn nánfēng.

Wind is blowing from the North, and later from the South.

(most, high, temperature, 28, degree)

最高气温 28 度。

Zuì gāo qìwēn èrshíbā dù.

The high temperature is 28℃.

(today, night, clear, has, small, rain)

今天夜间晴有小雨。

Jīntiān yèjiān qíng yǒu xiǎoyǔ.

There will be a clear night, but with a light drizzle.

(most, low, temperature, 15, degree)	The low temperature will be 15°.
最低气温 15 度。	
Zuì dī qìwēn shíwǔ dù.	

季节	jìjié	season
春天	chūntiān	spring
夏天	xiàtiān	summer
秋天	qiūtiān	fall
冬天	dōngtiān	winter

China's temperate climate is similar to that of the continental United States, however, area contrasts are greater. The winter in Northern China is bitterly cold and dry as Siberian winds attack the region. Temperatures usually do not rise above freezing from December to March. Spring is characterized by strong winds that come from Inner Mongolia. Summer temperatures always exceed 80°F, and in the North China Plain approach 90°F. Most rain falls in the summer months of July and August. Autumn, which lasts from September to mid-November, is probably the most comfortable time to be in the North. Temperatures range from around 40°F to 65°F, but don't forget to take an extra layer of clothing at night.

In Central China down to Shanghai, winters are short but cold. Summers, lasting from April to October, are hot and humid. Temperatures will often hit the 100° mark. The mountainous plateaus and basins to the southwest also enjoy tropical climates. Due to higher elevations, summer months are cooler and winters are milder. The Sichuan Basin is characterized by high humidity and cloudiness.

Southeastern China has a subtropical climate. Summer temperatures average 80°F. The weather is humid, hot and rainy from mid-April to September. Between July and November, numerous typhoons will strike the coastal region, bringing high winds and heavy rains.

Manchuria's climate is similar to that of North China. January temperatures are about 0°F while July temperatures are in the 70s. Desert and steppe climates prevail in the Mongolian Steppe and greater northwest. Winter temperatures are around 14°F and in July, it usually hits 70°F.

Family and Addressing People

家庭与称呼

The Chinese Family

Based upon strong Confucian values, the Chinese family is a very cohesive unit. As evidenced by the various forms of address, Chinese pay particular attention to respecting elders and loving the young.

Prior to the implementation of Deng Xiaoping's Market Reform policy in 1978, most couples would move into the house of the male's parents following marriage, making the house a very rènao(bustling)place. While this practice still exists, it is quite common for a young couple to buy their own house. (An average house in China would be considered an apartment by western standards.) Regardless of whether or not they live with their parents, grown-up children have the duty to support and help their parents.

In 1973, China began to promote family planning as means of survival. According to State statistics, if the family planning policy had not been initiated, China's population would have already passed the 1.5 billion mark. (It currently stands at 1.295 billion.) In cities, families are allowed to have just one child. In rural areas, a family is allowed to have a second child in exceptional cases, but only after a significant amount of time has passed between births. Under family planning, it is illegal for college students to engage in sexual activity. The minimal marital age for men is 22 and 20 for women, while Beijing city dwellers can tie the knot at 25 for men and 23 women.

Prior to 1949, the role of women was to perform housework. Not anymore. Women have entered the workforce at alarming rates and are making significant contributions to the development of the country.

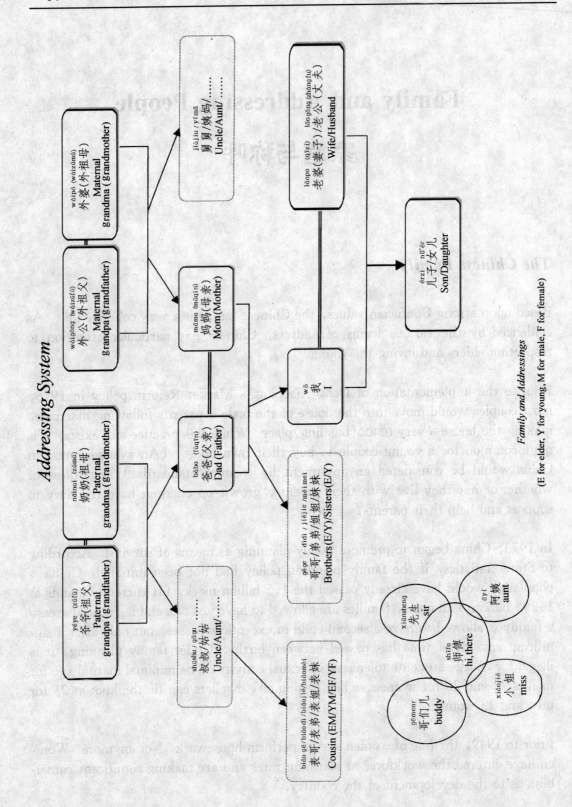

Addressing System

Family and Addressings

(E for elder, Y for young, M for male, F for female)

Holidays

节 日

(lover, festival)		
情人节	Qíngrén Jié	Valentine's Day (Feb. 14)

Over the past few years, more and more younger generation Chinese are celebrating Valentine's Day. Couples will go out to celebrate, gifts are exchanged, etc. The soaring rose prices on Valentine's Day can evidence this newfound interest in a traditionally Western holiday. Fortunately, the original price is only one *yuan*, or 12 cents.

(spring, festival)		
春节	Chūn Jié	Spring Festival, Chinese New Year

The most important holiday in China is Spring Festival, or the Chinese New Year. The exact date of Spring Festival, which lasts 15 days, is determined by the lunar calendar and usually falls in late January or early February. New Year's Eve and New Year's Day are family celebrations similar to Thanksgiving and Christmas in the West. Families get together and eat big meals, play games, sit around and talk, etc. Traditionally, the festival celebrated the earth coming back to life and the start of plowing and sowing.

Traditions and Superstitions

A few days prior to Spring Festival, families will perform a type of "Spring Cleaning" so as to clean the house from evil spirits. It is believed that if sweeping is done on New Year's Day, it will sweep away good luck. After New Year's Day, the floors can be swept but the dust can not cross the threshold of the door, as it will sweep the luck of the family away. The dust must be picked up in the house and then thrown out.

Lighting firecrackers is the Chinese way of sending out the old year and bringing in the new one. At 12 midnight, every house door should be opened to let the old year out and the new one in.

Lucky Chinese characters are hung on doors, sometimes upside down, to bring good luck to the family. Some characters are hung upside down because the Chinese word dào, which means arrive, has the same pronunciation as dào, upside down. The most common character is fú, which means blessing.

All debts should be paid before New Year's Day and nothing should be lent, as it is believed that the person doing the lending will not be paid back for an entire year.

It is very unlucky to say curse words or unlucky words like sì(four), which sounds like sǐ, the word for death. The telling of ghost or scary stories is also taboo.

If one cries on New Year's day, it is believed that person will cry throughout the entire year.

It is lucky to hear birds sing or see red-colored birds.

It is considered unlucky to greet anyone in the bedroom. Even the sick and elderly do their best to get dressed and visit guests in the living room.

Knives and scissors are not used on New Year's Day because they might cut off good fortune.

Foods
It is customary to prepare a tremendous amount of food during Spring Festival to show wealth.

A whole chicken is eaten for completeness and prosperity and fish for togetherness and abundance. Noodles are eaten because they are long and represent long life.

In southern China, niángāo, a sweet rice pudding and zòngzi, rice wrapped in reed leaves are eaten; while in northern China, steamed-wheat bread called mántou and Chinese dumplings are popular.

The Lion Dance
The Lion Dances are done during the first few days of the New Year to bring good luck to the places that they visit. Performed by two dancers, the dance is accompanied by firecrackers, loud drums and cymbals so as to help the lion dispel evil spirits.

Fortune Sticks
For centuries, Chinese have been using the *Kau Chime* method of telling fortunes during the New Year. A person will shake a bamboo case containing 78 numbered sticks. When one of the sticks falls out, it is cross-referenced with a bunch of old Chinese texts and it is believed that this will give the person a general idea of their future.

Red Envelopes
Red Envelopes filled with money are the main gift of Spring Festival. The money symbolizes the hope of future prosperity. The envelopes are usually decorated with lucky symbols or Chinese characters of auspicious remark.

(Spring Festival, happy)		
春节愉快!	Chūn Jié yúkuài!	Happy New Year!

(wish, get rich)		
恭喜发财!	Gōngxǐ fācái!	I wish that you become rich!

(spend, year, good)		
过年好!	Guò nián hǎo!	Have a great New Year!

(give, you, new year's visit)		
给您拜年!	Gěi nín bàinián!	Wish you a happy New Year!

(wish, you, new, year, happy)		
祝您新年愉快!	Zhù nín xīnnián yúkuài!	Happy New Year!

(women, festival)		
妇女节	Fùnǚ Jié	Women's Day (March 8)

March 8th is International Women's Day. Women are given the day or half the day off.

(English)		
圣帕特里克节	Shèng Pàtèlǐkè Jié	St. Patrick's Day (March 17)

Most Chinese do not celebrate St. Patrick's Day. However, in major cities, there are celebrations at local pubs where green beer is served.

(again, live, festival)		
复活节	Fùhuó Jié	Easter

Most Chinese do not celebrate Easter.

(labor, festival)		
劳动节	Láodòng Jié	Labor Day (May 1)

May 1st is International Labor Day and like in all other Communist countries, is celebrated in China. Workers are given the entire week off.

(mother, festival)		
母亲节	Mǔqīn Jié	Mother's Day (2nd Sunday in May)

On Mother's Day, family members get together and children give presents to their mothers. However, it is not celebrated to the extent as it is in Western countries.

(children, festival)		
儿童节	Értóng Jié	Children's Day (June 1)

On Children's Day, parents (usually mothers) are given half a day off to celebrate with their children.

(father, festival)		
父亲节	Fùqīn Jié	Father's Day (2nd Sunday in June)

On Father's Day, families get together and children give presents to their fathers. Like Mother's Day, Father's Day is not celebrated to the extent as it is in Western countries.

(middle, autumn, festival)		
中秋节	Zhōngqiū Jié	Mid-Autumn Festival

The Mid-Autumn Festival is one of the most important festivals celebrated in China. In ancient times, family members would convene on the 15th day of the eighth lunar month, the exact middle of autumn, to make offerings to the moon.

The Song dynasty (960—1280 AD) was taken over by the Mongolians and needed a way to start a rebellion without being discovered. Song leaders decided to place little messages describing their attack into cakes that they made for the Mid-Autumn Festival, knowing that the Mongolians would never inspect the tiny pastries. On the night of the festival, the attack was successfully carried out and the Ming Dynasty (A.D. 1368—1644) was established.

Today, the "Moon Festival" is celebrated by eating mooncakes with friends and family while watching the bright, beautiful full moon. It is customary to give mooncakes as presents around the time of the festival, especially to colleagues and business partners.

(country, celebrate, festival)		
国庆节	Guóqìng Jié	National Day (Oct. 1)

October 1ˢᵗ marks the founding of the People's Republic of China. Parades are held and fireworks are lit. People are given one week off from work.

万圣节	Wànshèng Jié	Halloween (Oct. 31)

Most Chinese do not celebrate Halloween. Like St. Patrick's Day, there are parties thrown at local bars and restaurants in major cities. Sorry, no trick-or-treating.

(holy, birth, festival)		
圣诞节	Shèngdàn Jié	Christmas (Dec. 25)

Christmas has become more and more popular amongst the younger generation Chinese. Some decorate their houses with Christmas trees and Christmas lights. Friends get together for meals, drinking, and gift giving. Christmas has also become commercialized in China. Big department stores have holiday sales and are decorated to get people in the holiday spirit.

(new, year, before, night)		
新年前夜	xīnnián qiányè	New Year's Eve (Dec. 31)

Over the past few years, New Year's Eve celebrations have become more and more popular in China. Parties are thrown at restaurants and bars.

Chinese Zodiac

生 肖

Legend has it that when Buddha convened the animal kingdom to determine how to restore order to the world, only twelve animals showed up. These animals came to represent the Chinese Zodiac, each presiding over one year based upon the order of their arrival.

Knowing the signs of the zodiac is a way to find out a person's age without directly asking. Being able to calculate the age of a person based upon their Chinese Zodiac sign will display that you have a deep understanding of the Chinese culture.

鼠	shǔ	rat

Aggressive, power hungry, have a sense of fair play, generous
1924, 1936, 1948, 1960, 1972, 1984, 1996, 2008
A rat is compatible with a monkey, ox or dragon. Beware of the horse!

| 牛 | niú | ox |

Power individuals with stubborn personalities; natural-born leaders
1925, 1937, 1949, 1961, 1973, 1985, 1997, 2009
An ox is compatible with a rat, snake or cock. Beware of the sheep!

| 虎 | hǔ | tiger |

Carefree, charming, quick-tempered, sensitive
1926, 1938, 1950, 1962, 1974, 1986, 1998, 2010
A tiger is compatible with a horse, dragon and dog. Rats, rabbits, sheep, pigs, cocks, and fellow tigers are also ok.

| 兔 | tù | rabbit |

Prudent, value security and tranquility
Avoid conflict and emotional involvement.
1927, 1939, 1951, 1963, 1975, 1987, 1999, 2011
Rabbits are compatible with sheep, pigs and dogs. Avoid dragons. Beware of rats and cocks!

| 龙 | lóng | dragon |

Bossy, loud and unfaithful; very popular and successful
1928, 1940, 1952, 1964, 1976, 1988, 2000, 2012
Dragons are compatible with snakes, cocks, monkeys and rats. Avoid the rabbit, ox and other dragons. Beware of dogs!

蛇	shé	snake

Clever, known for abstract thought and idealism
1929, 1941, 1953, 1965, 1977, 1989, 2001, 2013
Snakes are compatible with oxen and cocks. Rabbits, rats, horses, sheep, dogs, dragons, and fellow snakes are ok. Beware of monkeys and do not come near pigs or tigers!

马	mǎ	horse

Hard-working, considers him/herself to be superior
1930, 1942, 1954, 1966, 1978, 1990, 2002, 2014
Horses are compatible with tigers, dogs or sheep. Can do well with dragons, snakes, monkeys, cocks and pigs. Bewear of fellow horses and avoid rats at all costs!

羊	yáng	sheep

Warmhearted, honest, disorganized, and vulnerable
1931, 1943, 1955, 1967, 1979, 1991, 2003, 2015
Sheep find good partners in horses, pigs and rabbits. Monkeys, cocks, snakes, dragons, tigers and fellow sheep are also ok. Stay away from the rat and absolutely do not get involved with dogs and oxen!

猴	hóu	monkey

Intelligent and entertaining, dangerous and deceptive
1932, 1944, 1956, 1968, 1980, 1992, 2004, 2016
Monkeys go well with dragons or rats. Sheep, dogs or rabbits are acceptable. Snakes and pigs should be avoided. Beware of tigers!

鸡	jī	cock

Courageous, arrogant, reckless. Pay attention to details.
1933, 1945, 1957, 1969, 1981, 1993, 2005, 2017
Cocks get along well with oxen, snakes, and dragons. Pigs, monkeys, tigers and sheep are acceptable. Rats, dogs and fellow cocks are bad news. Beware of rabbits!

狗	gǒu	dog

Quiet, intelligent, extroverted, dedicated
1934, 1946, 1958, 1970, 1982, 1994, 2006, 2018
Dogs go extremely well with rabbits, tigers and horses. Snakes, pigs, dogs and monkeys are acceptable. Stay away from dragons and sheep at all costs!

猪	zhū	pig

Honest and reliable, deep thirst for knowledge. Successful in financial affairs.
1935, 1947, 1959, 1971, 1983, 1995, 2007, 2019
Pigs are compatible with sheep and rabbits. Dragons, tigers, cocks, dogs, horses, oxen and rats also make suitable matches. Monkeys and fellow pigs should be avoided. Stay away from snakes!

(you, are, born in the year of, what)	What is your Chinese zodiac sign?
Q) 你是属什么的？	
Nǐ shì shǔ shénme de?	
(I, am, born in the year of, **dragon**)	I was born in the Year of the **Dragon**.
A) 我是属龙的。	
Wǒ shì shǔ **lóng** de.	

(you, compare, I, small/big, one, cycle)	You are one cycle older/younger than I am. (We have the same zodiac sign, but were born in different years. He is 24, I am 36, or the other way round.)
你比我小/大一轮。	
Nǐ bǐ wǒ xiǎo/dà yì lún.	

(oneself, life, year)		
本命年	běnmìngnián	the year of one's zodiac sign
(this year, is, my, oneself, life, year)	It is currently the year of the zodiac sign in which I was born. (I was born in the year of the dragon and it is the year of the dragon.)
今年是我的本命年。	
Jīnnián shì wǒ de běnmìngnián.	

Emotions

情　感

害怕	hàipà	afraid
(I, afraid, ghost)		I am afraid of ghosts.
我害怕鬼。		
Wǒ hàipà guǐ.		

生气	shēngqì	angry
(you, still, feel angry about , me, QW)		Are you still mad at me?
你还生我的气吗？		
Nǐ hái shēng wǒ de qì ma?		

无聊	wúliáo	bored
(I, feel, very, bored, we, go out)		I feel really bored. Let's go out.
我觉得很无聊，咱们出去吧。		
Wǒ juéde hěn wúliáo, zánmen chūqu ba.		

平静	píngjìng	calm, at peace
(he, very, be excited, emotion, not, able, calm)		He is so excited that he can't calm down.
他很激动，心情不能平静。		
Tā hěn jīdòng, xīnqíng bù néng píngjìng.		

(pleased, happy)		
愉快	yúkuài	cheerful

(wish, whole, country, people, Spring Festival, happy)	Wishing everybody a very happy and healthy Chinese New Year.
祝全国人民春节愉快。	
Zhù quán guó rénmín Chūn Jié yúkuài.	

舒服	shūfu	comfortable

(with, you, together, I, very, comfortable)	I am very comfortable with you.
跟你在一起，我很舒服。	
Gēn nǐ zài yìqǐ, wǒ hěn shūfu.	

(pity, remorse)		
怜悯	liánmǐn	compassion

(I, not, need, your, compassion)	I don't need your compassion.
我不需要你的怜悯。	
Wǒ bù xūyào nǐ de liánmǐn.	

好奇	hàoqí	curious

(I, with regard to, your, experience, very, curious)	I am curious about your past experiences.
我对你的经历很好奇。	
Wǒ duì nǐ de jīnglì hěn hàoqí.	

压抑	yāyì	depressed

(this, MW, movie, very, depressing)	This movie is very depressing.
这部电影很压抑。	
Zhè bù diànyǐng hěn yāyì.	

(lose, hope)		
失望	shīwàng	disappointed
(he, make, me, very, disappointed)	He disappoints me.
他让我很失望。	
Tā ràng wǒ hěn shīwàng.	

(sorrow, hurt)		
忧伤	yōushāng	distressed
(he, lose, love, seem, very, distressed)	After he lost his girlfriend, he was extremely distressed.
他失恋了，看上去十分忧伤。	
Tā shīliàn le, kàn shàngqu shífēn yōushāng.	

怀疑	huáiyí	doubt
(I, with regard to, your, words, express, doubt)	I doubt what you said is true.
我对你的话表示怀疑。	
Wǒ duì nǐ de huà biǎoshì huáiyí.	

不好意思	bù hǎoyìsi	embarrassed
(I, make, you, long time, wait, truly, embarrassed)	I am embarrassed to have made you wait such a long time.
我让你久等了，真不好意思。	
Wǒ ràng nǐ jiǔděng le, zhēn bù hǎoyìsi.	

心力交瘁	xīnlì jiāo cuì	emotionally and physically drained
(lately, busy with, open, company, almost, busy, emotionally and physically drained, PT)	I have been so busy lately starting a company that I am emotionally and physically exhausted.
最近忙着开公司，都忙得心力交瘁了。	
Zuìjìn mángzhe kāi gōngsī, dōu máng de xīnlì jiāo cuì le.	

(arouse, move)		
激动	jīdòng	excited
(see, you, I, very, excited)		I am very excited to see you.
看到**你**我**很激动**。		
Kàn dào nǐ wǒ hěn jīdòng.		

(heart, tide, surge)		
心**潮澎湃**	xīncháo péngpài	fanatic, ecstatic
(big, election, moment, candidates', supporters, fanatic)		During election time, supporters are really fanatic.
大选的时候，**候选人的**支持者们**心潮澎湃**。		
Dàxuǎn de shíhou, hòuxuǎnrén de zhīchízhěmen xīncháo péngpài.		

(afraid, fear)		
恐惧	kǒngjù	fear
(black, dark, make, him, fear)		He is afraid of the dark.
黑暗使他恐惧。		
Hēi'àn shǐ tā kǒngjù.		

气急败坏	qì jí bài huài	flustered, exasperated
(he, in a flustered manner, tell, me, happened, thing)		He angrily told me what had transpired.
他**气急败坏地告诉我发生**的事。		
Tā qì jí bài huài de gàosu wǒ fāshēng de shì.		

感激	gǎnjī	grateful
(you, help, PT, me, I, very, grateful)		I am very grateful that you helped me.
你帮了我，我**很感激**。		
Nǐ bāngle wǒ, wǒ hěn gǎnjī.		

(sad, hurt)		
悲伤	bēishāng	grieved, sorrowful
(his, dog, *marker of passive voice*, hit, death, he, very, grieved)		After his dog was run over, he was grieved.
他的**狗**被**撞死了，他很悲伤**。		
Tā de gǒu bèi zhuàng sǐ le, tā hěn bēishāng.		

(merry, happy)		
欢乐	huānlè	happiness
(life, fill, full, happiness)		Life is full of happiness.
生活**充满欢乐**。		
Shēnghuó chōngmǎn huānlè.		

(joyful, happy)		
快乐	kuàilè	happy
(you, seem, very, happy)		You seem very happy.
你**看起来**很**快乐**。		
Nǐ kàn qǐlai hěn kuàilè.		

(high, emotion)		
高兴	gāoxìng	happy
(very, happy, know, you)		It's my pleasure to meet you.
很**高兴**认识**你**。		
Hěn gāoxìng rènshi nǐ.		

痛快	tòngkuài	happy; extremely happy
(today, play, truly, very happy)		I had a great time today!
今天**玩儿得真痛快**!		
Jīntiān wánr de zhēn tòngkuài!		

(enmity, hate)

仇恨	chóuhèn	hatred

(don't, at, two, country, people, between, create, hatred)

不要在两国人民之间制造仇恨。

Búyào zài liǎng guó rénmín zhījiān zhìzào chóuhèn.

Don't create hatred between the peoples of two countries.

渴望	kěwàng	hope (very strong)

(he, hope, gain, freedom)

他渴望获得自由。

Tā kěwàng huòdé zìyóu.

He hopes (longs) for freedom.

(rush, move)

冲动	chōngdòng	impulsive

(he, at that time, impulsive, with, her, connect, PT, marriage)

他一时冲动跟她结了婚。

Tā yìshí chōngdòng gēn tā jiéle hūn.

He was very impulsive when he married her. (They were together only a few weeks prior.)

(self, inferior)

自卑	zìbēi	insecure

(she, because of, her, appearance, feel, insecure)

她为她的相貌感到自卑。

Tā wèi tā de xiàngmào gǎndào zìbēi.

She is insecure about her appearance.

嫉妒	jídù	jealousy

(he, always, jealous, comparison, him, stronger, person)

他总是嫉妒比他强的人。

Tā zǒngshì jídù bǐ tā qiáng de rén.

He is always jealous of people who possess stronger skills.

(open, heart)		
开心	kāixīn	joyful
(wish, you, play, happy)	Have a good time!	
祝你玩儿得开心！		
Zhù nǐ wǎnr de kāixīn!		

(quiet, lonely)		
寂寞	jìmò	lonely
(you, not, at, my, body, side, I, feel, very, lonely)	When you are not by my side, I am lonely.	
你不在我的身边，我觉得很寂寞。		
Nǐ bú zài wǒ de shēnbiān, wǒ juéde hěn jìmò.		

气愤	qìfèn	mad
(his, words, make, me, very, mad)	His words really made me mad.	
他的话让我很气愤。		
Tā de huà ràng wǒ hěn qìfèn.		

遗憾	yíhàn	pity
(heard, you, exam, again, not pass, I, very, feel, regretful)	I am sorry to hear that you did not pass the exam once again. (Knowing that the listener really wanted to pass the exam.)	
听说你考试又不及格，我深感遗憾。		
Tīngshuō nǐ kǎoshì yòu bù jígé, wǒ shēn gǎn yíhàn.		

(proud, arrogant)		
骄傲	jiāo'ào	proud
(to be, one, MW, American, I, very, proud)	I am very proud to be an American.	
身为一个美国人，我很骄傲。		
Shēn wéi yí ge Měiguórén, wǒ hěn jiāo'ào.		

(after, regret)		
后悔	hòuhuǐ	regret
(with, you, marry, I, very, regret)	I regret marrying you!	
跟你结婚，我很后悔。		
Gēn nǐ jiéhūn, wǒ hěn hòuhuǐ.		

(easy, relax)		
轻松	qīngsōng	relaxed
(pass, PT, test, his, heart, inside, very, relaxed)	Having passed the test, he felt at ease.	
通过了考试，他心里很轻松。		
Tōngguòle kǎoshì, tā xīn li hěn qīngsōng.		

(respect, respect)		
尊敬	zūnjìng	respect
(you, must, respect, your, parents)	You must respect your parents.	
你得尊敬你的父母。		
Nǐ děi zūnjìng nǐ de fùmǔ.		

(hard, pass)		
难过	nánguò	sad
(hear, his, teacher, die, news, he, very, sad)	He was very sad when he heard that his teacher had passed away.	
听到他老师去世的消息，他很难过。		
Tīngdào tā lǎoshī qùshì de xiāoxi, tā hěn nánguò.		

满意（不满意）	mǎnyì (bù mǎnyì)	satisfied (dissatisfied)
(I, with regard to, your, work, [not], satisfied)	I am (dis)satisfied with your work.	
我对你的工作(不)满意。		
Wǒ duì nǐ de gōngzuò (bù) mǎnyì.		

(firm, strong)		
坚强	jiānqiáng	strong (emotionally)
(we, at, difficulty, in front of, should, strong) 我们在困难面前应该坚强。 Wǒmen zài kùnnan miànqián yīnggāi jiānqiáng.		When faced with difficulty, we should be strong.

吃惊	chījīng	surprised
(his, appetite, make, me, surprised) 他的饭量使我吃惊。 Tā de fànliàng shǐ wǒ chījīng.		His appetite surprised me. (Eats like a horse)

(same, feeling)		
同情	tóngqíng	sympathetic
(his, misfortune, truly, make, people, sympathetic) 他的遭遇真让人同情。 Tā de zāoyù zhēn ràng rén tóngqíng.		His misfortunate really makes people sympathetic for him.

(sorrow, troubled)		
忧愁	yōuchóu	troubled
(these, problem, make, him, very, troubled) 这些问题使他很忧愁。 Zhèxiē wèntí shǐ tā hěn yōuchóu.		These questions have made him very troubled.

Human

人

(male, human)		
男人	nánrén	male
(female, human)		
女人	nǔrén	female
(small, kid)		
小孩	xiǎohái	child (under 10)
(age, young, human)		
年轻人	niánqīngrén	young person (teenager)
(reach, age, human)		
成年人	chéngniánrén	adult
(middle, age, human)		
中年人	zhōngniánrén	middle-aged person
(old, human)		
老人	lǎorén	elderly person

(outer, appearance)		
外貌	wàimào	outer appearance

美丽	měilì	beautiful
(Xinjiang, girl, very, beautiful, striking)		Xinjiang girls are strikingly beautiful.
新疆女孩非常美丽动人。		
Xīnjiāng nǔhái fēicháng měilì dòngrén.		

胖	pàng	fat
(his, mother, and, father, all, very, fat, he, why, so, skinny)		His mom and dad are both fat. How did he end up skinny?
他的妈妈和爸爸都很胖，他为什么那么瘦？		
Tā de māma hé bàba dōu hěn pàng, tā wèi shénme nàme shòu?		

虚弱	xūruò	feeble
(her, body, always, very, feeble)		Her body and health have always been feeble.
她的身体一直很虚弱。		
Tā de shēntǐ yìzhí hěn xūruò.		

(good, look)		
好看	hǎokàn	good-looking
(you, think, this, MW, girl, good-looking, QW)		Do you think that girl is good-looking?
你觉得这个女孩好看吗？		
Nǐ juéde zhè ge nǚhái hǎokàn ma?		

(outstanding person, handsome)		
英俊	yīngjùn	handsome
(girls, all, wish, find, MW, handsome, boyfriend)		All girls want to find a handsome boyfriend.
女孩都希望找个英俊的男朋友。		
Nǚhái dōu xīwàng zhǎo ge yīngjùn de nánpéngyou.		

(pale, white)		
苍白	cāngbái	pale
(he, get, illness, after, complexion, seem, very, pale)		After coming down with his illness, his complexion was very pale.
他得病以后脸色显得十分苍白。		
Tā dé bìng yǐhòu liǎnsè xiǎnde shífēn cāngbái.		

(pretty, shine)

漂亮	piàoliang	pretty

(your, girlfriend, today, make up, very, pretty)

你女朋友今天打扮得很漂亮。

Nǐ nǚpéngyou jīntiān dǎban de hěn piàoliang.

Your girlfriend is pretty today.

(sex, sense)

性感	xìnggǎn	sexy

(Madonna, is, MW, sexy, star)

麦当娜是个性感明星。

Màidāngnà shì ge xìnggǎn míngxīng.

Madonna is a sexy star.

(short, small)

矮小	ǎixiǎo	short

(Michael Fox, build, small, but, grow, very, handsome)

Michael Fox 身材矮小，但长得很帅。

Michael Fox shēncái ǎixiǎo, dàn zhǎng de hěn shuài.

Although Michael J. Fox is short, he is very handsome.

瘦	shòu	skinny

(his, height, very, tall, but, very, thin)

他个儿很高，但很瘦。

Tā gèr hěn gāo, dàn hěn shòu.

He is tall but very skinny.

潇洒	xiāosǎ	smooth, Casanova-like

(her, dad, that, year, very, smooth)

她爸爸当年相当潇洒。

Tā bàba dāngnián xiāngdāng xiāosǎ.

Her father was a real Casanova.

(powerful, strong)		
强壮	qiángzhuàng	strong
(lift, weight, teammates, each, each, body, strong)		Everyone who is a member of a weightlifting team has a strong body.
举重队员们个个身体强壮。		
Jǔzhòng duìyuánmen gègè shēntǐ qiángzhuàng.		

高	gāo	tall
(his, height, very, tall, basketball, play, very, good)		He is really tall, so he is good at basketball.
他的**个子很高**，篮球**打得很好**。		
Tā de gèzi hěn gāo, lánqiú dǎ de hěn hǎo.		

(hard, look)		
难看	nánkàn	ugly
(grow, ugly, definitely, not, is, person, own, fault)		Being ugly is not the person's fault.
长得**难看**并**不是人**自己的**错**。		
Zhǎng de nánkàn bìng bú shì rén zìjǐ de cuò.		

(long, hair)		
长发	cháng fà	long-haired
(I, like, watch, girl's, long hair, in , wind, float)		I like to watch girls' hair as it floats in the wind.
我喜欢看女孩的长发在风中飘动。		
Wǒ xǐhuan kàn nǚhái de cháng fà zài fēng zhōng piāodòng.		
(short, hair)		
短发	duǎn fà	short-haired
(now, very, popular, girl, cut, short hair)		It is very in vogue for young girls to have short hair these days.
现在**很流行女孩**剪**短发**。		
Xiànzài hěn liúxíng nǚhái jiǎn duǎn fà.		
(bald, head)		
光头	guāngtóu	shaved head
(summer, arrive, PT, I, want, cut, MW, bald head)		In the summer I want to shave my head.
夏天到了，**我想剪**个**光头**。		
Xiàtiān dào le, wǒ xiǎng jiǎn ge guāngtóu.		

(fake, hair)

假发	jiǎfà	toupee

(he, wear, wig, but, very, hard, tell)

他戴着假发，但是很难看出来。

Without looking very carefully, you wouldn't be able to tell that he wears a toupee.

Tā dàizhe jiǎfà, dànshì hěn nán kàn chūlai.

(nature, pattern)

性格	xìnggé	personality

(courage, dare)

勇敢	yǒnggǎn	brave, courageous

(we, should, courageously, face, reality)

我们应该勇敢地面对现实。

We should all courageously face reality.

Wǒmen yīnggāi yǒnggǎn de miànduì xiànshí.

(reverse, again, no, constant)

反复无常	fǎnfù wúcháng	capricious

(he, this, MW, person, capricious, make, people, hard to fathom)

他这个人反复无常，让人捉摸不定。

He changes his mind so much that people can never guess what he really wants.

Tā zhè ge rén fǎnfù wúcháng, ràng rén zhuōmō bú dìng.

小气	xiǎoqì	stingy

(he, very, cheap, even, one, piece, candy, still, not willing, treat, person, eat)

他很小气，连一颗糖也舍不得请人吃。

He is so cheap that he is not even willing to part with a piece of candy.

Tā hěn xiǎoqì, lián yì kē táng yě shěbudé qǐng rén chī.

幼稚	yòuzhì	childish, immature
(your, behavior, too, immature, should, mature, a little) 你的**行为**太幼稚了,应该**成熟**一点儿。	Your behavior is way too immature. You need to grow up a little.	
Nǐ de xíngwéi tài yòuzhì le, yīnggāi chéngshú yìdiǎnr.		

(protect, defend)		
保守	bǎoshǒu	conservative
(we, parents, this, one, generation, people, mindset, all, very, conservative) 我们**父母**这一代**人**思想都很**保守**。	The mindset of our parents' generation is very conservative.	
Wǒmen fùmǔ zhè yí dài rén sīxiǎng dōu hěn bǎoshǒu.		

狡猾	jiǎohuá	cunning, sneaky, foxy
(he, is, MW, sneaky, businessman, you, should, be careful) 他是个**狡猾的**商人,**你要小心**。	He is a very cunning businessman, you should be careful.	
Tā shì ge jiǎohuá de shāngrén, nǐ yào xiǎoxīn.		

沉着	chénzhuó	composed
(exam, should, compose) 考试应该沉着。	When you take a test, you should keep your composure.	
Kǎoshì yīnggāi chénzhuó.		

(self, conceit)		
自负	zìfù	conceited

(self-confidence, pass, PT, limit, will, become, conceited)	Too much self-confidence can make a person conceited.
自信过了头就会变成自负。	
Zìxìn guòle tóu jiù huì biànchéng zìfù.	

(diligent, labor)		
勤劳	qínláo	diligent, hard-working
(diligence, is, Chinese, virtue)		Diligence is the virtue of Chinese.
勤劳是中国人的美德。		
Qínláo shì Zhōngguórén de měidé.		

(nice, good)		
善良	shànliáng	good-hearted
(I, like, her, beauty, but, I, more, like, her, good-heartedness)		I find her attractive, but her good-heartedness is what I really like about her.
我喜欢她的漂亮, 但我更喜欢她的善良。		
Wǒ xǐhuan tā de piàoliang, dàn wǒ gèng xǐhuan tā de shànliáng.		

绝情	juéqíng	heartless
(on, some, problem, he, do, very, heartless)		On certain things he is just heartless.
在某些事情上他做得非常绝情。		
Zài mǒuxiē shìqing shang tā zuò de fēicháng juéqíng.		

诚实	chéngshí	honest, honesty
(I, very, appreciate, your, honesty)		I really appreciate your honesty.
我很欣赏你的诚实。		
Wǒ hěn xīnshǎng nǐ de chéngshí.		

(temper, fire, explode)		
脾气火暴	píqi huǒbào	hot-tempered
(he, hot-tempered, don't, provoke, him)	He has a really bad temper. Please do not provoke him.	
他脾气火暴,别惹他。		
Tā píqi huǒbào, bié rě tā.		

(modest, humble)		
谦虚	qiānxū	humble
(although, test, get, PT, first, he, still, very, modest)	Although he scored the highest on the test, he is still humble.	
虽然考试得了第一,他还是很谦虚。		
Suīrán kǎoshì déle dì yī, tā háishi hěn qiānxū.		

(English)		
幽默	yōumò	humorous
(he, always, love, make joke, very, humorous)	He always cracks jokes, very humorous.	
他总是爱开玩笑,特别幽默。		
Tā zǒngshì ài kāi wánxiào, tèbié yōumò.		

(hollow, fake)		
虚伪	xūwěi	hypocritical
(I, very, dislike, like, him, same, hypocritical, people)	I really dislike people who are hypocritical like he is.	
我很讨厌像他那样虚伪的人。		
Wǒ hěn tǎoyàn xiàng tā nàyàng xūwěi de rén.		

(hesitant, not decide)		
犹豫不决	yóuyù bù jué	indecisive
(he, this, MW, person, do, thing, indecisive, no, charisma)	He is a very indecisive person with no courage and determination.	
他这个人做事犹豫不决，没有魄力。		
Tā zhè ge rén zuò shì yóuyù bù jué, méiyǒu pòlì.		

冷静	lěngjìng	level-headed
(handle, problem, need, level-headed)	When dealing with a problem, you should be level-headed.	
处理问题要冷静。		
Chùlǐ wèntí yào lěngjìng.		

成熟	chéngshú	mature
(woman, like, mature, man)	Women like mature men.	
女人喜欢成熟的男人。		
Nǚrén xǐhuan chéngshú de nánrén.		

单纯	dānchún	naive
(young, girl, all, very, naive)	Young girls are very naive.	
年轻女孩儿都很单纯。		
Niánqīng nǚháir dōu hěn dānchún.		

淘气	táoqì	naughty
(little, kid, born, naughty, but, lively, cute)	Little kids are naughty, but cute.	
小孩子天生淘气，但是活泼可爱。		
Xiǎoháizi tiānshēng táoqì, dànshì huópo kě'ài.		

(have/haven't, politeness)		
有/没礼貌	yǒu/méi lǐmào	polite, impolite
(she, very, has/hasn't, politeness) 她很有/没礼貌。 Tā hěn yǒu/méi lǐmào.		She is very polite/impolite.

(proud, arrogant)		
骄傲	jiāo'ào	proud, arrogant
(he, very, arrogant, anyone, all, not, willing, show interest in) 他很骄傲,谁都不愿理睬。 Tā hěn jiāo'ào, shéi dōu bú yuàn lǐcǎi.		He is so arrogant that he is not willing to talk to others.

现实	xiànshí	realistic
(people, grow up, after, then, will, change, very, realistic) 人长大以后就会变得很现实。 Rén zhǎngdà yǐhòu jiù huì biàn de hěn xiànshí.		When people grow up they become more realistic.

果断	guǒduàn	resolute, decisive
(until, key, moment, need, resolute, make, decision) 到关键时刻,要果断做决定。 Dào guānjiàn shíkè, yào guǒduàn zuò juédìng.		At the critical moment, one should be resolute when making decisions.

(*English*)		
浪漫	làngmàn	romantic, romanticism
(they, although, already, are, mid-aged person, but, still, preserve, young, when, romantic) 他们虽然已是中年人，但仍然保持着年轻时候的浪漫。		Although they are middle-aged, they have still managed to keep their younger-aged romanticism alive.
Tāmen suīrán yǐ shì zhōngniánrén, dàn réngrán bǎochízhe niánqīng shíhou de làngmàn.		

(self, selfish)		
自私	zìsī	selfish
(human, is, selfish, animal) 人是自私的动物。		Humans are selfish animals.
Rén shì zìsī de dòngwù.		

(rigid, serious)		
严肃	yánsù	serious
(he, this, MW, person, very, serious, work, when, never, joke around) 他这个人很严肃，工作的时候从不开玩笑。		He is a very serious person. When he is working, he never jokes around.
Tā zhè ge rén hěn yánsù, gōngzuò de shíhou cóng bù kāi wánxiào.		

(true, honest)		
真诚	zhēnchéng	sincere, sincerity
(my, sincerity, win, PT, her, heart) 我的真诚赢得了她的心。		My sincerity won her heart.
Wǒ de zhēnchéng yíngdéle tā de xīn.		

聪明	cōngming	smart
(he, very, smart, college entrance exam, score, PT, full, point)	He is very smart, scored perfect on the college entrance examination.	
他很聪明,高考得了满分。		
Tā hěn cōngming, gāokǎo déle mǎnfēn.		

势利	shìli	snobbish
(he, is, MW, snobbish, small, person, I, bear, not able, him)	He is such a snobbish person that I can't stand him.	
他是个势利小人,我受不了他。		
Tā shì ge shìli xiǎorén, wǒ shòu bu liǎo tā.		

稳重	wěnzhòng	stable
(stable, people, take care of things, very , dependable)	Stable people do things in a dependable manner.	
稳重的人办事很可靠。		
Wěnzhòng de rén bànshì hěn kěkào.		

(hard, strong)

坚强	jiānqiáng	strong-willed
(she, very, strong-willed, never, fear, any, difficulty)	She is very strong-willed, never afraid of difficulty.	
她很坚强,从不惧怕任何困难。		
Tā hěn jiānqiáng, cóng bú jùpà rènhé kùnnan.		

固执	gùzhi	stubborn
(he, this, MW, person, very, stubborn, a little, even, not, listen, person, persuade) 他这个人很**固执**，一点儿都不听人劝。		He is so stubborn, never willing to listen to other's advice.
Tā zhè ge rén hěn gùzhi, yìdiǎnr dōu bù tīng rén quàn.		

(warm, tender)		
温柔	wēnróu	tender, soft
(everybody, all, envy, him, has, MW, tender, wife) 人人都羡慕他有个**温柔**的老婆。		Everyone admires him because he has a tender wife.
Rénrén dōu xiànmù tā yǒu ge wēnróu de lǎopo.		

多疑	duōyí	not willing to trust people
(she, walk into, PT, one, time, trap, after, toward, any, stranger, all, has, some, suspicion) 她上了一次当以后，对任何**陌生人**都有些**多疑**。		After she was cheated once, she suspected every stranger that she came in contact with.
Tā shàngle yí cì dàng yǐhòu, duì rènhé mòshēng rén dōu yǒuxiē duōyí.		

(right, straight)		
正直	zhèngzhí	upright, honest
(he, is, MW, honest, judge) 他是个**正直**的法官。		He is a very upright, honest judge.
Tā shì ge zhèngzhí de fǎguān.		

热情	rèqíng	warm-hearted
(she, very, warm-hearted, always, happy, help others) 她很热情，总是乐于助人。 Tā hěn rèqíng, zǒngshì lèyú zhùrén.		She is very warm-hearted, always willing to lend a helping hand.

软弱	ruǎnruò	weak (mentally, emotionally)
(he, in, difficulty, front, seem, very, weak) 他在困难面前显得很软弱。 Tā zài kùnnan miànqián xiǎnde hěn ruǎnruò.		When staring problems in the face, he is weak.

Body Parts

身体部位

喉结	hóujié	adam's apple
胳膊	gēbo	arm
背	bèi	back
胡子	húzi	beard
乳房	rǔfáng	breast
屁股	pìgu	buttocks
胸	xiōng	chest
下巴	xiàba	chin
乳沟	rǔgōu	cleavage
耳朵	ěrduo	ear
肘	zhǒu	elbow
眼睛	yǎnjing	eyes
脸	liǎn	face
手	shǒu	hand
手指	shǒuzhǐ	finger
前臂	qiánbì	forearm
头	tóu	head
头发	tóufa	hair
脚后跟	jiǎohòugēn	heel

膝盖	xīgài	knee
腿	tuǐ	leg
嘴唇	zuǐchún	lips
小胡子	xiǎo húzi	moustache
口	kǒu	mouth
指甲	zhǐjia	nail
颈	jǐng	neck
鼻子	bízi	nose
手掌	shǒuzhǎng	palm
肩膀	jiānbǎng	shoulder
肚子	dùzi	stomach
牙齿	yáchǐ	teeth
大腿	dàtuǐ	thigh
脚趾	jiǎozhǐ	toe
腰	yāo	waist
手腕	shǒuwàn	wrist

(I, **foot**, hurt)	My **foot** hurts.
我**脚**疼。	
Wǒ **jiǎo** téng.	

(my, **ankle**, sprain)	I sprained my **ankle**.
我的**脚踝**扭伤了。	
Wǒ de **jiǎohuái** niǔ shāng le.	

(my, **leg**, bone, break)	**My leg** is broken.
我的腿骨折了。	
Wǒ de tuǐ gǔzhé le.	

(my, **nose**, bleeding)	**My nose** is bleeding.
我的鼻子流血了。	
Wǒ de bízi liú xiě le.	

(IO, your, **face**, wash, clean)	Wash your **face**.
把你的脸洗干净。	
Bǎ nǐ de liǎn xǐ gānjìng.	

Colors

颜 色

(this, MW, book, is, **red**)	This book is **red**.
这本书是红色的。	
Zhè běn shū shì **hóngsè** de.	

黑色	hēisè	black
蓝色	lánsè	blue
褐色	hèsè	brown
绿色	lǜsè	green
灰色	huīsè	gray
卡其色	kǎqísè	khaki
淡紫色	dàn zǐsè	lavender
橘色	júsè	orange
紫色	zǐsè	purple
红色	hóngsè	red
白色	báisè	white
黄色	huángsè	yellow

(this, MW, picture, very, colorful)	This picture is very colorful.
这幅画很鲜艳。	
Zhè fú huà hěn xiānyàn.	

深绿色的	shēn **lǜsè** de	dark green
浅绿色的	qiǎn **lǜsè** de	light green

Clothing

衣 服

(IO, **pants**, wear, on)	Put on your **pants**.
把**裤子**穿上。	
Bǎ **kùzi** chuān shàng.	
(IO, **pants**, take off)	Take off your **pants**.
把**裤子**脱掉。	
Bǎ **kùzi** tuō diào.	

(swim, clothing)		
游泳衣	yóuyǒngyī	bathing suit
(*English*)		
比基尼	bǐjīní	bikini
(female, style, shirt)		
女式衬衫	nǚshì chènshān	blouse
(outside, cover)		
外套	wàitào	coat
(link, clothes, skirt)		
连衣裙	liányīqún	dress
(cowboy, pants)		
牛仔裤	niúzǎikù	jeans
(sleep, clothes)		
睡衣	shuìyī	pajamas
裤子	kùzi	pants

(link, pants, sock)		
连裤袜	liánkùwà	panty-hose
(rain, clothes)		
雨衣	yǔyī	raincoat
(short, pants)		
短裤	duǎnkù	shorts
(short, sleeve, shirt)		
短袖衫	duǎnxiùshān	short-sleeved shirt
裙子	qúnzi	skirt
袜子	wàzi	socks
(west, clothes)		
西服	xīfú	suit
(wool, clothes)		
毛衣	máoyī	sweater
(sweat, shirt)		
汗衫	hànshān	sweatshirt
(*English*, shirt)		
T 恤衫	T xùshān	T-shirt
(tight, body, pants)		
紧身裤	jǐnshēnkù	tights
(inside, pants)		
内裤	nèikù	underwear

(IO, **leather shoes**, wear, on)	Put on your **shoes**.
把皮鞋穿上。	
Bǎ píxié chuān shàng.	
(IO, **leather shoes**, take off)	Take off your **shoes**.
把皮鞋脱掉。	
Bǎ píxié tuō diào.	

(breast, cover)		
乳罩	rǔzhào	bra
(rain, shoes)		
雨鞋	yǔxié	galoshes
(high, heel, shoes)		
高跟鞋	gāogēnxié	high heels
(leather, shoes)		
皮鞋	píxié	shoes
(sport, shoes)		
运动鞋	yùndòngxié	sneakers

(IO, **shoelaces**, tie, on)		Tie your **shoelaces**.
把鞋带系上。		
Bǎ **xiédài** jì shàng.		
(IO, **shoelaces**, untie, open)		Untie your **shoelaces**.
把鞋带解开。		
Bǎ **xiédài** jiě kāi.		
(leather, strip)		
皮带	pídài	belt
(sleeve, button)		
袖扣	xiùkòu	cuff links
(collar, strip)		
领带	lǐngdài	tie

(IO, **gloves**, wear, on)		Put the **gloves** on.
把手套戴上。		
Bǎ **shǒutào** dài shàng.		
(IO, **gloves**, pick, off)		Take off the **gloves**.
把手套摘下来。		
Bǎ **shǒutào** zhāi xiàlai.		
帽子	màozi	cap
(invisible, shape, glasses)		
隐形眼镜	yǐnxíng yǎnjìng	contact lenses
(eye, mirror)		
眼镜	yǎnjìng	glasses
(hand, cover)		
手套	shǒutào	gloves
(surround, cloth)		
围巾	wéijīn	scarf
(sun, [eye], mirror)		
太阳(**眼**)镜	tàiyáng(yǎn)jìng	sunglasses
(hand, watch)		
手表	shǒubiǎo	wrist watch

抹_____。	mǒ _____.	To put on _____.
(eyebrow, pen)		
眉笔	méibǐ	eyeliner
(eye, shadow)		
眼影	yǎnyǐng	eye shadow

(powder, base)		
粉底	fěndǐ	foundation
(lip, paste)		
唇膏	chúngāo	lipstick
(eyelash, paste)		
睫毛膏	jiémáogāo	mascara
(fragrant, water)		
香水	xiāngshuǐ	perfume/cologne

(hand, carry, bag)		
口袋	kǒudài	pocket
(hand, carry, bag)		
手提包	shǒutíbāo	pocket bag

(this, MW, sweater, is, **pure, cashmere**)	This sweater is **cashmere**.
这件毛衣是**纯羊毛**的。	
Zhè jiàn máoyī shì **chún yángmáo** de.	
(this, MW, clothing, is, **50%, wool, 50%, cotton**)	This piece of clothing is **50% wool, 50% cotton**.
这件衣服是**百分之五十羊毛, 百分之五十棉料**。	
Zhè jiàn yīfu shì **bǎi fēn zhī wǔshí yángmáo, bǎi fēn zhī wǔshí miánliào**.	

(English)		
尼龙	nílóng	nylon
(extend, shrink, nylon)		
伸缩尼龙	shēnsuō nílóng	polyester
(real, silk)		
真丝	zhēnsī	pure silk

(pure, cotton)		
纯棉	chúnmián	pure cotton
(wool, material)		
毛料	máoliào	wool

(he/she, dress, very, _____	He/She dresses very ____.
他/她穿着很____。	
Tā/Tā chuānzhuó hěn ____.	

得体	détǐ	appropriate for age
(protect, old)		
守旧	shǒujiù	conservative
体面	tǐmiàn	dapper
(enter, times)		
入时	rùshí	fashionable
前卫	qiánwèi	fashionable
(tempt, tease)		
挑逗	tiǎodòu	provocative
(sex, feeling)		
性感	xìnggǎn	sexy

(he, wear, clothes, very, has, taste)	He has good taste in clothes.
他穿衣服很有品位。	
Tā chuān yīfu hěn yǒu pǐnwèi.	

(he, wear, all, is, broken, clothes, broken, shirt)	His clothes are all rags.
他穿的都是破衣烂衫。	
Tā chuān de dōu shì pò yī làn shān.	

(white, clothes, very, easy, dirty)	White clothes get dirty easily.
白色的衣服很容易脏。	
Báisè de yīfu hěn róngyì zāng.	

(don't, IO, clothes, messily, throw, this way, easily, wrinkle)	Don't throw your clothes everywhere. They get wrinkled easily that way.
别把衣服乱扔，这样容易皱。	
Bié bǎ yīfu luàn rēng, zhèyàng róngyì zhòu.	

(this, MW, clothes, I, wear, too, big/small)	The clothing is too big/small for me.
这件衣服我穿太大/小了。	
Zhè jiàn yīfu wǒ chuān tài dà/xiǎo le.	

(this, MW, skirt's, waist, too, big/small)	The skirt is too big/small in the waist.
这条裙子的腰太大/小了。	
Zhè tiáo qúnzi de yāo tài dà/xiǎo le.	

(this, MW, pants, very, fat)	These pants are very baggy.
这条裤子很肥。	
Zhè tiáo kùzi hěn féi.	

(this, MW, suit, very, fit, my, body)	This suit fits me perfect.
这套西服非常合我的身。	
Zhè tào xīfú fēicháng hé wǒ de shēn.	

(this, kind, material, clothes, must, dry, clean)	Clothing of such material must be dry-cleaned.
这种料子的衣服必须干洗。	
Zhè zhǒng liàozi de yīfu bìxū gānxǐ.	

(IO, your, shirt, tuck, good)	Tuck your shirt in.
把你的衬衫掖好。	
Bǎ nǐ de chènshān yē hǎo.	

(my, jeans, already, by, me, wear, break)	I've worn this pair of jeans so much that they have holes in them.
我的牛仔裤已经被我穿破了。	
Wǒ de niúzǎikù yǐjing bèi wǒ chuān pò le.	

(your, socks, wear, opposite)	Your socks are on inside out.
你的袜子穿反了。	
Nǐ de wàzi chuān fǎn le.	

(your, shirt's, button, button, not straight)	You buttoned your shirt wrong.
你衬衣的扣子扣歪了。	
Nǐ chènyī de kòuzi kòu wāi le.	

(my, shirt, stain, full, PT, ketchup)	My shirt has ketchup all over it.
我的衬衫沾满了番茄酱。	
Wǒ de chènshān zhān mǎnle fānqiéjiàng.	

(your, clothes, wrinkled) 你的**衣服**皱皱巴巴的。 Nǐ de yīfu zhòuzhoubābā de.	Your clothes are wrinkled.

(my, shirt, broken, PT, MW, hole) 我的**衬衫**破了个洞。 Wǒ de chènshān pòle ge dòng.	My shirt has a hole in it.

(my, pants, rip, PT, MW, opening) 我的**裤子**撕了个口子。 Wǒ de kùzi sīle ge kǒuzi.	My pants are ripped.

(I, must, wash, clothes) 我得洗**衣服**了。 Wǒ děi xǐ yīfu le.	I have to wash my clothes.

(your, pants', zipper, open) 你**裤子**的拉链开了。 Nǐ kùzi de lāliàn kāi le.	Your fly is down.

(your, **shirt**, and, your, **scarf**, very, suit each other) 你的**衬衫**和你的**头巾**很般配。 Nǐ de **chènshān** hé nǐ de **tóujīn** hěn bānpèi.	Your **shirt** and your **scarf** go well together.

(IO, your, ____ hang, up) 把你的____挂起来。 Bǎ nǐ de ____ guà qǐlai.	Hang up your ____.

Foods

食　物

水果	shuǐguǒ	fruits
椰子	yēzi	coconut
苹果	píngguǒ	apple
香蕉	xiāngjiāo	banana
樱桃	yīngtáo	cherry
葡萄	pútáo	grape
猕猴桃	míhóutáo	kiwi
柠檬	níngméng	lemon
橘子	júzi	orange
桃子	táozi	peach
梨子	lízi	pear
菠萝	bōluó	pineapple
草莓	cǎoméi	strawberry
西瓜	xīguā	watermelon

(eat, apple, before, should, peel, skin)	You should peel the skin of the apple before eating.
吃苹果之前要削皮。	
Chī píngguǒ zhīqián yào xiāo pí.	

(watermelon, rot) 西瓜烂了。 Xīguā làn le.	The **watermelon** is rotten.

(milk, make, product)		
乳制品	rǔzhìpǐn	dairy products
(yellow, oil)		
黄油	huángyóu	butter
奶酪	nǎilào	cheese
(chicken, eggs)		
鸡蛋	jīdàn	eggs
(man-made, cream)		
人造奶油	rénzào nǎiyóu	margarine
(sour, milk)		
酸奶	suānnǎi	yogurt

蔬菜	shūcài	vegetables
朝鲜蓟	cháoxiǎnjì	artichoke
芦笋	lúsǔn	asparagus
西兰花	xīlánhuā	broccoli
菜花	càihuā	cauliflower
芹菜	qíncài	celery
玉米	yùmǐ	corn
黄瓜	huánggua	cucumber
茄子	qiézi	eggplant
大蒜	dàsuàn	garlic
青椒	qīngjiāo	green pepper
尖椒	jiānjiāo	hot pepper
生菜	shēngcài	lettuce

洋葱	yángcōng	onion
泡菜	pàocài	pickle
土豆	tǔdòu	potato
小红萝卜	xiǎo hóng luóbo	radish
菠菜	bōcài	spinach
刀豆	dāodòu	string bean
白薯	báishǔ	sweet potato
西红柿	xīhóngshì	tomato

肉	ròu	meat
(cattle, meat)		
牛肉	niúròu	beef
(chicken, meat)		
鸡肉	jīròu	chicken
(duck, meat)		
鸭肉	yāròu	duck
鱼	yú	fish
(sheep, meat)		
羊肉	yángròu	lamb
(pig, meat)		
猪肉	zhūròu	pork
(snake, meat)		
蛇肉	shéròu	snake

海鲜	hǎixiān	seafood
螃蟹	pángxiè	crab
蛤蜊	gélí	clam

(dragon, shrimp)

龙虾	lóngxiā	lobster
牡蛎	mǔlì	oyster

(*English*, fish)

三文鱼	sānwényú	salmon
扇贝	shànbèi	scallop
鲜贝	xiānbèi	shellfish
虾仁	xiārén	shrimp
海螺	hǎiluó	conch
鱿鱼	yóuyú	squid

(gold, gun, fish)

金枪鱼	jīnqiāngyú	tuna

(shell, fish)

甲鱼	jiǎyú	soft-shelled turtle

(adjust, ingredients)

调料	tiáoliào	condiments

(miss, our, dish, too, bland; please, give, us, add, a little, **salt**) 小姐，**我们的**菜太淡了。**请给我们加一点儿盐**。	Waitress, our dish is a little bland. Please bring us some **salt**.
Xiǎojiě, wǒmen de cài tài dàn le. Qǐng gěi wǒmen jiā yìdiǎnr **yán**.	
Jiā can be used with all condiments. Sǎ and zhàn are specifically used for powdered and liquid condiments respectively.	

(spicy, pepper)		
辣椒	làjiāo	hot pepper
生姜	shēngjiāng	ginger
大蒜	dàsuàn	garlic

(on, this, MW, dish, on, sprinkle, a little, **salt**)	Put some **salt** on this dish.
在这道菜上撒一点儿盐。	
Zài zhè dào cài shang sǎ yìdiǎnr **yán**.	

(pepper, powder)		
胡椒粉	hújiāofěn	black pepper

(flavor, essence)		
味精	wèijīng	MSG
盐	yán	salt
糖	táng	sugar

(**French fries**, very, bland, should, dip, a little, **ketchup**)	The **French fries** are bland; you should put some **ketchup** on them.
薯条很淡,应该蘸一点儿番茄酱。	
Shǔtiáo hěn dàn, yīnggāi zhàn yìdiǎnr **fānqiéjiàng**.	

(spicy, sauce)		
辣酱	làjiàng	hot sauce

(tomato, sauce)		
番茄酱	fānqiéjiàng	ketchup
芥末	jièmo	mustard
香油	xiāngyóu	sesame oil

酱油	jiàngyóu	soya sauce
(strawberry, sauce)		
草莓酱	cǎoméijiàng	strawberry jam
(sweet, sour, sauce)		
甜醋酱	tiáncùjiàng	sweet and sour sauce
醋	cù	vinegar

烤 （鸭）	kǎo （yā）	to roast （duck）
煮 （鸡蛋）	zhǔ （jīdàn）	to boil （eggs）
涮 （羊肉）	shuàn （yángròu）	to instant boil （mutton）
炸 （薯条）	zhá （shǔtiáo）	to fry （french fries）
煎 （鸡蛋）	jiān （jīdàn）	to pan （eggs）
炒 （饭）	chǎo （fàn）	to sauté （rice）
蒸 （饺子）	zhēng （jiǎozi）	to steam （dumplings）
烧 （茄子）	shāo （qiézi）	to stew （eggplant）

糖	táng	candy
(mouth, fragrant, candy)		
口香糖	kǒuxiāngtáng	chewing gum
(English)		
巧克力	qiǎokèlì	chocolate
(stick, stick, candy)		
棒棒糖	bàngbàngtáng	lollipop
(Enlish, bean)		
MM 豆	MM dòu	M&Ms

(English)		
麦利素	màilìsù	skittles
糖葫芦	tánghúlu	sugar-coated haws on a stick, Chinese snack

(little, eat)		
小吃	xiǎochī	snacks
(flat round cake, dry)		
饼干	bǐnggān	biscuits, cookies
(English)		
趣多多	Qùduōduō	Chips Ahoy
(English)		
奥里奥	Àolǐào	Oreos
(Enlish)		
乐之	Lèzhī	Ritz crackers
(convenient, noodles)		
方便面	fāngbiànmiàn	instant noodles
(explode, corn, flower)		
爆米花	bàomǐhuā	popcorn
(potato, piece)		
薯片	shǔpiàn	potato chips
(English)		
品客	Pǐnkè	Pringles
(English)		
乐事	Lèshì	Lay's

(*English*)		
麦当劳	Màidāngláo	McDonald's
(apple/pineapple, *English*)		
苹果/**菠萝派**	píngguǒ/bōluópài	apple/pineapple pie
巨无霸	jùwúbà	Big Mac
(*English*)		
吉士汉堡包	jíshì hànbǎobāo	Cheeseburger
(McDonald's, happy, chicken)		
麦乐鸡	màilèjī	Chicken nuggets
(double, level, *English*)		
双层吉士汉堡包	shuāngcéng jíshì hànbǎobāo	Double-cheeseburger
(surpass, value, set, meal)		
超值套餐	chāozhí tàocān	extra-value meal
(McDonald's, fragrant, fish)		
麦香鱼	màixiāngyú	Fish sandwich
(potato, strip)		
薯条	shǔtiáo	French fries
(*English*)		
汉堡包	hànbǎobāo	Hamburger
(happy, playground, meal)		
开心**乐园**餐	kāixīn lèyuán cān	Kid's Meal
(McDonald's, spicy, chicken, leg, hamburger)		
麦辣鸡腿汉堡	Màilàjītuǐ hànbǎo	Spicy chicken sandwich
(*English*)		
新地	Xīndì	Sundae

Beverages

饮　料

(soft, beverages)		
软饮料	**ruǎnyǐnliào**	**soft drinks**
(English)		
可口可乐	kěkǒu kělè	Coke
健怡可乐	jiànyí kělè	Diet Coke
(English)		
芬达	fēndá	Fanta
(mineral, spring, water)		
矿泉水	kuàngquánshuǐ	mineral water
(hundred, things, can, laugh)		
百事可乐	bǎishì kělè	Pepsi
(7, happy)		
七喜	qīxǐ	7-up
(snow, green)		
雪碧	xuěbì	Sprite
(gas, water)		
汽水	qìshuǐ	soda

(cow, milk)		
牛奶	niúnǎi	milk
奶昔	nǎixī	milk shake

(strip, fat, milk)		
脱脂牛奶	tuōzhī niúnǎi	skim milk
(coconut, juice)		
椰汁	yēzhī	coconut juice
(apple, juice)		
苹果汁	píngguǒzhī	apple juice
(grape, juice)		
葡萄汁	pútáozhī	grape juice
(orange, juice)		
橙汁	chéngzhī	orange juice
(pineapple, juice)		
菠萝汁	bōluózhī	pineapple juice
(tomato, juice)		
番茄汁	fānqiézhī	tomato juice

(ice, green, tea)		
冰绿茶	bīng lǜchá	green tea (iced)
(ice, tea)		
冰茶	bīngchá	iced-tea
(ice, red, tea)		
冰红茶	bīng hóngchá	red tea (iced)

(foam, coffee)		
泡沫咖啡	pàomò kāfēi	cappuccino
(coffee)		
咖啡	kāfēi	coffee
(strong, condensed, coffee)		
浓缩咖啡	nóngsuō kāfēi	espresso

(hot, *English*)		
热巧克力	rè qiǎokèlì	hot chocolate
(fast, melt, coffee)		
速溶咖啡	sùróng kāfēi	instant coffee

酒	jiǔ	alcohol

啤酒	píjiǔ	beer
(*English*)		
贝克	Bèikè	Beck's
(*English*)		
百威	Bǎiwēi	Budweiser
(*English*)		
嘉士伯	Jiāshìbó	Carlsberg
(*English*)		
科罗娜	Kēluónà	Corona
(*English*, beer)		
扎啤	zhāpí	draught beer
(happy, strength)		
喜力	Xǐlì	Heineken
(blue, ribbon)		
蓝带	Lándài	Pabst Blue Ribbon
(city in China)		
青岛	Qīngdǎo	Tsingdao
(old name of Beijing)		
燕京	Yānjīng	Yanjing

(meal, after, sweet, alcohol)		
餐后甜酒	cān hòu tiánjiǔ	liquors
(English, English)		
干邑白兰地	Gānyì báilándì	Cognac
(English)		
人头马	Réntóumǎ	Remy Martin

(English, alcohol)		
金酒	Jīnjiǔ	Gin
(English, English)		
必发达金	Bìfādájīn	Beefeater's
(English, English)		
哥顿金	Gēdùnjīn	Gordon's
(English, English)		
格兰金	Gélánjīn	Grant's

(coffee, sweet, alcohol)		
咖啡甜酒	kāfēi tiánjiǔ	Kahlua

(English, alcohol)		
朗姆酒	Lǎngmǔjiǔ	Rum
(English)		
白家得	Báijiādé	Bacardi
(English, boat, captain)		
摩根船长	Mógēn Chuánzhǎng	Captain Morgan's

(*English*)		
特基拉	Tèjīlā	Tequilla
(*English*)		
银快活	Yínkuàihuo	Jose cuervo

(*English*)		
伏特加	fútèjiā	Vodka
(Sweden, vodka)		
瑞典伏特加	Ruìdiǎn fútèjiā	Absolut
(Finland, vodka)		
芬兰伏特加	Fēnlán fútèjiā	Finlandia
皇冠	Huángguān	Smirnoff
(Russian, red, brand)		
苏联红牌	Sūlián Hóngpái	Stolichnaya

(*English*)		
威士忌	wēishìjì	Whiskey
(Canada, club)		
加拿大俱乐部	Jiānádà Jùlèbù	Canadian Club
(*English*, 12, years)		
芝华士 12 年	Zhīhuáshì shí'èr nián	Chivas Regal 12 years
(*English*)		
格兰威	Gélánwēi	Grant's
(*English*)		
占边	Zhànbiān	Jim Beam

(English)		
杰克·丹尼	Jiékè Dānní	Jack Daniels
(English)		
珍宝	Zhēnbǎo	J&B
(English)		
占美臣	Zhànměichén	Jameson
(red, square)		
红方	Hóngfāng	Johnny Walker (Red)
(black, square)		
黑方	Hēifāng	Johnny Walker (Black)

(chicken, tail, alcohol)		
鸡尾酒	jīwěijiǔ	cocktail
(black, Russia)		
黑色俄罗斯	Hēisè Éluósī	Black Russian
(bloody, English)		
血玛丽	Xiě Mǎlì	Bloody Mary
(English)		
黛克瑞	Dàikèruì	Daiquiri
(English)		
金汤力	Jīntānglì	Gin and Tonic
青草蜢	Qīngcǎoměng	Grasshopper
(long, island, ice, tea)		
长岛冰茶	Chángdǎo Bīngchá	Long Island Ice Tea

(*English*)		
曼哈顿	Mànhādùn	Manhattan
(*English*)		
玛格丽特	Mǎgélìtè	Margarita
(*English*)		
辛辣马丁尼	Xīnlà Mǎdīngní	Martini Dry
椰林风光	Yēlín Fēngguāng	Pina Colada
红粉佳人	Hǒngfěn Jiārén	Pink lady
丝刀	Sīdāo	Screwdriver
(day, rise, dragon, *English*)		
日升龙舌兰	Rìshēng Lóngshélán	Tequila sunrise
(*English*, sour)		
威士忌酸	Wēishìjìsuān	Whiskey sour

(*English*, alcohol)		
香槟酒	xiāngbīnjiǔ	champagne
(grapes, alcohol)		
葡萄酒	pútáojiǔ	wine
二锅头	èrguōtóu	Chinese alcohol

(this, alcohol, very, strong) 这酒很冲/烈。	This alcohol is very strong.
Zhè jiǔ hěn chòng /liè.	

(this, alcohol, proof, not, high) 这酒度数不高。	This alcohol is not strong.
Zhè jiǔ dùshù bù gāo.	

(this, whisky, 40, degree)	This whiskey is 80 proof.
这威士忌40度。	
Zhè wēishìjì sìshí dù.	

(waitress, I, want, one, cup, beer)	Waitress, I'd like a cup of beer.
小姐，我要一杯扎啤。	
Xiǎojiě, wǒ yào yì bēi zhāpí.	

(waiter, I, want, one, can, cola)	Waiter, I'd like a can of cola.
服务员，我要一罐儿可乐。	
Fúwùyuán, wǒ yào yí guànr kělè.	

(mister, I, want, one, can, 7-up)	Waiter, I'd like a can of 7-Up.
先生，我要一听七喜。	
Xiānsheng, wǒ yào yì tīng qīxǐ.	

(I, want, one, small/large, cup, orange, juice)	I would like one small/large glass of OJ.
我要一小/大杯橙汁。	
Wǒ yào yī xiǎo /dà bēi chéngzhī.	

(I, want, ice-cold, beer)	I'd like an ice-cold beer.
我要冰镇啤酒。	
Wǒ yào bīngzhèn píjiǔ.	

| (Sprite, I, want, cold)

雪碧，我要凉的。

Xuěbì, wǒ yào liáng de. | I want cold Sprite. |

| (please, you, add, a little, ice cube)

请你加一点儿冰块儿。

Qǐng nǐ jiā yìdiǎnr bīngkuàir. | Please add some ice cubes. |

| (miss, give, tea, inside, add, a little, hot, water)

小姐，给茶里加一点儿热水。

Xiǎojiě, gěi chá li jiā yìdiǎnr rè shuǐ. | Miss, please add some water to my tea. |

| (mister, please, you, add, a little, sugar)

先生，请你加一点儿糖。

Xiānsheng, qǐng nǐ jiā yìdiǎnr táng. | Sir, please bring more sugar. |

| (once, drunk, release, thousand, worry)

一醉解千愁。

Yí zuì jiě qiān chóu. | Once you are drunk, all your worries go away. |

| (alcohol, after, spit out, true, words)

酒后吐真言。

Jiǔ hòu tǔ zhēn yán. | A drunk man's words are a sober man's thoughts. |

(contend, alcohol)		
拼酒	pīn jiǔ	compare who can drink most
(with, me, compare who can drink most, you, still, weak, a little)	When compared with me, your drinking level is weak.	
跟我拼酒，你还嫩点儿。		
Gēn wǒ pīn jiǔ, nǐ hái nèn diǎnr.		

(awake, alcohol)		
灌醉	guàn zuì	to be forced to drink
(I, dont't, like, by, person, forced to drink)	I dont't like to be forced to drink.	
我不喜欢被人灌醉。		
Wǒ bù xǐhuan bèi rén guàn zuì.		

(awake, alcohol)		
醒酒	xǐng jiǔ	to sober up
(I, 8 o'clock, will, with, boss, meet, I, must, sober up)	I am going to meet my boss at 8. I've gotta sober up!	
我八点要跟老板见面，我得醒醒酒。		
Wǒ bā diǎn yào gēn lǎobǎn jiànmiàn, wǒ děi xǐngxing jiǔ.		

(alcohol, strength)		
酒劲儿	jiǔjìnr	affect of alcohol
(damn it, my, affect of alcohol, come up; you, step-up, drive, vehicle)	Shit! The alcohol has made me faded. You should drive.	
糟了，我的酒劲儿上来了。你来开车。		
Zāo le, wǒ de jiǔjìnr shànglai le. Nǐ lái kāichē.		

| (feeling, not intimate, sip; feeling, deep, chug) | If you are not close with the person with whom you are drinking, sip (your drink). If you are comfortable, chug. |
| 感情浅, 添一添; 感情深, 一口闷。 | |

Gǎnqíng qiǎn, tiǎn yì tiǎn; gǎnqíng shēn, yì kǒu mēn.

This phrase is said when making a toast as a way to cajole, almost force the other party to chug. How can you tell the person who is making a toast to you that the relationship between you is not profound?

Restaurant

餐 馆

(meal, hall)		
餐厅	cāntīng	restaurant
(food, hall)		
食堂	shítáng	cafeteria
(alcohol, *English*)		
酒吧	jiǔbā	bar

(food, tool)		
餐具	cānjù	utensils
碗	wǎn	bowl
椅子	yǐzi	chair
筷子	kuàizi	chopsticks
(Westerner, not, able, use, chopstick) 西方人不会使筷子。 Xīfāngrén bú huì shǐ kuàizi.		Westerners can't use chopsticks.
杯子	bēizi	cup
(meal, table)		
餐桌	cānzhuō	dining table
(please, set, properly, table) 请摆好餐桌。 Qǐng bǎi hǎo cānzhuō.		Please set the table.

叉子	chāzi	fork
刀子	dāozi	knife
(meal, towel, paper)		
餐巾纸	cānjīnzhǐ	napkins
盘子	pánzi	plate
碟子	diézi	small plate; saucer
勺子	sháozi	spoon
(suck, pipe)		
吸管	xīguǎn	straw
(table, cloth)		
餐布	cānbù	table cloth
(please, IO, tablecloth, lay, good) 请把餐布铺好。	Please put the tablecloth on the table.	
Qǐng bǎ cānbù pū hǎo.		
(tea, cup)		
茶杯	chábēi	tea cup
(tea, pot)		
茶壶	cháhú	tea pot
(waitress, can, give, teapot, continue, a little, water, QW) 小姐，可以给茶壶续点儿水吗？	Waitress, please refill our teapot.	
Xiǎojiě, kěyǐ gěi cháhú xù diǎnr shuǐ ma?		
(tooth, piece of bamboo)		
牙签	yáqiān	toothpick

(my, teeth, gap, inside, have, something, please, give, me, one, MW, toothpick)	I have food in between my teeth. Please pass me a toothpick.
我牙缝里有东西，请给我一根牙签儿。	
Wǒ yá fèng li yǒu dōngxi, qǐng gěi wǒ yì gēn yáqiānr.	

(morning, meal)		
早饭/餐	zǎofàn/cān	breakfast
(noon, meal)		
午饭/餐	wǔfàn/cān	lunch
(evening, meal)		
晚饭/餐	wǎnfàn/cān	dinner

(China, food)		
中餐	zhōngcān	Chinese food
(fast, food)		
快餐	kuàicān	fast food
(west, food)		
西餐	xīcān	Western food

(dish, list)		
菜单	càidān	menu
(miss, look, a little, your, menu)	Waitress, can I have a look at your menu?	
小姐，看一下你们的菜单。		
Xiǎojiě, kàn yíxià nǐmen de càidān.		

凉菜	liángcài	cold dishes
小葱拌豆腐	xiǎocōng bàn dòufu	bean curd with shallots
拍黄瓜	pāi huánggua	cucumbers in sauce
五香花生米	wǔxiāng huāshēngmǐ	five spices boiled peanuts
糖拌西红柿	táng bàn xīhóngshì	tomatoes with sugar

热菜	rècài	hot dishes
韭菜炒鸡蛋	jiǔcài chǎo jīdàn	fried Chinese chives and eggs
鸡蛋西红柿	jīdàn xīhóngshì	fried eggs and tomatoes
地三鲜	dìsānxiān	fried sliced potatoes, pepper and eggplant
蒜茸生菜	suànróng shēngcài	romaine lettuce with minced garlic
醋熘土豆丝	cù liū tǔdòu sī	shredded potatoes with vinegar
烧茄子	shāo qiézi	stewed eggplant
清炒豆苗	qīngchǎo dòumiáo	stir-fried bean sprouts
家常豆腐	jiācháng dòufu	homely tofu
麻婆豆腐	mápó dòufu	pock-marked grandma's tofu (spicy)
红烧豆腐	hóngshāo dòufu	stewed tofu

腰果鸡丁	yāoguǒ jīdīng	diced chicken with cashewnuts
宫宝鸡丁	gōngbǎo jīdīng	diced chicken with peanuts (spicy)

鱼香肉丝	yúxiāng ròusī	fish flavored shredded pork
京酱肉丝	jīngjiàng ròusī	shredded pork in Beijing sauce
古老肉	gǔlǎoròu	sweet and sour pork

糖醋里脊	tángcù lǐjǐ	sweet and sour pork tenderloin
红烧排骨	hóngshāo páigǔ	stewed spareribs

葱爆羊肉	cōng bào yángròu	quick fried mutton with onion
孜然羊肉	zīrán yángròu	strange flavored mutton

咖喱牛肉	gālí niúròu	beef curry
铁板牛肉	tiěbǎn niúròu	beef served on a sizzling iron plate
水煮牛肉	shuǐ zhǔ niúròu	boiled beef with hot peppers
蚝油牛肉	háoyóu niúròu	fried beef in oyster sauce

(main, food)		
主食	zhǔshí	staple food (eaten after entree)
饺子	jiǎozi	Chinese dumplings
馒头	mántou	Chinese steamed bread
包子	bāozi	Chinese steamed stuffed bun (usually pork)
(fried, noodles)		
炒面	chǎomiàn	fried noodles
炸酱面	zhájiàngmiàn	fried noodles served with bean sauce
鸡蛋炒饭	jīdàn chǎo fàn	fried rice with egg
牛肉炒饭	niúròu chǎo fàn	fried rice with minced beef
牛肉面	niúròumiàn	noodles served with beef
米饭	mǐfàn	rice
扬州炒饭	Yángzhōu chǎo fàn	Yangzhou style fried rice
粥	zhōu	porridge (very popular in China)

汤	tāng	soup
酸辣汤	suānlàtāng	hot and sour soup
榨菜肉丝汤	zhàcài ròusītāng	hot pickled mustard and shredded meat soup
三鲜汤	sānxiāntāng	three flavored soup
西红柿鸡蛋汤	xīhóngshì jīdàn tāng	tomato and egg soup

(sweet, refreshments)		
甜点	tiándiǎn	desserts
(ice, *English*)		
冰淇淋	bīngqílín	ice cream
(ice, stick)		
冰棍儿	bīnggùnr	popsicle
(*English*)		
布丁	bùdīng	pudding
(this, MW, dish, very, _____)		
这道菜很_____.	Zhè dào cài hěn _____.	This dish is very _____.
(difficult, eat)		
难吃	nán chī	bad-tasting
苦	kǔ	bitter
淡	dàn	bland
脆	cuì	crispy
(good, eat)		
好吃	hǎo chī	delectable
烫	tàng	hot (temperature)

咸	xián	salty
酸	suān	sour
辣	là	spicy
甜	tián	sweet

香	xiāng	aromatic, fragrant
(this, MW, dish, smell, very, aromatic) **这道菜闻起来很香。** Zhè dào cài wén qǐlai hěn xiāng.		This dish smells great!

地道	dìdao	authentic
(Rocky's, dumplings, make, very, authentic, like, Chinese, make, same) Rocky 的**饺子**包得**很地道,像**中国人 包得一样。 Rocky de jiǎozi bāo de hěn dìdao, xiàng Zhōngguórén bāo de yíyàng.		Rocky's dumplings are very authentic, just like a Chinese makes.

煳	hú	burnt
(this, roast duck, roast, time, too, long, all, burn, PT, no, way, eat) 这烤鸭烤的**时间太长了,**都煳了。**没 法儿吃。** Zhè kǎoyā kǎo de shíjiān tài cháng le, dōu hú le. Méifǎr chī.		This duck has been roasted so long that it is burnt. It is inedible!

(fire, time)		
火候	huǒhou	duration and degree of cooking

(miss, this, MW, dish, cook, still, not, reach, duration and degree of cooking; can, again, boil, a little while, QW)	Waitress, this dish is not fully cooked. Can you cook it a bit longer?
小姐，这道菜做得**还不到**火候。**能再煮一会儿吗**？	
Xiǎojiě, zhè dào cài zuò de hái bú dào huǒhou. Néng zài zhǔ yíhuìr ma?	

(down, rice)		
下饭	xiàfàn	go well with rice
(red, stew, sparerib, very, go well with rice)	Stewed spareribs go really well with rice.	
红烧排骨很**下饭**。		
Hóngshāo páigǔ hěn xiàfàn.		

绝	jué	superb
(Nima, make, gōngbǎo jīdīng, very, superb)	Nima makes a great *gongbao jiding*.	
Nima 做宫宝鸡丁很**绝**。		
Nima zuò gōngbǎo jīdīng hěn jué.		

嫩/老	nèn/lǎo	tender/tough
(this, meat, very, tender/old)	This meat is tender/tough.	
这肉太**嫩/老**了。		
Zhè ròu tài nèn/lǎo le.		

(Chinese food, you, eat, accustomed, QW)	Are you accustomed to eating Chinese food?
Q) 中餐你吃得**惯**吗？	
Zhōngcān nǐ chī de guàn ma?	

(I, still, not, accustomed)	I am still not accustomed.
A) 我还没习惯呢。	
Wǒ hái méi xíguàn ne.	

(this, MW, table, very, dirty)	This table is dirty.
A) 这张桌子很脏。	
Zhè zhāng zhuōzi hěn zāng.	
(no problem, not clean, not clean, eat, PT, no, sickness)	No problem. If it's not clean, it doesn't matter. You won't get sick.
B) 没事儿，不干不净，吃了没病。	
Méishìr, bù gān bú jìng, chīle méi bìng.	
Used as a joke to comfort someone when meeting unsanitary conditions when eating.	

(you, want, eat, what)	What do you feel like eating?
Q) 你想吃什么？	
Nǐ xiǎng chī shénme?	
(give, what, eat, what)	I'll eat whatever I can get my hands on.
A) 给什么，吃什么。	
Gěi shénme, chī shénme.	
Used as a joke to express that you are not a picky eater. A polite way of allowing the other person decide what you eat.	

Two foreigners walk into a restaurant in Beijing. Let's listen . . .

A = Waitress

B = Foreigner

C = Foreigner

(you, order, some, what) A) 你们点点儿**什么**？	What would you like to eat? (very informal)
Nǐmen diǎn diǎnr shénme?	

(we, still, not, think, good, able, wait, a while, QW) B) 我们**还没**有**想好**，**能**等一**会儿**吗？	We have not yet decided. Please give us a moment.
Wǒmen hái méiyǒu xiǎng hǎo, néng děng yíhuìr ma?	

(miss, order, dish; you, here, have, what, speciality; please, you, give, us, recommend, a little) C) 小姐，点菜！**你们**这儿**有**什么**特色菜**？请你给我们**推荐**一下。	Waitress, we'd like to order. What are your special dishes? Could you please recommend one?
Xiǎojiě, diǎn cài! Nǐmen zhèr yǒu shénme tèsècài? Qǐng nǐ gěi wǒmen tuījiàn yíxià.	

(you, like, what, type of food; sweet, spicy, or...) A) 你们**喜欢**什么**口味儿**？甜的，**辣的**，还是……	What type of food do you like? Sweet, spicy, or...
Nǐmen xǐhuan shénme kǒuwèir? Tián de, là de, háishi…	

(all, OK; for, us, serve, a few, MW, best, dish) B) 都**可以**。给**我们**上几个**最好**的**菜**吧。	We eat everything. Give us your best dishes.
Dōu kěyǐ. Gěi wǒmen shàng jǐ ge zuì hǎo de cài ba.	

(no problem; then, just, come, cashew chicken, stir-fried bean sprouts) **A)** 没问题。那就来腰果鸡丁，清炒豆苗吧。	No problem. That willl have to be our cashew chicken and stir-fried bean sprouts.
Méi wèntí. Nà jiù lái yāoguǒ jīdīng, qīngchǎo dòumiáo ba.	

(you, drink, a little, what) **A)** 你们喝点儿什么？	What would you like to drink?
Nǐmen hē diǎnr shénme?	

(I, want, one, bottle, ice-cold, beer) **B)** 我要一瓶冰镇啤酒。	I would like a bottle of cold beer.
Wǒ yào yì píng bīngzhèn píjiǔ.	

(I, want, one, can, Coke; you, have, ice cubes, QW) **C)** 我来一听可乐。你们有冰块儿吗？	I would like a can of Coke. Do you have ice cubes?
Wǒ lái yì tīng kělè. Nǐmen yǒu bīngkuàir ma?	

(have; staple food, order, what) **A)** 有。主食要什么？	Yes. What would you like as your staple food?
Yǒu. Zhǔshí yào shénme?	

(two, bowl, rice; we, still, have, thing, please, fast, a little) **C)** 两碗米饭。我们还有事儿，请快一点儿。	Two bowls of rice. We have something to do (we're in a rush). Please hurry up.
Liǎng wǎn mǐfàn. Wǒmen hái yǒu shìr, qǐng kuài yìdiǎnr.	

(OK, please, a little, wait) **A)** 好，请稍等。	Ok, please wait a moment.
Hǎo, qǐng shāoděng.	

Waitress quickly gives the two gentlemen their beverages. Ten minutes later ……

(miss, you, here, serve dishes, why, so, slow) B) 小姐，你们这儿上菜怎么这么慢？	Waitress, why is it taking you so long to serve our food?
Xiǎojiě, nǐmen zhèr shàng cài zěnme zhème màn?	
(sorry, right away, come) A) 对不起，马上就来。	I'm sorry, coming right up.
Duìbuqǐ, mǎshàng jiù lái.	

Two minutes later, ...

(mister, cashew chicken, stir-fried bean sprouts, arrive) A) 先生，腰果鸡丁、清炒豆苗来了。	Sir, your cashew chicken and stir-fried bean sprouts.
Xiānsheng, yāoguǒ jīdīng、qīngchǎo dòumiáo lái le.	
(now, serve, rice) C) 现在上米饭吧。	Please serve the rice now.
Xiànzài shàng mǐfàn ba.	

Ten minutes later, ...

(miss, please, you, again, come, two, bowl, rice; help, us, grab, some, napkin) C) 小姐，请你再来两碗米饭。帮我们拿一些餐巾纸。	Waitress, could you please bring us two more bowls of rice. Please grab us a few napkins.
Xiǎojiě, qǐng nǐ zài lái liǎng wǎn mǐfàn. Bāng wǒmen ná yìxiē cānjīnzhǐ.	
(OK) A) 好的。	Ok. Sure.
Hǎo de.	

Twenty minutes later, . . .

(miss, settle, account) **B)** 小姐，结账。	Waitress, check please.
Xiǎojiě, jiézhàng.	
(altogether, 32, MW, money; you, need, receipt, QW) **A)** 一共三十二块钱。你们**需要**发票**吗**？	Altogether 32 *yuan*. Do you need a receipt?
Yígòng sānshí'èr kuài qián. Nǐmen xūyào fāpiào ma?	
(no need; you, able, discount, QW) **C)** 不用了。**你们能打折吗**？	No, that is not necessary. Can you give us a little discount?
Búyòng le. Nǐmen néng dǎzhé ma?	
(today, not, able; next time) **A)** 今天**不可以**。**下次吧**。	Not today. Next time.
Jīntiān bù kěyǐ. Xià cì ba.	
(miss, give, us, bring, several, MW, box, and, plastic bag, OK, QW; we, want, pack-up) **B)** 小姐，给我们拿几个饭盒和塑料袋好吗？**我们要打包**。	Waitress, can you please bring us some take-out containers and a plastic bag? We are going to make a doggy bag.
Xiǎojiě, gěi wǒmen ná jǐ ge fànhé hé sùliàodài hǎo ma? Wǒmen yào dǎbāo.	

Waitress brings them bag and containers.

(thank you; good bye) **B)** 谢谢你了。**再见**。	Thank you. Bye-bye.
Xièxie nǐ le. Zàijiàn.	

(slow, go, welcome, next time, honor us with your presence)	Take it easy. Please come again.
A) 慢走，欢迎**下次**光临。	
Màn zǒu, huānyíng xià cì guānglín.	

Other useful sentences：

(miss, our, dish, cold, able, give, us, heat, a little, QW)	Waitress, our food is cold. Can you please heat it up for us?
小姐，**我们**的菜凉了，能给我们热一下吗？	
Xiǎojiě, wǒmen de cài liáng le, néng gěi wǒmen rè yíxià ma?	

(miss, day lily, already, cold, PT, fast, a little)	Waitress, our day lily is already cold. Please hurry up!
小姐，**黄花菜**都凉了，快一点儿！	
Xiǎojiě, huánghuācài dōu liáng le, kuài yìdiǎnr!	

Day lily is a vegetable that is served cold. Similar to the English joke, "Hurry up, the salad is getting cold". *Huánghuācài dōu liáng le* should be used as a joke or only when you are really mad as it has the potential to annoy the waitress.

(miss, we, lack, one, MW, fork)	Waitress, we're short of a fork.
小姐，**我们**少一把叉子。	
Xiǎojiě, wǒmen shǎo yì bǎ chāzi.	

(my, tea cup, crack)	My, tea cup is cracked.
我的茶杯破了。	
Wǒ de chábēi pò le.	

(this, dish, portion, very/not, sufficient)	This portion is very big/small.
这菜的分量很/不足。	
Zhè cài de fènliàng hěn/bù zú.	

(miss, our, dish, not, enough, we, want, again, order, few, MW, dishes)	Waitress, our food is not enough. We would like to order some more.
小姐，我们的菜不够，我们想再点几个菜。	
Xiǎojiě, wǒmen de cài bú gòu, wǒmen xiǎng zài diǎn jǐ ge cài.	

(miss, our, dish, inside, has, one, MW, hair, able, explain, a little, QW)	Waitress, there is a hair in our food. Can you please explain why?
小姐，我们菜里有一根头发，能解释一下吗？	
Xiǎojiě, wǒmen cài li yǒu yì gēn tóufa, néng jiěshi yíxià ma?	

(you, are, at, here, eat, or, are, take out)	Are you going to eat in or take out?
A）你们是在这儿吃，还是带走？	
Nǐmen shì zài zhèr chī, háishi dàizǒu?	
(we, take out)	We are going to take out.
B）我们带走。	
Wǒmen dàizǒu.	

(miss, you, deliver, food, QW)	Waitress, do you have delivery service?
A）小姐，你们送餐吗？	
Xiǎojiě, nǐmen sòng cān ma?	

(please, ask, you [polite], live, where) B) 请问您住哪儿? Qǐngwèn nín zhù nǎr?	Where do you live?
(I, at, Chang'an Avenue, 15, number) A) 我在长安街 15 号。 Wǒ zài Cháng'ān Jiē shíwǔ hào.	I live on 15 Chang'an Avenue.
(no, problem; you [polite], want, what) B) 没问题。您要什么? Méi wèntí. Nín yào shénme?	No problem. What can I get for you?
(I, want, Gōngbǎo jīdīng, not, want, too, spicy) A) 我要宫宝鸡丁,不要太辣。 Wǒ yào gōngbǎo jīdīng, búyào tài là.	I want *gongbao jiding*, but not too spicy.
(OK; right away, for, you [polite], deliver, over) B) 好。马上给您送过去。 Hǎo. Mǎshàng gěi nín sòng guòqu.	Ok. We'll deliver that to you right away.

Eating in China

Chinese are famous for paying special attention to preparing and eating food. The earliest Chinese restaurant can be traced back over 2, 000 years and the first Chinese cookbook was written over 2, 500 years ago.

The way that Chinese prepare foods also tells us a lot about the country's desire to conserve energy. For instance, ingredients are cut before they are cooked so that they can cook faster. (That also explains why eating can be done without knives.) Chinese woks have a curved shape so a small amount of heat covers a large area. Bamboo steamers, used in cooking traditional *baozi*, can be stacked up so that one source of heat can be maximized.

Chinese cuisine can be broken down into a few regional styles. In the north, dishes are prepared with a lot of onions and garlic and wheat is preferred over rice. One of China's most famous dishes calls the north its home, Beijing Roast Duck, which is served with soft tortilla-like shells and plum sauce. The use of Hot Pots is very popular in China and the best mutton comes from Inner Mongolia's Jining City. The city of Harbin is famous for its fish, caviar, and pickled cucumbers. Due to historical and geographical reasons, Russian-style dishes are also quite popular.

The coastal city of Shanghai is famous for its seafood and *xiao long bao* or dim sum. Many light snacks are also available.

The Chinese culinary capital is Canton, or Guangzhou. Canton is world renowned for its abundant amount of delicately flavored seafood. In fact, persons from this region open most Chinese restaurants outside of the mainland.

Western China's climate has made the growing season short and food is very carefully preserved. Sichuan cuisine is very spicy and the most famous dish is *mapo doufu* or mama's tofu. Make sure that you have a beverage close by when eating!

Foods from Hunan Province are by far the spiciest in all of China. The most famous Hunan dish is *duojiao yutou*, fish head with sliced hot peppers.

Eating is one of the most popular social activities in China. It is the custom to order more than what one can possibly eat, so don't be surprised if you end up with a lot of food left. Chinese never go Dutch. Usually the person who suggests that they go out to eat will pay, unless they are friends in which case there is an understanding 'I paid last time so it is your turn now. '

Other customs include:

➤ The main guest always sits farthest from the main door. He/she also sits facing this door so that when new people enter the room, he/she is the first person that is seen.

➤ Tea should be poured to the oldest person or most important person (boss, official, etc.) first.

➤ When being poured beverages, tapping your index and middle finger together on the table at least two times will represent "thank you". The reason for this custom dates back to Emperor Qian Long of the Qing Dynasty(1644-1911). One day, Qian Long decided to get away from "Emperor" lifestyle so he traveled to southern

China. He did not want his identity to be revealed to the southerners and demanded his servants to treat him as an equal, meaning that they were not allowed to kneel down to him during their excursion, standard procedure for that epoch. In the south, the group met new friends and was invited to eat dinner with them. At the table, Qian Long poured one of his servants a cup of tea. Since the servant was not allowed to kneel down to the Emperor as it would show his subordination, he tapped his fingers on the table as a way of showing respect. Since then, this method has been used to show respect and thanks to a person for pouring beverages.

➤ The head of the fish should face the oldest person to show respect.

➤ Persons should not eat until the main guest starts to eat.

Beijing Roast Duck
Roasting ducks can be traced back over 1, 500 years to the period of the Northern and Southern Dynasties (420-581 AD). It is also known that about 800 years later, the Mongolian Emperor of the Yuan Dynasty ate roast duck as a banquet delicacy.

Today, prior to being cooked, the duck is shown to the customers. Before being served the main course, other cold and hot duck dishes are eaten. Tender on the inside and crisp on the outside, Beijing Roast Duck is served in thin slices which are rolled up in a thin pancake and eaten with cucumbers, scallions, and a sweet plum sauce. Following the main course, the skeleton of the duck is placed into broth to make duck soup.

Vehicles

交通工具

(fly, machine)		
飞机	fēijī	airplane
(save, nurse, vehicle)		
救护车	jiùhùchē	ambulance
(self, move, vehicle)		
自行车	zìxíngchē	bicycle
船	chuán	boat
(public, steam, vehicle)		
公共汽车	gōnggòng qìchē	bus
(steam, vehicle)		
汽车	qìchē	car
(open, car roof, car)		
敞篷车	chǎngpéngchē	convertible
(lift, heavy, machine)		
起重机	qǐzhòngjī	crane
(save, fire, vehicle)		
救火车	jiùhuǒchē	fire truck
(direct, rise, machine)		
直升机	zhíshēngjī	helicopter

(*English*, vehicle)		
吉普车	jípǔchē	jeep
(luxurious, sedan, vehicle)		
豪华轿车	háohuá jiàochē	limousine
(bread, taxi)		
面的	miàndī	small yellow van (a kind of cheap taxi in China)
(police, vehicle)		
警车	jǐngchē	police car
(three, wheel, vehicle)		
三轮车	sānlúnchē	tricycle
(dive, water, boat)		
潜水艇	qiánshuǐtǐng	submarine
(ground, iron)		
地铁	dìtiě	subway
(rent, vehicle)		
出租车	chūzūchē	taxi
(*English*)		
坦克	tǎnkè	tank
(clean, obstruct, vehicle)		
清障车	qīngzhàngchē	tow truck
(drag, pull, machine)		
拖拉机	tuōlājī	tractor
(fire, vehicle)		
火车	huǒchē	train
(*English*, vehicle)		
卡车	kǎchē	truck

	奥迪	Àodí	Audi
	宝马	Bǎomǎ	BMW
	别克	Biékè	Buick
	卡迪拉克	Kǎdílākè	Cadillac
	克莱斯勒	Kèláisīlè	Chrysler
	大宇	Dàyǔ	Daewoo
	法拉利	Fǎlālì	Ferrari
	福特	Fútè	Ford
	本田	Běntián	Honda
	现代	Xiàndài	Hyundai
	五十铃	Wǔshílíng	Isuzu
	铃志	Língzhì	Lexus
	林肯	Línkěn	Lincoln
	马自达	Mǎzìdá	Mazda
	奔驰	Bēnchí	Mercedes-Benz
	三菱	Sānlíng	Mitsubishi

	尼桑	Nísāng	Nissan
	欧宝	Ōubǎo	Opel
	标致	Biāozhì	Peugeot
	保时捷	Bǎoshíjié	Porsche
	红旗	Hóngqí	Red Flag（Chinese）
	雷诺	Léinuò	Renault
	劳斯莱斯	Láosīláisī	Rolls-Royce
	丰田	Fēngtián	Toyota
	夏利	Xiàlì	Xiali（Chinese）
	大众	Dàzhòng	Volkswagen
	沃尔沃	Wò'ěrwò	Volvo

（you, can, drive, QW）	Can you drive?
Q) 你会开车吗？	
Nǐ huì kāichē ma?	
（I, 16, year, already, can）	I've been driving since I was 16.
A) 我十六岁就会了。	
Wǒ shíliù suì jiù huì le.	

(I, can't, drive, car, I, only, can, ride, bicycle)	I can't drive a car. I can only ride a bike.
A）我不会开车，我只会骑自行车。	
Wǒ bú huì kāichē, wǒ zhǐ huì qí zìxíngchē.	

(I, like, drive, car, go for a spin)	I like joy riding, going for a spin.
我喜欢开车兜风。	
Wǒ xǐhuan kāichē dōufēng.	

Cabs and Directions

出租车与问路

东	dōng	east
北	běi	north
南	nán	south
西	xī	west
东北	dōngběi	northeast
西北	xīběi	northwest
东南	dōngnán	southeast
西南	xīnán	southwest

(bike, lane)		
自行车道	zìxíngchēdào	bike lane

(bump)		
撞	zhuàng	collide, accident
(several, MW, car, collide, PT, together, die, PT, three, MW, person) 几辆车撞在了一起，死了三个人。		There was an accident involving several cars, killing three.
Jǐ liàng chē zhuàng zàile yìqǐ, sǐle sān ge rén.		
(one, MW, big, truck, bump, PT, a, MW, ride, bike) 一辆大卡车撞了一个骑自行车的。		A truck hit a person riding a bike.
Yí liàng dà kǎchē zhuàngle yí ge qí zìxíngchē de.		

(ten, character, road, mouth)		
十字路口	shízì lùkǒu	four-way intersection

The shape of a 4-way intersection looks exactly like the Chinese character 十.

(high, speed, public, road)		
高速公路	gāosù gōnglù	highway

(left, vehicle, lane)		
左车道	zuǒchēdào	left lane

(pass, vehicle, lane)		
超车道	chāochēdào	passing lane

(person, move, lane)		
人行道	rénxíngdào	pedestrian lane

(refuse, load)		
拒载	jù zài	to refuse to take a passenger
(master, Wangfujing, go, QW) A) 师傅，王府井去吗？		Mister, can you take me to Wangfujing?
Shīfu, Wángfǔjǐng qù ma?		
(come on board) B) 上来吧。		Get in. Let's go.
Shànglai ba.		
(thank, you [polite], just now, take, PT, two, MW, vehicle, all, refuse, carry) A) 谢谢您，刚才打了两辆车，都拒载。		Thank you. I just tried to take two other cabs but they both refused.
Xièxie nín, gāngcái dǎle liǎng liàng chē, dōu jù zǎi.		

(right, vehicle, lane)		
右车道	yòuchēdào	right lane

丁字路口	dīngzì lùkǒu	T-intersection
The shape of a T-intersection looks exactly like the Chinese character 丁.		

(road, fee)		
路费	lùfèi	toll
(hand in, fee, station)		
交费站	jiāofèizhàn	toll gate

交通	jiāotōng	traffic

(traffic, accident)		
交通事故	jiāotōng shìgù	traffic accident
(here, often, appear, traffic, accidents)		There are a lot of accidents around here.
这里经常出交通事故。		
Zhèli jīngcháng chū jiāotōng shìgù.		

(clog/stuff, vehicles)		
堵/塞车	dǔ/sāi chē	traffic jam
(able, not, able, clog, cars)		Are we going to hit (heavy) traffic?
Q) 会不会堵车?		
Huì bu huì dǔ chě?		

(now, is, off, work, high, peak, definitely, traffic jam) **A)** 现在是下班高峰，肯定堵车。	It is rush hour, and traffic will definitely be heavy.	
Xiànzài shì xiàbān gāofēng, kěndìng dǔ chē.		

(traffic, smooth)		
交通**畅通**	jiāotōng chàngtōng	free-flowing traffic
(weekend, traffic, fairly, smooth) 周末**交通**比较**畅通**。	traffic is not too bad on the weekends.	
Zhōumò jiāotōng bǐjiào chàngtōng.		

(red, green, light)		
红绿灯	hónglǜdēng	traffic light
(pass, road, before, first, look, traffic light) 过马路前**先**看红绿灯。	Before crossing the street, you should check the traffic light.	
Guò mǎlù qián xiān kàn hónglǜdēng.		
(dash through, red light, very, dangerous) 闯红灯很危险。	It will be dangerous to run the red light.	
Chuǎng hóngdēng hěn wēixiǎn.		

(traffic, rules)		
交通规则	jiāotōng guīzé	traffic regulations
(you, if, not, follow, traffic regulation, will, be fined) 你要是不遵守交通规则，**会**被罚款。	If you do not follow traffic regulations, you will be fined.	
Nǐ yàoshi bù zūnshǒu jiāotōng guīzé, huì bèi fákuǎn.		

(master, arrive, airport, how much, money)	Sir, how much to go to the airport?
Q）师傅，到机场多少钱？	
Shīfu, dào jīchǎng duōshao qián?	

(add, highway, fee, altogether, 150, MW)	Including tolls, 150 *kuai*.
A）加高速公路费一共 150 块。	
Jiā gāosù gōnglù fèi yígòng yìbǎi wǔshí kuài.	

(master, pull, work, QW)	Sir, are you on duty?
A）师傅，拉活儿吗？	
Shīfu, lāhuór ma?	

(you, go, where)	Where are you going?
B）你去哪儿？	
Nǐ qù nǎr?	

(I, go, Great Wall Hotel, you, know, how, go, QW)	I am going to the Great Wall Hotel. Do you know how to get there?
A）我去长城饭店，你知道怎么走吗？	
Wǒ qù Chángchéng Fàndiàn, nǐ zhīdào zěnme zǒu ma?	

(I, not, know)	I don't know.
B）我不知道。	
Wǒ bù zhīdào.	

(no, relation, I, can, for, you, bring, road)	No problem, I can show you the way.
A）没关系，我可以给你带路。	
Méi guānxi, wǒ kěyǐ gěi nǐ dàilù.	

(I, have, little, cold, can, IO, window, roll, up, QW)	I'm a little cold. Could you please put up the window?
我有点儿冷，可以把窗户摇上吗？	
Wǒ yǒudiǎnr lěng, kěyǐ bǎ chuānghu yáo shàng ma?	

(car, inside, truly, hot, trouble, you, IO, window, roll, down)	It's a little hot in here. Could you please put down the windows?
车里真热，麻烦您把窗户摇下来。	
Chē li zhēn rè, máfan nín bǎ chuānghu yáo xiàlai.	

(able, open, heater / AC, QW)	Can you put on the heat / air?
能开暖气 / 空调吗？	
Néng kāi nuǎnqì / kōngtiáo ma?	

(this, song, good, listening, trouble, you, IO, volume, open, big, a little)	This song is really good. Could you please raise the volume?
这歌儿好听，麻烦您把音量开大一点儿。	
Zhè gēr hǎotīng, máfan nín bǎ yīnliàng kāi dà yìdiǎnr.	

(my, head, hurt, please, you, IO, radio, shut off)	I have a headache. Please shut off the radio.
我头疼，请你把收音机关了。	
Wǒ tóuténg, qǐng nǐ bǎ shōuyīnjī guān le.	

(just, at, front, intersection, keep side way, stop)	At the next intersection, please pull over.
就在前边的路口，靠边儿停。	
Jiù zài qiánbian de lùkǒu, kàobiānr tíng.	

(please, you, don't, make a detour, far)	Please don't take the long way. (I know the way.)
请你别绕远儿。	
Qǐng nǐ bié ràoyuǎnr.	

(trouble, you, at, front, convenient store, stop, a little while, I, get out, buy, pack, cigarette)	Can you stop for a second at the next convenient store? I want to buy a pack of cigarettes.
麻烦你在前边小卖部停一下，我下去买包烟。	
Máfan nǐ zài qiánbian xiǎomàibù tíng yíxià, wǒ xiàqu mǎi bāo yān.	

(please, you, IO, safety belt, tighten)	Please fasten your seatbelt.
请你把安全带系上。	
Qǐng nǐ bǎ ānquándài jì shàng.	

(master, you, able, not, able, not, smoke, cigarettes)	Mister, would you mind not smoking please?
师傅，你能不能不抽烟？	
Shīfu, nǐ néng bu néng bù chōuyān?	

(master, I, 5:30, before, must, arrive, there; you, think, there is show, QW)	Mister, I have to get there before 5:30. Do you think that is possible?
A) 师傅，我5:30之前得到那儿。你看有戏吗？	
Shīfu, wǒ wǔ diǎn sānshí zhīqián děi dào nàr. Nǐ kàn yǒu xì ma?	

(that, string, road, very, not, good, go, probably not)	That road is horrible (traffic is bad), probably not.
B) 那条路特不好走,**够呛**。	
Nà tiáo lù tè bù hǎo zǒu, gòuqiàng.	

(please, you, strike, meter)	Please use your meter.
请你打表。	
Qǐng nǐ dǎ biǎo.	

(you, don't, cheat, me, your, name, on, your, monitor card, on, be careful, I, go, your, company, report, you)	Don't cheat me. Your name is written on your monitor's card. Be careful, I will report you to your company.
你别骗**我**,你的**名字在你的**监督卡上,当心**我**去**你们**公司举报你。	

Nǐ bié piàn wǒ, nǐ de míngzi zài nǐ de jiāndūkǎ shang, dāngxīn wǒ qù nǐmen gōngsī jǔbào nǐ.

The majority of cab drivers are very friendly people. However, there are some that will try to cheat passengers. If you strongly feel that you are being cheated, saying the above will usually make the driver think twice. On the dashboard of every licensed taxi, there should be a monitor's card that tells the driver's name, number and company.

(I, have, emergency, able, not, able, drive, fast, a little)	I am in a rush. Could you please hurry up?
我有急事儿,**能不能**开快一点儿?	
Wǒ yǒu jíshìr, néng bu néng kāi kuài yìdiǎnr?	

(master, you, drive, very, fast, please, slow, a little) 师傅，你开得太快了，请慢一点儿。 Shīfu, nǐ kāi de tài kuài le, qǐng màn yìdiǎnr.	Driver, you are driving too fast. Could you please drive a little slower?

(here, to, we, go, place, need, how, long, time) 这里到我们去的地方要多长时间？ Zhèli dào wǒmen qù de dìfang yào duō cháng shíjiān?	How long is it going to take to get there from here?

(master, you, drive, truly, **stable**) 师傅，你开得真稳。 Shīfu, nǐ kāi de zhēn **wěn**.	Mister, you drive very **stable**.

狂	kuáng	crazy, like a maniac
牛	niú	great
快	kuài	fast
慢	màn	slow
面	miàn	turtle-like
晃	huàng	unstable

(excuse me, please, ask, go, **US embassy**, how, go)	Excuse me, could you please tell me how to get to the **U.S. embassy**?
Q) 对不起，请问去美国大使馆怎么走？	
Duìbuqǐ, qǐngwèn qù **Měiguó dàshǐguǎn** zěnme zǒu?	
(towards, **front**, walk, 100, meters, then, right, turn)	Go **straight** 100 meters, then make a right.
A) 往前走一百米，然后右拐。	
Wǎng **qián** zǒu yìbǎi mǐ, ránhòu yòu guǎi.	

(at, front, four-way intersection, left, turn)	At the four-way intersection ahead, make a left.
A) 在**前边**的十字路口左拐。	
Zài qiánbian de shízì lùkǒu zuǒ guǎi.	

(towards , north, walk, 50, meter, right, side, has, MW, McDonald's, back, side , right there)	Go north 50 meters, on your right-hand there is a McDonald's. It's right back of there.
A) 往**北**走**五十米**,**右边有个麦当劳**,后边就是。	
Wǎng běi zǒu wǔshí mǐ, yòubian yǒu ge Màidāngláo, hòubian jiù shì.	

(pass, one, MW, traffic light, towards, right, walk, 30, meter, about, then, left, turn)	Past this traffic light, go right about 30 meters, then make a left.
A) 过一个**红绿灯**,往右走三十米左右再左拐。	
Guò yí ge hónglǜdēng, wǎng yòu zǒu sānshí mǐ zuǒyòu zài zuǒ guǎi.	

Transportation in China

China is called the "Bicycle Kingdom" for good reason. Nearly everyone owns one and uses it to go to work or to school. During morning and afternoon rush hour, two-wheeled vehicles can be seen as far as your vision will take you. All streets have bike lanes, and the laws for riding are strictly enforced by policemen who are monitoring traffic at virtually every corner. The fine for riding through a red light is about one dollar.

The cost of an average new bicycle is around 150 *yuan*, or about 20 dollars. There is also a used bicycle market where a decent bike can be picked up for a few bucks. If your bicycle has a problem, there is no need to worry. There are stands set up every few blocks with "skilled" repairmen. The cost for pumping up a tire is 0.2 *yuan*, or three cents.

Besides bicycles, buses are the most popular form of transportation in Chinese cities. The fare is dependent upon the distance you travel, ranging from six to 15 cents. The bus system is convenient, but of course very, very crowded.

In major cities, there are subway lines that are sometimes really crowded, but are more efficient than buses. The fare is 3 *yuan* or 24 cents per ride.

Ten years ago it was difficult to catch a cab. Not anymore. The streets are roaming with taxis. The initial fare is 10 *yuan* in Beijing, and then is calculated at a rate of either 1.2, 1.6, or 2.00 yuan per kilometer, depending upon the type of vehicle. There are also many *hei che* or "black car", which are vehicles  owned by private citizens who take passengers just like a regular cab would. In recent years, the government has been intent of getting rid of these illegal vehicles because of insurance and tax evasion reasons.

Although it is getting more popular to travel by air, the train system is by far the most widely used means of transport between Chinese cities. The passenger lines, which run throughout every province except Tibet, have four different types of seats. The cheapest and least comfortable are the hard seat and soft seat. The hard sleeper provides the passenger with a small bed, while the soft sleeper is largest and most comfortable. For a trip between Beijing and Tianjin, which takes about an hour and a half, the hard or soft seat is an option. However, if you are taking an overnight trip, the hard or soft sleeper is highly advisable.

The Beijing Taxi Driver

When Wang Junjian, one of Beijing's over 70,000 licensed taxi drivers, wakes up every morning at around six o'clock, the only thing on his mind is the 200 renminbi ($24) that he needs to earn throughout the course of the day in order to break even. By the time he has warmed up his 1997 36-horsepower Xia Li (around 74,000 RMB/ $9,000), his wife Wang Yan and parents have prepared the breakfast that they will eat together: traditional Chinese noodles in a water-based broth and *Man Tou*, a rather bland (by Western standards) traditional Chinese pastry. While the others are eating, Wang Yan prepares for her husband a big thermos of green tea that he will take on the road. "In the morning I am full of life", Wang says, "I really enjoy chatting with my family". In order to take advantage of the morning rush hour, at 7 o'clock Wang heads off to work and a minimum of 12 hours will pass before Wang sees his family again, and by then the pressure of Beijing's nerve racking traffic has taken its toll.

Tea thermos in hand, Wang says good-bye to his family and walks out of their two-bedroom, 70m^2 Chaoyang District (Northeastern Beijing) residence. According to Wang, there are two ways of *la huor*, or picking up passengers. Some drivers have specific spots that they go to and wait for people while others will drive around until they find customers. The latter technique is called "*sao lu* (*searching road*)" in cab driver language. Wang prefers the latter. "I don't really care how I get customers", he exclaims. "Before the traffic gets too packed up, I'd like to have taken a few customers. Besides, when the traffic is really bad, it is better to have someone in the car with you, for both financial and boredom reasons. And boy can it get backed-up! What does the last sentence mean?"

After hustling the streets and alleys of Beijing for a few hours, Wang will stop for a quick lunch. Fried eggs and tomatoes and a bowl of plain white rice, no beverage. Total cost: six renminbi or 70 cents. "I don't have a lot of time to talk with my friends or family during the day, but that really doesn't bother me", he confesses, "If you think about it, my life is very interesting. In what other field can you meet new people every hour? People from Beijing, outside of Beijing, and of course foreign friends. And my passengers realize that when my Xia Li reaches their destination, our relationship will also come to an end so they are rather willing to speak their minds. I have heard many interesting stories over the past five years."

Besides speaking with his customers, Wang enjoys listening to classical Chinese novel and English-learning cassettes issued by his company a few years back in an attempt to better accommodate non-Chinese speaking passengers. "Hello! Do you need a taxi?" he blurts out in a hysterically funny but understandable English accent.

After lunch Wang will repeat the same routine. At around 8 o'clock, a fatigued

Wang returns home to his family. Although the other family members have already eaten, the entire family sits down at the table as Wang devours his eggplant, pork, and rice. Following dinner, Wang and his wife watch a pirated copy of *American Beauty*. At around 11, he goes to sleep so that he can have the energy to do it all over again. "My life is pretty simple", he says. "I work during the day. When I come home I eat dinner and relax with my wife. On an exciting night I will play mahjong or cards with my friends. In the summer, I like to take a stroll around the block".

Do you know?

The initial charge for a Beijing taxi is 10 renminbi ($ 1.25) for the first four kilometers. Every kilometer over 4 is charged at a rate of 1.20, 1.60 or 2.00 renminbi respectively based upon the make of the car. On all taxis, there should be a sticker posted stating its rate. For every 5 minutes that the vehicle is idle, the price of one kilometer will be added.

There are over 70,000 licensed taxis in Beijing. Additionally, there are an estimated over 20,000 *hei* (black) or illegal cabs.

On the dashboard of every cab, there should be a monitor card displayed. If you feel that you have been given great or poor service, you can call the company to make your comments heard.

The average car insurance cost for cab drivers is 2700 renminbi/year or around $ 325. The cost of gas is about 2.5 renminbi per liter or about 20 cents. There also is a road fee of 110 renminbi or $ 13US per month.

Education

教　育

书	shū	book
(map, manual)		
地图册	dìtúcè	atlas
(oneself, chronicle)		
自传	zìzhuàn	autobiography
传记	zhuànjì	biography
词典	cídiǎn	dictionary
(hundred, subject, comprehensive, book)		
百科全书	bǎikē quánshū	encyclopedia
(little, speak)		
小说	xiǎoshuō	novel
(class, book)		
课本	kèběn	textbook
(turn, open / close up, book)	Open / close the book.	
翻开/合上书。		
Fān kāi / hé shàng shū.		
(turn, to, 3rd, page)	Turn to page three.	
翻到第三页。		
Fān dào dì sān yè.		

(state, request)		
申请	shēnqǐng	to apply, application
(he, apply, PT, Harvard University)	He applied to Harvard University.	
他申请了哈佛大学。		
Tā shēnqǐngle Hāfó Dàxué.		
(she, apply, to, PT, Harvard University)	She got into Harvard.	
她申请到了哈佛大学。		
Tā shēnqǐng dàole Hāfó Dàxué.		

(black, board)		
黑板	hēibǎn	blackboard
(IO, blackboard, wipe, clean)	Wipe the blackboard.	
把黑板擦干净。		
Bǎ hēibǎn cā gānjìng.		

(book, slender piece of bamboo)		
书签	shūqiān	bookmark
(at, 20th, page, clip, one, MW, bookmark)	Put a bookmark at page 20.	
在第二十页夹一个书签。		
Zài dì èrshí yè jiā yí ge shūqiān.		

(school, yard)		
校园	xiàoyuán	campus
(I, next year, will, live, at, campus, outside)	I am going to live off campus next year.	
我明年要住在校园外。		
Wǒ míngnián yào zhù zài xiàoyuán wài.		

(powder, writing utensil)		
粉笔	fěnbǐ	chalk

(commit, fraud)		
作弊	zuòbì	to cheat on a test
(test, cheat, when, movement, should, little, a little) 考试**作弊**的时候，**动作**应该小一点儿。	When cheating on a test, you should keep a low profile.	
Kǎoshì zuòbì de shíhou, dòngzuò yīnggāi xiǎo yìdiǎnr.		

(same, study)		
同学	tóngxué	classmate
(he, is, my, same, class, classmate) 他是我同班**同学**。	He is my classmate.	
Tà shì wǒ tóngbān tóngxué.		

(teach, room)		
教室	jiàoshì	classroom

(hug, Buddha's feet)		
抱佛脚	bào fó jiǎo	to cram (for a test)
(he, usually, not, study, arrive, test, when, then, temporarily, hug Buddha's feet) 他**平时**不学习，到考试的时候**就**临时**抱佛脚**。	He usually doesn't study. When the test approaches, he crams.	
Tā píngshí bù xuéxí, dào kǎoshì de shíhou jiù línshí bào fó jiǎo.		

(wax, writing utensil)		
蜡笔	làbǐ	crayons

(study, point)		
学分	xuéfēn	credits
(I, already, accumulate, PT, 30, credit) 我已经修了三十学分。 Wǒ yǐjing xiūle sānshí xuéfēn.		I have already earned 30 credits.

(escape, class)		
逃课	táo kè	to cut class
(you, for what, escape, class) 你为什么逃课？ Nǐ wèi shénme táo kè?		Why did you cut class?

(class, scheme)		
课程	kèchéng	curriculum

(study, position)		
学位	xuéwèi	degree
(you, take, PT, what, degree) Q) 你拿到了什么学位？ Nǐ ná dàole shénme xuéwèi?		What is your degree?
(I, take, is, law, Ph.D, degree) A) 我拿到的是法律博士学位。 Wǒ ná dào de shì fǎlǜ bóshì xuéwèi.		I have a Ph.D in law.

文凭	wénpíng	diploma
(you, when, take, diploma, PT)	When did you graduate?	
你什么时候拿到文凭的？		
Nǐ shénme shíhou ná dào wénpíng de?		

(lodge, house)		
宿舍	sùshè	dormitory
(I, live, in, foreign students, dorm)	I live in the foreign students dorm.	
我住在留学生宿舍。		
Wǒ zhù zài liúxuéshēng sùshè.		

(cease, study)		
辍学	chuòxué	to drop out of school
(he, because, economic, condition, not, good, drop out of school)	Due to financial considerations, he dropped out of school.	
他因为经济条件不好辍学了。		
Tā yīnwèi jīngjì tiáojiàn bù hǎo chuòxué le.		

(off, class)		
下课	xiàkè	to end class
(I, 3:30, end, class)	My class is over at 3:30.	
我三点半下课。		
Wǒ sān diǎn bàn xiàkè.		

橡皮	xiàngpí	eraser
(use, eraser, IO, this, MW, word, wipe, off) **用橡皮把这个词擦掉。** Yòng xiàngpí bǎ zhè ge cí cā diào.		Erase this word.

(study, card)		
学习卡片	xuéxí kǎpiàn	flash cards

(book, idiot)		
书呆子	shūdāizi	geek person who always studies

(sticky, water)		
胶水儿	jiāoshuǐr	glue
(at, stamp, on, paste, a little, glue) **在邮票上沾点儿胶水儿。** Zài yóupiào shang zhān diǎnr jiāoshuǐr.		Put some glue on the stamp.

(year, level)		
年级	niánjí	grade
(you, this year, read, how many, grade) **Q) 你今年读几年级？** Nǐ jīnnián dú jǐ niánjí?		What grade are you in?
(you, this year, university, how many) **Q) 你今年大几？** Nǐ jīnnián dà jǐ?		What year are you in university?

(I, this year, read, _____)	This year, I am (in, a)_____.
A）我今年读_____。	
Wǒ jīnnián dú _____.	

(one－six, grade)		
一－六年级	yī－liù niánjí	1st-6th grade
(primary, one－three)		
初一－三	chūyī－sān	7th-9th grade
(high, one－three)		
高一－三	gāoyī－sān	10th-12th grade
(university, one-four)		
大一－四	dàyī－sì	freshman / sophomore / junior / senior

(result, achievement)		
成绩	chéngjì	grades
(his, grade, excellent)		
他成绩优良。	His grades are really good.	
Tā chéngjì yōuliáng.		

(finish, course of study)		
毕业	bìyè	graduate

(on, class)		
上课	shàngkè	to have class
(you, what time, have class)		
你几点上课?	What time do you have class?	
Nǐ jǐ diǎn shàngkè?		

(fluorescent, writing utensil)		
荧光笔	yíngguāngbǐ	hi-liter
(this, MW, sentence, use, hi-liter, mark up, sign, express, emphasis) 这句话用荧光笔做上记号，表示强调。 Zhè jù huà yòng yíngguāngbǐ zuò shàng jìhào, biǎoshì qiángdiào.		Hi-light this sentence for emphasis.

(practice, work)		
作业	zuòyè	homework
(our, teacher, everyday, all, assign, very, much, homework) 我们老师每天都布置很多作业。 Wǒmen lǎoshī měi tiān dōu bùzhì hěn duō zuòyè.		Our teacher assigns us a lot of homework everyday.
(we, tomorrow, must, hand in, homework) 我们明天必须交作业。 Wǒmen míngtiān bìxū jiāo zuòyè.		We have to hand in our homework assignment.

开除	kāichú	to be kicked out of school
(he, by, school, expel) 他被学校开除了。 Tā bèi xuéxiào kāichú le.		He was kicked out of school.

(early, retreat)		
早退	zǎotuì	to leave early

(he, today, because, body, not, comfortable, leave early)	He left class early today because he did not feel well.
他今天因为**身体不舒服**早退了。	
Tā jīntiān yīnwèi shēntǐ bù shūfu zǎotuì le.	

(picture, book, establishment)		
图书馆	túshūguǎn	library
(I, from, library, borrow, PT, one, MW, book)		I borrowed a book from the library.
我从图书馆借了一本书。		
Wǒ cóng túshūguǎn jièle yì běn shū.		
(I, will, go, library, renew, one, MW, book)		I will go to the library to renew a book.
我要去**图书馆**续借一本书。		
Wǒ yào qù túshūguǎn xùjiè yì běn shū.		
(I, must, go , return, book)		I must return a book. (to a library)
我得去还书。		
Wǒ děi qù huán shū.		

(do, note)		
做笔记	zuò bǐjì	to take notes

(note, book)		
笔记本	bǐjìběn	notebook

(release, study)		
放学	fàngxué	School is out (for the day, morning, vacation)

纸	zhǐ	paper

钢笔	gāngbǐ	pen

(lead, writing utensil)		
铅笔	qiānbǐ	pencil

(pencil, box)		
铅笔盒	qiānbǐhé	pencil box

(turn, pencil, knife)		
转笔刀	zhuànbǐdāo	pencil sharpener

(loot, steal)		
剽窃	piáoqiè	to plagiarize
(he, because, plagiarize, PT, other person's, thesis, by, school, expel)		He was expelled from school for plagiarizing somebody else's thesis.
他因为剽窃了别人的论文被学校开除了。		
Tā yīnwèi piáoqièle biéren de lùnwèn bèi xuéxiào kāichú le.		

(school, leader)		
校长	xiàozhǎng	principal

(teach, instruct)		
教授	jiàoshòu	professor
(our, school, have, very, many, foreign teacher)		Our school has many foreign teachers.
我们学校有很多外教。		
Wǒmen xuéxiào yǒu hěn duō wàijiào.		

休息	xiūxi	recess, break
(we, every, MW, hour, have, 10 minutes, recess)		Every hour we have a ten-minute break.
我们每个小时有十分钟休息。		
Wǒmen měi ge xiǎoshí yǒu shí fēnzhōng xiūxi.		

(recommendation, letter)		
推荐信	tuījiànxìn	recommendation letter
(my, teacher, for, me, write, PT, one, MW, recommendation letter)		My teacher wrote me a letter of recommendation.
我老师给我写了一封推荐信。		
Wǒ lǎoshī gěi wǒ xiěle yì fēng tuījiànxìn.		

尺子	chǐzi	ruler

(prize, study, gold)		
奖学金	jiǎngxuéjīn	scholarship
(he, receive, PT, full amount, scholarship)		He was awarded a full scholarship.
他拿到了全额奖学金。		
Tī ná dàole quán'é jiǎngxuéjīn.		

(book, bag)		
书包	shūbāo	schoolbag

(cut, knife)		
剪刀	jiǎndāo	scissors

(study, period)		
学期	xuéqī	semester

学生	xuésheng	student
(I, am, Chinese Department, student)		I study in the Chinese Department.
我是中文系的学生。		
Wǒ shì Zhōngwénxì de xuésheng.		
(male, student / female, student)		
男生/女生	nánshēng / nǚshēng	boy / girl student

学习	xuéxí	study
(good, good, study, day, day, towards, up)		Study hard and make progress everyday. (Mao Zedong)
好好学习,天天向上。		
Hǎohǎo xuéxí, tiāntiān xiàng shàng.		

(abroad, study)		
留学	liúxué	study abroad

(I, plan, next year, go, Stanford, study abroad) 我打算明年去斯坦福留学。	I plan on studying abroad at Stanford next year.	
Wǒ dǎsuan míngnián qù Sītǎnfú liúxué.		

(summer, vacation)		
暑假	shǔjià	summer vacation
(Chinese, student, July, August, release, summer vacation) 中国学生七、八月放暑假。	Chinese students have their summer vacation from July to August.	
Zhōngguó xuésheng qī、bāyuè fàng shǔjià.		

胶带	jiāodài	tape
(use, tape, IO, this, MW, book, stick, a little) 用胶带把这本书粘一下。	Tape this book.	
Yòng jiāodài bǎ zhè běn shū zhān yíxià.		

老师	lǎoshī	teacher
(I, from, my, teacher, there, learn, PT, very, many, things) 我从我老师那儿学会了很多东西。	I learned a lot from my teacher.	
Wǒ cóng wǒ lǎoshī nàr xué huìle hěn duō dōngxi.		

(test, trial)		
考试	kǎoshì	test

(I, will, test, GRE)		I will take the GRE.
我要考 GRE。		
Wǒ yào kǎo GRE.		
(he, test, not, pass)		He didn't pass the test.
他考试没过。		
Tā kǎoshì méi guò.		
(he, test, pass)		He passed the test.
他考试及格了。		
Tā kǎoshì jígé le.		
(I, test, PT, 89, point)		I got an 89 on my test.
我考了八十九分儿。		
Wǒ kǎole bāshíjiǔ fēnr.		
(semester, end, test)		
期末考试	qīmò kǎoshì	final exam
(semester, middle, test)		
期中考试	qīzhōng kǎoshì	midterm exam
(measure, test)		
测验	cèyàn	quiz

(discuss, article)		
论文	lùnwén	thesis
(your, thesis, write, what, topic)		What are you writing your thesis about?
你的论文写什么题目？		
Nǐ de lùnwén xiě shénme tímù?		

(grade, sheet)		
成绩单	chéngjìdān	transcript

(I, four o'clock, will, with, tutor, study)	I am going to study with my tutor at 4.
我四点要跟辅导学习。	
Wǒ sì diǎn yào gēn fǔdǎo xuéxí.	

(cold, vacation)		
寒假	hánjià	winter vacation

(children, kid, garden)		
幼儿园	yòu'éryuán	kindergarten
(small, study)		
小学	xiǎoxué	elementary school
(elementary, middle)		
初中	chūzhōng	junior high school
(high, middle)		
高中	gāozhōng	senior high school
(vocation, school)		
职业学校	zhíyè xuéxiào	vocational school
(big, study)		
大学(北京大学)	dàxué (Běijīng Dàxué)	university (Peking Univ.)
(study, institute)		
学院	xuéyuàn	institute, college

本科 / 学士	běnkē / xuéshì	undergraduate / Bachelor's
硕士	shuòshì	Master's
博士	bóshì	Ph.D.

(you, study, is, what, major)	What is your major?
Q) 你学的是**什么**专业？	
Nǐ xué de shì shénme zhuānyè?	
(my, major, is _____)	My major is / was _____.
A) 我的**专业**是_____。	
Wǒ de zhuānyè shì _____.	

(you, select, is, what, major)	What is / was your minor?
Q) 你**选修**的是**什么**专业？	
Nǐ xuǎnxiū de shì shénme zhuānyè?	
(my , minor, is _____)	My minor is / was _____.
A) 我的**选修专业**是_____。	
Wǒ de xuǎnxiū zhuānyè shì _____.	

(this, MW, major, very, popular)	This major is very popular.
这个专业很热门儿。	
Zhè ge zhuānyè hěn rèménr.	

| (accounting, studies) | | |
| 会计学 | kuàijìxué | Accounting |

(agriculture, studies)		
农学	nóngxué	Agriculture
(people, category, studies)		
人类学	rénlèixué	Anthropology
(construction, studies)		
建筑学	jiànzhùxué	Architecture
(sky, culture, studies)		
天文学	tiānwénxué	Astronomy
(business, studies)		
商学	shāngxué	Business
(industrial, business, administration)		
工商管理	gōngshāng guǎnlǐ	Business Administration
(change, studies)		
化学	huàxué	Chemistry
(electric, image, studies)		
电影学	diànyǐngxué	Cinematography
(computer, science)		
计算机科学	jìsuànjī kēxué	Computer Science
(east, Asia, research)		
东亚研究	Dōngyà yánjiū	East Asian Studies
(economy, studies)		
经济学	jīngjìxué	Economics
(education, studies)		
教育学	jiàoyùxué	Education

(project, procedure, studies)		
工程学	gōngchéngxué	Engineering
(gold, melt)		
金融	jīnróng	Finance
(ground, theory)		
地理	dìlǐ	Geography
(calendar, history)		
历史	lìshǐ	History
(international, business, studies)		
国际商学	guójì shāngxué	International Business
(Jewish, studies)		
犹太学	Yóutàixué	Jewish Studies
(news, studies)		
新闻学	xīnwénxué	Journalism
(law, rule)		
法律	fǎlǜ	Law
(language, studies)		
语言学	yǔyánxué	Linguistics
(literature, studies)		
文学	wénxué	Literature
(great, concern, economics)		
宏观经济学	hóngguān jīngjìxué	Macroeconomics
(operation, sales, studies)		
营销学	yíngxiāoxué	Marketing

(number, studies)		
数学	shùxué	Mathematics
(small, concern, economics)		
微观经济学	wēiguān jīngjìxué	Microeconomics
(sound, music)		
音乐	yīnyuè	Music
(wise, studies)		
哲学	zhéxué	Philosophy
(body, cultivate)		
体育	tǐyù	Physical Education
(object, theory, studies)		
物理学	wùlǐxué	Physics
(administration, govern, studies)		
政治学	zhèngzhìxué	Political Science
(heart, theory , studies)		
心理学	xīnlǐxué	Psychology
(society, studies)		
社会学	shèhuìxué	Sociology
(statistics, studies)		
统计学	tǒngjìxué	Statistics
(woman, studies)		
妇女学	fùnǚxué	Women's Studies
(animal, studies)		
动物学	dòngwùxué	Zoology

The Chinese Educational System

Before Liberation in 1949, an alarming 80% of Chinese were illiterate. Since then, the government has placed great importance on educational policies and great strides have been made. Today, the cost of education is affordable, but is on the rise.

Most Chinese children enter kindergarten at the age of two or three. Parents pay around RMB 1,500 tuition cost out of their own pocket, around US$ 200 annually. At age six or seven, the student will enter primary school. The tuition cost is about US$ 1,200 for six years. At age 12-13, the student will enter junior high school for three years and tuition costs are similar to those of primary school.

Following middle school, students have a choice between entering Senior high school, entering a vocational school where they can learn a specific trade, or leaving school altogether in search of work. Leaving school altogether is an option that is more common in rural areas. Senior high school is three years and tuition costs are slightly higher than those of junior high school.

The only word used to describe the competition to enter a Chinese university is fierce. Every June 7th, 8th and 9th there is a college entrance examination called Gāo kǎo, which is administered nationwide. College hopefuls have the option of choosing Science or Liberal Arts examination. If the student selects Science, he/she will participate in the Math, English, Physics, Chemistry, and Chinese examinations. If the student chooses Liberal Arts, he/she will take the Math, History, Politics, Chinese and English tests. Needless to say, the period leading up to the examination is a very nervous one for students and parents alike, especially following the implementation of the "one family, one child" policy in 1978.

College tuition costs have been rising steadily over the past few years and have become a major concern for Chinese families. For example, a student entering Beijing Language and Culture University will pay around US$ 750 annually for tuition, dormitory, and book fees. That figure does not include meal costs, an additional few hundred dollars per year. Although the amount seems rather small, one must consider that the annual income of most Chinese urban dwellers does not exceed a few thousand dollars and is substantially less in the countryside. In recent years, the government has introduced measures to provide financing to help those who have financial difficulties to realize their educational dreams.

Electronics

电　器

(air, adjust)		
空调	kōngtiáo	air conditioner
(IO, air conditioner, temperature, adjust, high / low, a little) 把空调温度调高 / 低一点儿。 Bǎ kōngtiáo wēndù tiáo gāo / dī yìdiǎnr.		Raise / lower the air.
(IO, temperature, adjust to, most, low) 把温度调到最低。 Bǎ wēndù tiáo dào zuì dī.		Put the air on high.

(noisy, clock)		
闹钟	nàozhōng	alarm clock
(IO, alarm clock, set, to, 8, o'clock) 把闹钟上到八点。 Bǎ nàozhōng shàng dào bā diǎn.		Set the alarm for eight.

(leave, words, machine)		
留言机	liúyánjī	answering machine

(call, machine)		
呼机	hūjī	beeper

(have, thing, page, me)	If necessary, you can page me.
有事呼我。	
Yǒu shì hū wǒ.	

(count, calculate, machine)		
计算器	jìsuànqì	calculator

(shoot, image, machine)		
摄像机	shèxiàngjī	camcorder
(he, use, camcorder, shoot, PT, his, brother's, wedding)		He recorded his brother's wedding with his camcorder.
他用摄像机拍下了他哥哥的婚礼。		
Tā yòng shèxiàngjī pāi xiàle tā gēge de hūnlǐ.		

(reflect, image, machine)		
照相机	zhàoxiàngjī	camera
(digit, camera)		
数字照相机	shùzì zhàoxiàngjī	digital camera
(IO, film, load into, camera, inside)		Load the film into the camera.
把胶卷装进照相机里。		
bǎ jiāojuǎn zhuāng jìn zhàoxiàngjī li.		
(IO, film, take, out)		Take the film out of the camera.
把胶卷取出来。		
Bǎ jiāojuǎn qǔ chūlai.		
(wash, film)		
冲胶卷	chōng jiāojuǎn	to develop film

(*English*, machine)		
CD 机	CD jī	CD player / Discman

(electric, brain)		
电脑	diànnǎo	computer
(smooth, disc)		
光盘	guāngpán	CD ROM
(core, piece)		
芯片	xīnpiàn	computer chip
(soft, disk)		
软盘	ruǎnpán	floppy disk
(hard, disc)		
硬盘	yìngpán	hard disc
(key, board)		
键盘	jiànpán	keyboard
(notebook, computer)		
笔记本电脑	bǐjìběn diànnǎo	laptop
(display, machine)		
显示器	xiǎnshìqì	monitor
(mouse, mark)		
鼠标	shǔbiāo	mouse
(palm, on, treasure)		
掌上宝	zhǎngshàngbǎo	palm pilot
(print, machine)		
打印机	dǎyìnjī	printer

(sweep, instrument)		
扫描仪	sǎomiáoyí	scanner

(main, machine)		
主机	zhǔjī	mainframe

(leave, copy left as record)		
留底	liúdǐ	back-up

| (my, computer, not, very, reliable, you, write, complete, thing, better, leave, MW, back-up)
我的电脑不太保险, 你写完东西最好留个底。
Wǒ de diànnǎo bú tài bǎoxiǎn, nǐ xiě wán dōngxi zuìhǎo liú ge dǐ. | | My computer is not reliable; when you are done you'd better back up your file. |

(English)		
拷贝	kǎobèi	copy

| (IO, this, MW, file, copy to, floppy disc, on)
把这个文件拷贝到软盘上。
Bǎ zhè ge wénjiàn kǎobèi dào ruǎnpán shang. | | Copy this file onto a floppy disk. |

删除 / 掉	shānchú / diào	delete
(IO, this, one, line / MW, character, delete) 把这一行 / 个字删掉。 Bǎ zhè yì háng / ge zì shān diào.		Delete this line / character.

(down, load)		
下载	xiàzǎi	download
(my, thesis, is, from, Net, on, download, PT) 我的论文是从网上下载的。 Wǒ de lùnwén shì cóng wǎngshang xiàzǎi de.		I downloaded my thesis from the Internet.

(English)		
伊妹儿	yīmèir	E-mail
(I, must, check, my, E-mail) 我得查我的伊妹儿。 Wǒ děi chá wǒ de yīmèir.		I have to check my E-mail.
(I, today, receive, PT, four, MW, E-mail) 我今天收到了四个伊妹儿。 Wǒ jīntiān shōudàole sì ge yīmèir.		I received four E-mails today.
(he, give, me, send, PT, one, MW, E-mail) 他给我发了一个伊妹儿。 Tā gěi wǒ fāle yí ge yīmèir.		He sent me an E-mail.

(install, assemble)		
安装	ānzhuāng	install
Install; both ānzhuāng and zhuāng are used, zhuāng is more colloquial.		
(my, computer, should , install, one, MW, kill, virus, software) 我的电脑应该装一个杀毒软件。 Wǒ de diànnǎo yīnggāi zhuāng yí ge shādú ruǎnjiàn.		I should install virus-killing software into my computer.

(*English*)		
猫	māo	modem
(this, MW, computer's, modem, is, 56K)	This computer has a 56K modem.	
这台电脑的猫是 56K 的。		
Zhè tái diànnǎo de māo shì wǔshíliù K de.		

(strike, print)		
打印	dǎyìn	print
(IO, this, MW, article, print out)	Print this article.	
把这篇文章打印出来。		
Bǎ zhè piān wénzhāng dǎyìn chūlai.		

(protect, save)		
保存	bǎocún	save
(IO, this, MW, document, save, to, my, floppy disk, inside)	Please save this document onto my disk.	
把这个文件保存到我的软盘里。		
Bǎ zhè ge wénjiàn bǎocún dào wǒ de ruǎnpán li.		

扫描	sǎomiáo	scan
(help, me, scan, several, MW, photo, OK, QW)	Can you help me scan these pictures?	
帮我扫描几张相片，好吗？		
Bāng wǒ sǎomiáo jǐ zhāng xiàngpiàn, hǎo ma?		

(illness, toxic)		
病毒	bìngdú	virus

(my, computer's, C drive, infect, PT, virus)		There is a virus in my C drive.
我电脑的 C 盘染了病毒。		
Wǒ diànnǎo de C pán rǎnle bìngdú.		

(electric, pool)		
电池	diànchí	batteries

(this, battery, no, power, need, fill, a little, power)		This battery is out of juice. It needs to be recharged.
这电池没电了，需要充一下电。		
Zhè diànchí méi diàn le, xūyào chōng yíxià diàn.		

(English, machine)		
DVD 机	DVD jī	DVD player

(electric, move, shave, beard, knife)		
电动剃须刀	diàndòng tìxūdāo	electric razor

(electric, step)		
电梯	diàntī	elevator/escalator

(transmit, real, machine)		
传真机	chuánzhēnjī	facsimile

(I, will, give, you, send, MW, fax)	I will send you a fax.	
我会给你发个传真。		
Wǒ huì gěi nǐ fā ge chuánzhēn.		

(electric, wind, fan)		
电风扇	diànfēngshàn	electric fan

(blow, wind, machine)		
吹风机	chuīfēngjī	hair dryer

(electric, iron)		
电熨斗	diànyùndǒu	iron
(IO, clothes, iron, a little)	Iron the clothes.	
把衣服熨一下。		
Bǎ yīfu yùn yíxià.		

(electric, light)		
电灯	diàndēng	lamp
(IO, light, adjust, light / dark, a little)	Make the light brighter / dim the light.	
把灯调亮 / 暗一点儿。		
Bǎ dēng tiáo liàng / àn yìdiǎnr.		

(micro, wave, oven)		
微波炉	wēibōlú	microwave oven

(please, IO, this, MW, hamburger, place, into, microwave, inside, heat, a little)	Please heat the hamburger up in the microwave.
请把这个汉堡包放进微波炉里热一下。	
Qǐng bǎ zhè ge hànbǎobāo fàng jìn wēibōlú li rè yíxià.	

(repeat, print, machine)		
复印机	fùyìnjī	photocopier
(IO, this, MW, article, photocopy, three, copy)		Make three copies of this article.
把这篇文章复印三份。		
Bǎ zhè piān wénzhāng fùyìn sān fèn.		

(plug in, wire, board)		
插线板	chāxiànbǎn	plug bar
(IO, plug, plug into, plug bar, on)		Plug the chord into the plug bar.
把插头插到插线板上。		
Bǎ chātóu chā dào chāxiànbǎn shang.		

(receive, sound, machine)		
收音机	shōuyīnjī	radio

(electric, ice, box)		
电冰箱	diànbīngxiāng	refrigerator
(IO, beer, from, refrigerator, inside, take, out)		Take the beer out of the refrigerator.
把啤酒从冰箱里拿出来。		
Bǎ píjiǔ cóng bīngxiāng li ná chūlai.		

(IO, coke, place, in, refrigerator, inside)	Put the coke in the refrigerator.
把可乐放进冰箱里。	
Bǎ kělè fàng jìn bīngxiāng li.	

(remote, control, machine)		
遥控器	yáokòngqì	remote control
(fast, advance, a little)	Fast forward.	
快进一下儿。		
Kuàijìn yíxiàr.		
(IO, sound, shut)	Mute the sound.	
把声音关了。		
Bǎ shēngyīn guān le.		
(IO, sound, open, big / small, a little)	Raise / lower the volume.	
把声音开大 / 小一点儿。		
Bǎ shēngyīn kāi dà / xiǎo yìdiǎnr.		
(IO, this, section, again, play, a little)	Rewind.	
把这一段重放一下儿。		
Bǎ zhè yí duàn chóngfàng yíxiàr.		
(start, play, movie)	Play.	
开始放电影吧。		
Kāishǐ fàng diànyǐng ba.		
(change, to, ESPN channel)	Switch the channel to ESPN.	
换到 ESPN 台。		
Huàn dào ESPN tái.		

(change, to, 4 channel)		Turn to channel 4.
换到四频道。		
Huàn dào **sì** píndào.		

(plug in, seat)		
插座	chāzuò	socket
(you, here, have, extra, socket, QW; I, want, use, computer)		Is there an extra socket here? I would like to use my computer.
你们这儿有多余的插座吗？我想用电脑。		
Nǐmen zhèr yǒu duōyú de chāzuò ma? Wǒ xiǎng yòng diànnǎo.		

(voice, box)		
音箱	yīnxiāng	speaker

(record, sound, machine)		
录音机	lùyīnjī	tape recorder

(electric, words)		
电话	diànhuà	telephone
(incoming, electric, display)		
来电显示	láidiàn xiǎnshì	caller ID
(no, answer)		
没有应答	méiyǒu yìngdá	no answer
(phone, *English*)		
电话卡	diànhuàkǎ	phone card

(my, [phone], card, almost, use, over)		My (telephone) card is just about done.
我的（电话）卡快用完了。		
Wǒ de (diànhuà) kǎ kuài yòng wán le.		

(hand, machine)		
手机	shǒujī	mobile phone

(I, not, equip, mobile phone)		I don't have a cell phone.
我没配手机。		
Wǒ méi pèi shǒujī.		

(his, cell phone, not, on)		His cell phone is not turned on.
他的手机没开机。		
Tā de shǒujī méi kāijī.		

(no, signal)		No signal.
没有信号。		
Méiyǒu xìnhào.		

(voice, mail)		
声音邮件	shēngyīn yóujiàn	voice mail

(if, you, with, me, connect, not, on, head, then, leave, MW, voice mail)		If you can't get a hold of me, leave a message on my voice mail.
如果你跟我接不上头，就留个声音邮件。		
Rúguǒ nǐ gēn wǒ jiē bu shàng tóu, jiù liú ge shēngyīn yóujiàn.		

(I, will, give, you, make, phone call)		I'll give you a call.
我会给你打电话。		
Wǒ huì gěi nǐ dǎ diànhuà.		

(have, person, give, me, make, PT, phone call, QW)	Did anyone call me?
有人给我打过电话吗？	
Yǒu rén gěi wǒ dǎguo diànhuà ma?	

(please, relay to, him, I, give, him, make, PT, phone call)	Please tell him that I called.
请转告他，我给他打过电话。	
Qǐng zhuǎngào tā, wǒ gěi tā dǎguo diànhuà.	

(phone, occupy, line)	The line is busy.
电话占线。	
Diànhuà zhànxiàn.	

(I, give, him, call, PT, but, no, person, answer)	I called him but there was no answer.
我给他打过，但没人接。	
Wǒ gěi tā dǎguo, dàn méi rén jiē.	

(where, have, public, phone)	Where can I find a public phone?
哪儿有公用电话？	
Nǎr yǒu gōngyòng diànhuà?	

(you, want, make, long distance, or, local call)	Do you want to make a local or long distance call?
你想打长途还是市话？	
Nǐ xiǎng dǎ chángtú háishi shìhuà?	

(phone, no, dial tone)	There is no dial tone.
电话没有拨号音。	
Diànhuà méiyǒu bōhàoyīn.	

(phone, bell, sound)	The phone is ringing.
电话铃响了。	
Diànhuàlíng xiǎng le.	

(your, phone number, is, how many)	What is your phone number?
你的电话号码是多少?	
Nǐ de diànhuà hàomǎ shì duōshao?	

(my, phonebook, lose)	I lost my phonebook.
我的电话本儿丢了。	
Wǒ de diànhuàběnr diū le.	

(phone, has, confused, noise)	The phone has static.
电话有杂音。	
Diànhuà yǒu záyīn.	

(electric, view)		
电视	diànshì	television
(have, wire, television)		
有线电视	yǒuxiàn diànshì	cable television

(high, definition, degree, television)		
高清晰度电视	gāoqīngxīdù diànshì	high definition television

(satellite, television)		
卫星电视(卫视)	wèixīng diànshì (wèishì)	satellite television

(letter, screen)		
字幕	zìmù	subtitles

(I, watch, not, understand, Chinese, movies, this, movie, have, English, subtitles, QW)	
我看不懂中国电影，这片儿有英文字幕吗？	I can't watch Chinese movies. Does this movie have English subtitles?
Wǒ kàn bu dǒng Zhōngguó diànyǐng, zhè piānr yǒu Yīngwén zìmù ma?	

屏幕	píngmù	monitor, screen

(this, MW, screen, is, how many, inch)	
Q) 这个屏幕是多少吋的？	How big is this screen?
Zhè ge píngmù shì duōshao cùn de?	

(29, inch)	
A) 29 吋。	29'.
Èrshíjiǔ cùn.	

(strike, character, machine)		
打字机	dǎzìjī	typewriter

(suck up, dust, machine)		
吸尘器	xīchénqì	vacuum cleaner

(use, vacuum cleaner, IO, carpet, suck up, clean)		Vacuum the rugs.
用吸尘器把地毯吸干净。		
Yòng xīchénqì bǎ dìtǎn xī gānjìng.		

(movie, disc, machine)		
影碟机	yǐngdiéjī	VCD Player

(record, image, machine)		
录像机	lùxiàngjī	VCR

(game, machine)		
游戏机	yóuxìjī	video game machine
(now, children, play, video game machine, addicted)		Kids these days are really addicted to video games.
现在的小孩玩儿游戏机上瘾。		
Xiànzài de xiǎohái wánr yóuxìjī shàngyǐn.		

(with, body, listen)		
随身听	suíshēntīng	walkman

(wash, clothes, machine)		
洗衣机	xǐyījī	washing machine
(IO, want, wash, clothes, throw, in, washing machine, inside)		Put the clothes that need to be washed in the washing machine.
把要洗的衣服扔进洗衣机里。		
Bǎ yào xǐ de yīfu rēng jìn xǐyījī li.		

(IO, wash, good, clothes, from, washing machine, inside, take, out, hang up)	Take the washed clothes out of the washing machine and hang them up.
把洗好的衣服从洗衣机里拿出来, 晾起来。	
Bǎ xǐ hǎo de yīfu cóng xǐyījī li ná chūlai, liàng qǐlai.	

(drink, water, machine)		
饮水机	yǐnshuǐjī	water machine (mineral)

(IO, **electronic**, turn, open)	Turn on the _____.
把电器打开。	
Bǎ diànqì dǎ kāi.	

(IO, **electronic**, close)	Turn off the _____.
把电器关上。	
Bǎ diànqì guān shàng.	

(IO, **electronic**, plug, on)	Plug the **electronic** in.
把电器插上。	
Bǎ diànqì chā shàng.	

(IO, plug, pull, down)	Pull the plug out.
把插头拔下来。	
Bǎ chātóu bá xiàlai.	

A *sample phone call*

(please, ask, **Yang Kang**, in, QW) **A)** 请问杨康在吗? Qǐngwèn **Yáng Kāng** zài ma?	Is **Yang Kang** there?
(he, go out; your, honorable, surname) **B)** 他出去了。您贵姓? Tā chūqu le. Nín guìxìng?	He went out. May I have your name?
(no, honorable, surname, Zhang; I, can, for him, leave, MW, note, QW) **A)** 免贵姓张。我能给他留个言吗? Miǎn guì xìng Zhāng. Wǒ néng gěi tā liú ge yán ma?	My surname is Zhang. Can I leave a message?
(you[polite], say) **B)** 您说吧。 Nín shuō ba.	Go ahead.
(trouble, you [polite], tell, him, US general election, result, in a while, still, can't come out, OK, QW) **A)** 麻烦您告诉他, 美国大选结果一时半会儿还出不来, 好吗? Máfan nín gàosu tā, Měiguó dàxuǎn jiéguǒ yì shí bàn huìr hái chū bu lái, hǎo ma?	Would you please tell him that the result of the US election will not turn out soon, OK?
(no, problem, still, have, other, matters, QW) **B)** 没问题, 还有别的事儿吗? Méi wèntí, hái yǒu bié de shìr ma?	No problem, anything else?
(no, thank you [polite]; hang up) **A)** 没有了, 谢谢您。挂了。 Méiyǒu le, xièxie nín. Guà le.	No, thank you. Good bye.

Paging a person

(hello, please, ask, you [polite], page, what number) **A)** 您好,请问您呼多少? Nín hǎo, qǐngwèn nín hū duōshao?	Which number are you calling?
(please, page, 592754) **B)** 请呼 592754。 Qǐng hū wǔ-jiǔ-èr-qī-wǔ-sì.	Please call 592754.
(your, hohorable, surname) **A)** 您贵姓? Nín guìxìng?	What's your name? (formal)
(my, surname, Cheng, "gongcheng", "cheng") **B)** 我姓程,工程的程。 wǒ xìng Chéng, "gōngchéng" de "chéng".	My surname is Cheng, the Cheng that appears in the word Gōngchéng (project).
(please, you [polite], leave, words) **A)** 请您留言。 Qǐng nín liúyán.	What is your message?
(if, convenient, please, return, phone call) **B)** "如果方便请回电话。" "Rúguǒ fāngbiàn qǐng huí diànhuà."	"If convenient, please call me back."
(your [polite], telephone, number, is, how many) **A)** 您的电话号码是多少? Nín de diànhuà hàomǎ shì duōshao?	What is your phone number?

B) 6555-1212。	6555-1212.
Liù-wǔ-wǔ-wǔ-yāo-èr-yāo-èr.	
(still, have, QW)	Is that all?
A) 还有吗?	
Hái yǒu ma?	
(no, thank you)	That's it. Thank you.
B) 没有了,谢谢。	
Méiyǒu le, xièxie.	
(again, see)	Goodbye.
A) 再见。	
Zàijiàn.	

Since the implementation of Deng Xiaoping's Market Reform policy in 1978, Chinese, for the first time, have been able to accumulate wealth. Obviously, money is no good unless it can be used to purchase things that bring happiness. Below is a list of appliance penetration into Chinese' households.

Television
Urban   140 per 100 households
Rural   38 per 100 households
Penetration rate in cities 99.3%.

Telephone
Nationwide penetration 20%

Cellular phone
Shenzhen, Guangzhou 25%, Beijing 8%, Nationwide 2%, Developed nation average 30%

Washing machine
Urban 87%

Rural 24 machines per 100 households

Refrigerator
Urban 90%
Rural 11 units per 100 households

Computer
Urban households 27%, Beijing, Shanghai, Chongqing, and Tianjin 40%

VCD Player
Urban 58%

Walkman
Urban 33%

Business

商 务

(money, property)		
资产	zīchǎn	asset

(broker, person [middle, between, person])		
经纪人(中间人)	jīngjìrén (zhōngjiānrén)	broker (middleman)
(broker, the fewer, we, earn, money, then, the more) 中间人越少，我们赚钱就越多。	The fewer the middlemen, the more money we make.	
Zhōngjiānrén yuè shǎo, wǒmen zhuàn qián jiù yuè duō.		

(before, count)		
预算	yùsuàn	budget
(this year, USA, increase, PT, defense, budget) 今年美国增加了国防预算。	America increased its defense budget this year.	
Jīnnián Měiguó zēngjiāle guófáng yùsuàn.		

(buying, power)		
购买力	gòumǎilì	buying power
(in, China, some, big, city, buying power, simply, startle, person) 在中国，一些大城市的购买力简直惊人。	In some big Chinese cities, people's buying power is amazing.	
Zài Zhōngguó, yìxiē dà chéngshì de gòumǎilì jiǎnzhí jīngrén.		

(receive, silver, table)		
收银台	shōuyíntái	cashier

(our, company, is, IBM, biggest, client)		
客户	kèhù	client
(our, company, is, IBM, biggest, client)		Our company is IBM's biggest client.
我们公司是 IBM 最大的**客户**。		
Wǒmen gōngsī shì IBM zuì dà de kèhù.		

(draw money, ticket)		
支票	zhīpiào	check
(you[polite], accept, check, QW)		Do you accept checks?
您接受**支票**吗？		
Nín jiēshòu zhīpiào ma?		

(save/check, account)		
储蓄/**支票**账户	chǔxù/zhīpiào zhànghù	savings account/checking account
(my, savings/checking, account, overdraw)		My savings/checking account is overdrawn.
我的**储蓄**/支票账户透支了。		
Wǒ de chǔxù/zhīpiào zhànghù tòuzhī le.		

(goods, arrive, pay, funds)		
货到付款	huò dào fù kuǎn	COD

(compensate for, pledge)		
抵押	dǐyā	collateral

(take loan, buy, car, can, use, house, serve as, collateral)	You can put up your house as collateral when buying a car.
贷款买车可以用房子作抵押。	
Dàikuǎn mǎi chē kěyǐ yòng fángzi zuò dǐyā.	

(compensate, repay)		
赔偿	péicháng	compensation, to compensate

(compete, contend)		
竞争	jìngzhēng	competition, to compete

(consume, person)		
消费者	xiāofèizhě	consumer

(businessman, should, more, for, consumer, take into consideration)	Businesspeople should take more interest in the consumer.
商家应该多为消费者着想。	
Shāngjiā yīnggāi duō wèi xiāofèizhě zhuóxiǎng.	

(consume, product)		
消费品	xiāofèipǐn	commodity

消费	xiāofèi	consumption, to consume

(Labor Day, National Day, have holiday, seven, day, is, for, stimulate, people, consume)	The Labor Day and National Day holidays are for stimulating consumption.
"五·一"、"十·一"放假七天是为了刺激人们消费。	
"Wǔ-yī"、"Shí-yī" fàngjià qī tiān shì wèile cìjī rénmen xiāofèi.	

(version, right)

版权	bǎnquán	copyright

(can, download, music, give rise to, PT, very, many, piracy, problem)	Downloadable music has given rise to a lot of copyright disputes.
可下载音乐引起了很多版权问题。	
Kěxiàzǎi yīnxuè yǐnqǐle hěn duō bǎnquán wèntí.	

成本	chéngběn	cost

(in, developing country, build, factory, can, lower, labor costs)	Setting up a plant in a developing country can cut labor costs.
在发展中国家办厂可以降低劳动力成本。	
Zài fāzhǎn zhōng guójiā bàn chǎng kěyǐ jiàngdī láodònglì chéngběn.	

(hundred, product, store)

百货商场	bǎihuò shāngchǎng	department store

萧条	xiāotiáo	depression

(this, century, 30s, economic, big, depression, towards, entire, world, hit, very big)	The Great Depression of the 1930s had a great effect on the entire world.
本世纪三十年代的经济大萧条对全球打击巨大。	
Běn shìjì sānshí niándài de jīngjì dà xiāotiáo duì quán qiú dǎjī jùdà.	

(make, discount)

打折	dǎ zhé	discount

(these, apple, very, expensive, you, able, not, able, discount)	These apples are very expensive. Can you reduce the price?
这些苹果很贵, 你能不能打折?	
Zhèxiē píngguǒ hěn guì, nǐ néng bu néng dǎ zhé?	

Note: This phrase might be the most useful in this entire book as just about everything in China can be discounted. It is just a matter of asking. I once got a discount on a book that I bought at an official university bookstore. At the time, I was only kidding around, but it worked!

效益	xiàoyì	efficiency
(very, many, SOE, economic, efficiency, not, good)	The efficiency of many state-owned enterprises is poor.	
很多国企的**经济**效益**不好**。		
Hěn duō guóqǐ de jīngjì xiàoyì bù hǎo.		

外汇	wàihuì	foreign exchange
(foreign exchange, in, China, for the time being, not, able, freely, exchange)	For the time being, foreign exchanges are not freely convertible in China.	
外汇在中国暂时不能自由兑换。		
Wàihuì zài Zhōngguó zànshí bù néng zìyóu duìhuàn.		

(rise, value)		
升值	shēngzhí	appreciation

(lower, value)		
贬值	biǎnzhí	depreciation

(one, country, currency, devaluation, able, increase, that, country's, exports)	The devaluation of a country's currency will increase that country's exports.	
一国货币贬值能增加该国的出口。		
Yì guó huòbì biǎnzhí néng zēngjiā gāi guó de chūkǒu.		

(exhange, rate)		
汇率	huìlǜ	exchange rate

(US Dollar, convert, RMB, exchange rate, recent, several, year, pretty, stable) 美元**兑**人民币的汇率近**几年比较**稳定。	Over the past few years, the exchange rate between the RMB and the US Dollar has been pretty stable.	
Měiyuán duì rénmínbì de huìlǜ jìn jǐ nián bǐjiào wěndìng.		

(current money, inflate)		
通货膨胀	tōnghuò péngzhàng	inflation
(USA, these, few, year, inflation, rate, very, low) 美国**这几年的**通货膨胀率非常**低**。	Over the past few years, America's inflation has been very low.	
Měiguó zhè jǐ nián de tōnghuò péngzhànglǜ fēicháng dī.		

(foundation, facility)		
基础设施	jīchǔ shèshī	infrastructure

(divide, period, pay, funds)		
分期付款	fēn qī fùkuǎn	installments, mortgage
(now, buy, house, majority, people, choose, installment, very, few, people, able, one time, pay off) 现在买房，**多数人选择**分期付款，**很少人能一次**付清。	Most people buying houses today use an installment plan, and very few people are able to pay it off in one lump sum.	
Xiànzài mǎi fáng, duōshù rén xuǎnzé fēn qī fùkuǎn, hěn shǎo rén néng yí cì fù qīng.		

(protect, risk)		
保险	bǎoxiǎn	insurance

(fire, insurance)		
火险	huǒxiǎn	fire insurance
(human being, body, insurance)		
人身保险	rénshēn bǎoxiǎn	life insurance
(medical, treatment, insurance)		
医疗保险	yīliáo bǎoxiǎn	medical insurance
(property, insurance)		
财产保险	cáichǎn bǎoxiǎn	property insurance

(knowledge, property, right)		
知识产权	zhīshi chǎnquán	intellectual property rights
(China, now, diligently, protect, intellectual property rights) 中国正在努力保护知识产权。 Zhōngguó zhèngzài nǔlì bǎohù zhīshi chǎnquán.		China is currently trying to protect intellectual property rights.

(profit, interest, [rate])		
利息(率)	lìxī(lǜ)	interest (rate)
(lower, interest rate, is, stimulating, consumption, measure, one of) 降低利率是刺激消费的措施之一。 Jiàngdī lìlǜ shì cìjī xiāofèi de cuòshī zhī yī.		Lowering interest rates is one way of stimulating consumption.

(cast, money)		
投资	tóuzī	investment, to invest

(we, now, really, need, attract, foreign, investment)	We really need to attract foreign investment.
我们现在非常需要吸引国外的投资。	
Wǒmen xiànzài fēicháng xūyào xīyǐn guówài de tóuzī.	

(release, ticket, [receive, evidence])		
发票(收据)	fāpiào(shōujù)	invoice (receipt)
(miss, you, able, make out, MW, receipt, QW)	Waitress, could you please give us a receipt?	
小姐,你能开张发票吗?		
Xiǎojiě, nǐ néng kāi zhāng fāpiào ma?		

(cut, employee)		
裁员	cáiyuán	to lay off employees
(takeover, usually, mean, layoff)	Takeovers usually mean that there will be layoffs.	
兼并通常意味着裁员。		
Jiānbìng tōngcháng yìwèizhe cáiyuán.		

(borrow, funds)		
贷款	dàikuǎn	loan
(take loan, buy, house, become, PT, very, many, young people's, fad)	Taking loans to buy houses has become a new trend of the younger generation.	
贷款买房成了很多年轻人的时尚。		
Dàikuǎn mǎi fáng chéngle hěn duō niánqīngrén de shíshàng.		

制造商(生产商)	zhìzàoshāng (shēngchǎnshāng)	manufacturer

（Microsoft, is, largest, software, producer）	Microsoft is the largest software pro-
微软是最大的**软件**生产商。	ducer.
Wēiruǎn shì zuì dà de ruǎnjiàn shēngchǎnshāng.	

(market, economy)		
市场经济	shìchǎng jīngjì	market economy

(market, share, amount)		
市场**份**额	shìchǎng fèn'é	market share

（Coke, occupy, PT, China, soft drink, 30％, market, share）	Coke has a 30％ share of China's soft drink market.
可口可乐**抢占**了**中国**软饮料 **30％** 的市场份额。	
Kěkǒukělè qiǎngzhànle Zhōngguó ruǎnyǐnliào bǎi fēn zhī sānshí de shìchǎng fèn'é.	

垄断	lǒngduàn	monopoly
（consumer, support, competition, oppose, monopoly）	Consumers favor competition, oppose monopolies.
消费者鼓励竞争，**反对**垄断。	
Xiāofèizhě gǔlì jìngzhēng, fǎnduì lǒngduàn.	

(famous, brand)		
名牌	míngpái	name brand
（Nike, is, every family knows, famous brand）	Nike is a household name.
耐克是家喻户晓的**名牌**。	
Nàikè shì jiā yù hù xiǎo de míngpái.	

(plan, economy)

计划经济	jìhuà jīngjì	planned economy

(China, now, at, from, planned economy, to, market economy, transformation period)

中国正处在从计划经济到市场经济的转型期。

China is currently in the process of going from a planned economy to a market economy.

Zhōngguó zhèng chǔzài cóng jìhuà jīngjì dào shìchǎng jīngjì de zhuǎnxíngqī.

利润	lìrùn	profit

(this year, this, MW, company, profit, reach, PT, two, one hundred million, *yuan*)

今年这家公司的利润达到了两亿元。

This company's profit was 200 million this year.

Jīnnián zhè jiā gōngsī de lìrùn dádàole liǎng yì yuán.

(decline, go backwards)

衰退	shuāituì	recession

(Japan, in, past, ten, year, happen, PT, economic, recession)

日本在过去十年发生了经济衰退。

Over the past ten years, Japan's economy has been going through a recession.

Rìběn zài guòqù shí nián fāshēngle jīngjì shuāituì.

(fragment, sale [businessman])

零售(商)	língshòu (shāng)	retail (retailer)

(our, wholesale, price, compare, retail, price, cheaper, 3, *yuan*)

我们的批发价格比零售价格便宜三元。

Our wholesale price is three *yuan* cheaper than our retail price.

Wǒmen de pīfā jiàgé bǐ língshòu jiàgé piányi sān yuán.

(receive, enter)		
收入	shōurù	revenues

(sales, amount)		
销售额	xiāoshòu'é	sales
(Dell, company's, computer, sales, amount, have, very, big, increase) 戴尔公司的电脑销售额有很大增长。		Dell's computer sales increased dramatically.
Dài'ěr Gōngsī de diànnǎo xiāoshòu'é yǒu hěn dà zēngzhǎng.		

(sell, goods, person)		
售货员	shòuhuòyuán	salesperson

(commerce, center)		
商业中心	shāngyè zhōngxīn	shopping mall
(Beijing, build, up, PT, very, many, shopping mall) 北京建起了很多商业中心。		There are a good number of shopping malls popping up in Beijing.
Běijīng jiàn qǐle hěn duō shāngyè zhōngxīn.		

(living, level)		
生活水平	shēnghuó shuǐpíng	standard of living
(Opening Up and Reform, make, Chinese, people, living standard, have, PT, obvious, improvement) 改革开放使中国人民的生活水平有了显著提高。		The Reform and Opening-up Policy has significantly increased the living standard of Chinese.
Gǎigé kāifàng shǐ Zhōngguó rénmín de shēnghuó shuǐpíng yǒule xiǎnzhù tígāo.		

(share, ticket)		
股票	gǔpiào	stock

(now, more and more, Chinese, start, speculate, stock)	Now, more and more Chinese are playing the stock market.
现在，越来越多的中国人开始炒股。	
Xiànzài, yuè lái yuè duō de Zhōngguórén kāishǐ chǎogǔ.	

(bear, market)		
熊市	xióngshì	bear market

(bull, market)		
牛市	niúshì	bull market

(on, market)		
上市	shàngshì	to go public

(Israel, already, has, hundred, MW, hi-tech, company, on, NASDAQ, go public)	One hundred Israeli high-tech companies have listed on the NASDAQ.
以色列已有 100 家高科技公司在纳斯达克上市。	
Yísèliè yǐ yǒu yìbǎi jiā gāokējì gōngsī zài Nàsīdákè shàngshì.	

基金	jījīn	mutual fund
(Baoying, is, China, best, mutual fund, management, company)	Baoying Fund Management Company is China's best fund management firm.
宝盈是中国最好的基金管理公司。	
Bǎoyíng shì Zhōngguó zuì hǎo de jījīn guǎnlǐ gōngsī.	

(stock, market)		
股票市场	gǔpiào shìchǎng	stock market

(China's, stock, market, still, very, not, developed) 中国的股票市场还很不发达。		China's stock market has not yet developed.
Zhōngguó de gǔpiào shìchǎng hái hěn bù fādá.		

(stock, trade, market)		
股票交易市场	gǔpiào jiāoyì shìchǎng	stock exchange

(New York, stock, trade, place)		
纽约股票交易所	Niǔyuē gǔpiào jiāoyìsuǒ	the New York Stock Exchange

(*English*, index)		
道·琼斯指数	Dào Qióngsī zhǐshù	Dow Jones Index

(Hang Seng, index)		
恒升指数	Héngshēng zhǐshù	Hang Seng Index

(*English*)		
纳斯达克	Nàsīdákè	NASDAQ

(standard, *English*, index)		
标准普尔指数	biāozhǔn Pǔ'ěr zhǐshù	Standard & Poors

(*English*)		
华尔街	Huá'ěrjiē	Wall Street

(customs, tax)		
关税	guānshuì	tariff

(sea, pass)		
海关	hǎiguān	customs

(when, goods, pass through, another, one, MW, country's, customs, when, usually, will, levy, certain, tariff) 当商品经过另一个国家的海关时，通常要征收一定的关税。		When goods pass through a country's customs, there are usually tariffs levied.
Dāng shāngpǐn jīngguò lìng yí ge guójiā de hǎiguān shí, tōngcháng yào zhēngshōu yídìng de guānshuì.		

税	shuì	Tax
(what, receive, tax)		
所得税	suǒdéshuì	income tax
(collect, tax)		
征税	zhēngshuì	to levy taxes
(this year, China, start, on, savings, interest, levy, tax) 今年中国开始对储蓄利息征税。 Jīnnián Zhōngguó kāishǐ duì chǔxù lìxī zhēngshuì.		This year, China has started to levy taxes on savings.
(pay, tax)		
纳税	nàshuì	to pay taxes
(any, citizen, and, enterprise, all, has, pay tax, obligation) 任何公民和企业都有纳税的义务。 Rènhé gōngmín hé qǐyè dōu yǒu nàshuì de yìwù.		Every person and business has the obligation of paying taxes.

(free of, tax)		
免税	miǎnshuì	duty free
(duty-free shop, thing, very, cheap) 免税商店的东西很便宜。 miǎnshuì shāngdiàn de dōngxi hěn piányi.		Items sold in duty-free shops are very cheap.
(pay, tax, person)		
纳税人	nàshuìrén	tax payer

(trade, exchange)		
贸易	màoyì	trade

(USA, and, Europe, trade, relationship, to some extent, deteriorate)	America and Europe's trade relationship to some extent has deteriorated.	
美国和欧洲的贸易关系有所恶化。		
Měiguó hé Ōuzhōu de màoyì guānxi yǒu suǒ èhuà.		

(out, port [trade])		
出口(贸易)	chūkǒu (màoyì)	export

(enter, port [trade])		
进口(贸易)	jìnkǒu (màoyì)	import

(Japan, need, import, big, amount, raw materials)	Japan must import a large amount of raw materials.	
日本需要进口大量原材料。		
Rìběn xūyào jìnkǒu dàliàng yuáncáiliào.		

(trade, deficit)		
贸易逆差	màoyì nìchā	trade deficit

(trade, surplus)		
贸易顺差	màoyì shùnchā	trade surplus

(usually, Japan, trade, surplus, USA, trade, deficit)	Japan usually has a trade surplus while the US usually runs a deficit.	
通常,日本贸易顺差,美国贸易逆差。		
Tōngcháng, Rìběn màoyì shùnchā, Měiguó màoyì nìchā.		

(business, label)		
商标	shāngbiāo	trade mark

(travel, check)		
旅行支票	lǚxíng zhīpiào	traveler's check

(travel, check, use, very, convenient, also, very, safe)	Traveler's checks are both convenient and safe.
旅行支票使用非常方便, 而且很安全。	
Lǚxíng zhīpiào shǐyòng fēicháng fāngbiàn, érqiě hěn ānquán.	

(bulk, deliver [salesman])		
批发(商)	pīfā (shāng)	wholesale (wholesaler)

(board of directors, council)		
董事会	dǒngshìhuì	board of directors
(board of directors, chief)		
董事长	dǒngshìzhǎng	chairman of the board
(chief, to execute, official)		
首席执行官	shǒuxí zhíxíngguān	CEO
(head, manager)		
总经理	zǒngjīnglǐ	general manager
(sales, manager)		
销售经理	xiāoshòu jīnglǐ	sales manager
(person, affair, manager)		
人事经理	rénshì jīnglǐ	human resources manager

澳元(澳大利亚元)	àoyuán	dollars (Australia)
加元(加拿大元)	jiāyuán	dollars (Canada)
新西兰元	Xīnxīlányuán	dollars (New Zealand)
美元	měiyuán	dollars (US)

何兰盾	Hélán dùn	florin (Netherlands)
比利时法郎	Bǐlìshí fǎláng	franc (Belgium)
法郎	fǎláng	franc (France)
瑞士法郎	Ruìshì fǎláng	franc (Switzerland)
瑞典克朗	Ruìdiǎn kèlǎng	krona (Sweden)
丹麦克朗	Dānmài kèlǎng	krona (Denmark)
挪威克朗	Nuówēi kèlǎng	krone (Norway)
意大利里拉	Yìdàlì lǐlā	lira (Italy)
德国马克	Déguó mǎkè	mark (Germany)
西班牙比赛塔	Xībānyá bǐsàitǎ	peseta (Sapin)
阿根廷比索	Āgēntíng bǐsuǒ	peso (Argentina)
智利比索	Zhìlì bǐsuǒ	peso (Chile)
英镑	yīngbàng	pound (Britain)
爱尔兰镑	Ài'ěrlán bàng	pound (Ireland)
卢布	lúbù	rouble (Russia)
印度卢比	Yìndù lúbǐ	rupee (India)
巴基斯坦卢比	Bājīsītǎn lúbǐ	rupee (Pakistan)
谢克尔	xièkè'ěr	shekel (Israel)
韩元	hányuán	won (Korea)
日元	rìyuán	yen (Japan)
人民币	rénmínbì	RMB *yuan* (China)

(black, market)		
黑市	hēishì	black exchange market
(if, you, need, **US dollars**, can, to, black market, go, change)	If you need **US dollars** you can go to the black market and exchange.	
如果**你**需要**美元**，可以**到黑市去换**。		
Rúguǒ nǐ xūyào **měiyuán**, kěyǐ dào hēishì qù huàn.		

Countries

国 家

(country, family)		
国家	Guójiā	**Countries**
(you, are, which, country, person) **Q)** 你是哪国人？ Nǐ shì nǎ guó rén?		Which country are you from?
(you, from, where, come) **Q)** 你从哪里来？ Nǐ cóng nǎli lái?		Where do you come from?
(I, am, from, **USA**, come) **A)** 我是从美国来的。 Wǒ shì cóng **Měiguó** lái de.		I come from the **US**.
(I, am, **USA**, person) **A)** 我是美国人。 Wǒ shì **Měiguó** rén.		I am **American**.

	阿富汗	Āfùhàn	Afghanistan
	阿尔巴尼亚	Ā'ěrbāníyà	Albania
	阿尔及利亚	Ā'ěrjílìyà	Algeria
	阿根廷	Āgēntíng	Argentina
	澳大利亚	Àodàlìyà	Australia

	奥地利	Àodìlì	Austria
	比利时	Bǐlìshí	Belgium
	波黑	Bōhēi	Bosnia & Herzegovina
	巴西	Bāxī	Brazil
	保加利亚	Bǎojiālìyà	Bulgaria
	加拿大	jiānádà	Canada
	智利	Zhìlì	Chile
	中国	Zhōngguó	China
	古巴	Gǔbā	Cuba
	丹麦	Dānmài	Denmark
	东帝汶	Dōngdìwèn	East Timor
	埃及	Āijí	Egypt
	埃塞俄比亚	Āisài'ébǐyà	Ethiopia
	芬兰	Fēnlán	Finland
	法国	Fǎguó	France
	德国	Déguó	Germany

	加纳	Jiānà	Ghana
	希腊	Xīlà	Greece
	荷兰	Hélán	Holland
	匈牙利	Xiōngyálì	Hungary
	(ice, island) 冰岛	Bīngdǎo	Iceland
	印度	Yìndù	India
	印尼(印度尼西亚)	Yìnní（Yìndùníxīyà)	Indonesia
	伊朗	Yīlǎng	Iran
	伊拉克	Yīlākè	Iraq
	爱尔兰	Ài'ěrlán	Ireland
	以色列	Yǐsèliè	Israel
	意大利	Yìdàlì	Italy
	日本	Rìběn	Japan
	约旦	Yuēdàn	Jordan
	哈萨克斯坦	Hāsākèsītǎn	Kazakhstan
	韩国	Hánguó	the Republic of Korea
	科威特	Kēwēitè	Kuwait
	马来西亚	Mǎláixīyà	Malaysia

	墨西哥	Mòxīgē	Mexico
	蒙古	Měnggǔ	Mongolia
	摩洛哥	Móluògē	Morocco
	新西兰	Xīnxīlán	New Zealand
	朝鲜	Cháoxiǎn	the Democratic People's Republic of Korea
	挪威	Nuówēi	Norway
	巴基斯坦	Bājīsītǎn	Pakistan
	巴拿马	Bānámǎ	Panama
	秘鲁	Bìlǔ	Peru
	菲律宾	Fēilùbīn	Philippines
	波兰	Bōlán	Poland
	葡萄牙	Pútáoyá	Portugal
	俄罗斯	Éluósī	Russia
	沙特阿拉伯	Shātè Ālābó	Saudi Arabia
	新加坡	Xīnjiāpō	Singapore
	南非	Nánfēi	South Africa
	西班牙	Xībānyá	Spain
	瑞典	Ruìdiǎn	Sweden
	瑞士	Ruìshì	Switzerland

	苏丹	Sūdān	Sudan
	泰国	Tàiguó	Thailand
	土耳其	Tǔ'ěrqí	Turkey
	阿拉伯联合酋长国	Ālābó Liánhéqiúzhǎngguó	UAE
	乌克兰	Wūkèlán	Ukraine
	英国	Yīngguó	United Kingdom
	美国	Měiguó	United States
	委内瑞拉	Wěinèiruìlā	Venezuela
	越南	Yuènán	Vietnam
	南斯拉夫	Nánsīlāfū	Yugoslavia

洲	zhōu	Continent
非洲	Fēizhōu	Africa
南极洲	Nánjízhōu	Antarctica
亚洲	Yàzhōu	Asia
欧洲	Ōuzhōu	Europe
拉丁美洲	Lādīng Měizhōu	Latin America
北美洲	Běiměizhōu	North America
大洋洲	Dàyángzhōu	Oceania
南美洲	Nánměizhōu	South America

Country Leaders

国家元首 *

澳大利亚	Àodàlìyà	Australia
霍华德	Huòhuádé	John Howard

中国	Zhōngguó	China
毛泽东	Máo Zédōng	Mao Zedong
周恩来	Zhōu Ēnlái	Zhou Enlai
邓小平	Dèng Xiǎopíng	Deng Xiaoping
江泽民	Jiāng Zémín	Jiang Zemin
朱镕基	Zhū Róngjī	Zhu Rongji

古巴	Gǔbā	Cuba
卡斯特罗	Kǎsītèluó	Fidel Castro

英国	Yīngguó	England
丘吉尔	Qiūjí'ěr	Winston Churchill
撒切尔	Sàqiè'ěr	Margaret Thatcher
布莱尔	Bùlái'ěr	Tony Blair

---

* Those names of the country leaders that people are familiar with are selected and listed here without any political purposes.

法国	Fǎguó	France
拿破仑	Nápòlún	Napoleon
戴高乐	Dàigāolè	De Gaule
希拉克	Xīlākè	Jacques Chirac

德国	Déguó	Germany
科尔	Kē'ěr	Helmut Kohl
施罗德	Shīluódé	Gerhard Schroeder

印度	Yìndù	India
甘地	Gāndì	Mohandas Gandhi
瓦杰帕伊	Wǎjiépàyī	Atal Behari Vajpayee

伊朗	yīlǎng	Iran
霍梅尼	Huòméiní	Ayatullah Khomeni
哈塔米	Hātǎmǐ	Mohammad Khatami

伊拉克	Yīlākè	Iraq
萨达姆·侯塞因	Sàdámǔ Hóusàiyīn	Saddam Hussein

以色列	Yǐsèliè	Israel
拉宾	Lābīn	Yitzhak Rabin
内塔尼亚胡	Nèitǎníyàhú	Benjamin Netanyahu
巴拉克	Bālākè	Ahud Barak
沙龙	Shālóng	Ariel Sharon

日本	Rìběn	Japan
小渊惠三	Xiǎoyuān Huìsān	Keizou Obuchi
森喜朗	Sēn Xǐlǎng	Yoshirou Mori
小泉纯一郎	Xiǎoquán Chúnyīláng	Junichiro Koizumi

韩国	Hánguó	Korea
金大中	Jīn Dàzhōng	Kim Dae Jung

朝鲜	Cháoxiǎn	North Korea
金日成	jīn Rìchéng	Kim Il Sung
金正日	Jīn Zhèngrì	Kim Jong Il

巴基斯坦	Bājīsītǎn	Pakistan
穆沙拉夫	Mùshālāfū	Pervez Musharaff

巴勒斯坦	Bālèsītǎn	Palestine
阿拉法特	Ālāfǎtè	Yasser Arafat

俄罗斯	Éluósī	Russia
叶利钦	Yèlìqīn	Boris Yeltsen
普京	Pǔjīng	Vladimir Putin

南非	Nánfēi	South Africa
曼德拉	Màndélā	Nelson Mandela
姆贝基	Mǔbèijī	Thabo Mbeki

美国	Měiguó	United States
华盛顿	Huáshèngdùn	George Washington
杰斐逊	Jiéfěixùn	Thomas Jefferson
林肯	Línkěn	Abraham Lincoln
罗斯福	Luósīfú	F. D. Roosevelt
肯尼迪	Kěnnídí	John F. Kennedy
尼克松	Níkèsōng	Richard Nixon
里根	Lǐgēn	Ronald Reagan
布什	Bùshí	George Bush
克林顿	Kèlíndùn	William J. Clinton
小布什	Xiǎo Bùshí	George. W. Bush

Language Studies

语言学习

(word, gender)		
词性	cíxìng	part of speech

(this, MW, word, is, what, part of speech)	What is this word's part of speech?
Q) 这个词是什么词性？	
Zhè ge cí shì shénme cíxìng?	

(this, MW, word, is, _____)	This word is a (an) _____.
A) 这个词是_____。	
Zhè ge cí shì _____.	

(describe, word)		
形容词	xíngróngcí	adjective
副词	fùcí	adverb
(connect, word)		
连词	liáncí	conjunctive word
(measure, word)		
量词	liàngcí	measure word
(name, word)		
名词	míngcí	noun
(introduce, word)		
介词	jiècí	preposition
(substitute, word)		
代词	dàicí	pronoun
(action, word)		
动词	dòngcí	verb

(this, MW, word, is, **word with a positive connotation**, QW) 这个词是**褒义词**吗？	Does this word have a **positive** connotation?
Zhè ge cí shì **bāoyìcí** ma?	

(neutral, word) 中性词	zhōngxìngcí	word with neutral meaning
(derogatory, word) 贬义词	biǎnyìcí	word with negative connotation

(this, MW, word, is, abstract word, or, concrete word) **Q**）这个词是抽象词还是具体词？	Is this word abstract or concrete?
Zhè ge cí shì chōuxiàngcí háishi jùtǐcí?	
(it, is, MW, abstract word/concrete word) **A**）它是个抽象词/具体词。	It is an abstract/a concrete word.
Tā shì ge chōuxiàngcí/jùtǐcí.	

(mouth, sound) 口音	kǒuyīn	accent
(he, has, a little, southern, accent) 他有一点儿南方口音。		He has a slight southern accent.
Tā yǒu yìdiǎnr nánfāng kǒuyīn.		
(his, accent, very, heavy) 他的口音很重。		He has a very heavy accent.
Tā de kǒuyīn hěn zhòng.		

(Chinese, character)		
汉字	Hànzì	Chinese characters
(simple, style, character)		
简体字	jiǎntǐzì	simplified characters
(complex, style, character)		
繁体字	fántǐzì	original complex characters
(you, able, write, Chinese characters, QW)		Can you write Chinese characters?
Q) 你会写汉字吗?		
Nǐ huì xiě Hànzì ma?		
(I, only, able, write, 300, MW)		I can only write 300.
A) 我只会写三百个。		
Wǒ zhǐ huì xiě sānbǎi ge.		
(many, pronunciation, character)		
多音字	duōyīnzì	character with multiple pronunciations
(乐, is, many, pronunciation, character, sometimes, read, "lè", sometimes, read, "yuè")		乐 is a character that has more than one pronunciation. Sometimes it is read "*lè*" and sometimes it is read "*yuè*".
乐是多音字,有的时候读"lè",有的时候读"yuè"。		
乐 shì duōyīnzì, yǒu de shíhou dú "lè", yǒu de shíhòu dú "yuè".		

(up, down, text)		
上下文	shàngxiàwén	context
(from, context, I, can, guess, this, MW, word's, meaning)		From the context, I can guess the meaning of this word.
从上下文我可以猜出这个词的意思。		
Cóng shàngxiàwén wǒ kěyǐ cāi chū zhè ge cí de yìsi.		

(dirty, word)		
脏话	zānghuà	curse word
(this, counted as, curse word, QW)	Is this a curse word?	
这算脏话吗?		
Zhè suàn zānghuà ma?		

词典	cídiǎn	dictionary
(this, MW, word, in, dictionary, inside, able, look up, QW)	Is this word in the dictionary?	
这个词在词典里能查到吗?		
Zhè ge cí zài cídiǎn li néng chá dào ma?		

正式	zhèngshì	formal (language)
(this, MW, word, very, formal, QW)	Is this word formal?	
这个词很正式吗?		
Zhè ge cí hěn zhèngshì ma?		

(language, law)		
语法	yǔfǎ	grammar
(I, don't, understand, this, MW, sentence's, grammar, you, can, explain, a little, QW)	I don't understand the grammar in this sentence. Can you explain it to me?	
我不懂这个句子的语法,你可以解释一下吗?		
Wǒ bù dǒng zhè ge jùzi de yǔfǎ, nǐ kěyǐ jiěshi yíxià ma?		

(Mr./Mrs. Wang, you [polite], can, analyze, a little, this, MW, sentence's, structure, QW)	Mr./Mrs. Wang, could you please analyze the structure of this sentence?
王老师, 您能分析一下这个句子的结构吗?	
Wáng lǎoshī, nín néng fēnxī yíxià zhè ge jùzi de jiégòu ma?	

(set, language)		
成语	chéngyǔ	idiom
(very, many, Chinese, idiom, have origins in, ancient time, story)	Many Chinese idioms have their origins in ancient China.	
很多中国的成语源于古代的故事。		
Hěn duō Zhōngguó de chéngyǔ yuányú gǔdài de gùshi.		

(mute, **English**)		
哑巴英语	yǎba Yīngyǔ	can only read and write, but not speak a language
(very, many, Chinese, study, is, mute, English, need, improve, listening, and, spoken)	Many Chinese can read and write English, but they need to improve their spoken and listening.	
很多中国人学的是哑巴英语, 需要提高听力和口语。		
Hěn duō Zhōngguórén xué de shì yǎba Yīngyǔ, xūyào tígāo tīnglì hé kǒuyǔ.		

(spell, sound)		
拼音	pīnyīn	*Pinyin* Romanization system
(*pinyin*, is, speak, good, Chinese, knock, door, brick)	*Pinyin* is your training wheels for speaking good Chinese.	
拼音是说好汉语的敲门砖。		
Pīnyīn shì shuō hǎo Hànyǔ de qiāoménzhuān.		

(produce, sound)		
发音	fāyīn	pronunciation
(my, pronunciation, clear, QW) 我的发音清楚吗？ Wǒ de fāyīn qīngchu ma?		Is my pronunciation clear?
(this, MW, word's, pronunciation, you, articulate, not, accurate) 这个单词的发音你咬得不准。 Zhè ge dāncí de fāyīn nǐ yǎo de bù zhǔn.		You didn't pronounce this word accurately.
(this, MW, sound, you, pronounce, not, is, very, to position) 这个音你发得不是很到位。 Zhè ge yīn nǐ fā de bú shì hěn dàowèi.		Your pronunciation of this word is not perfect.
(your, pronunciation, still, need, further, polish, practice) 你的发音还需要进一步磨炼。 Nǐ de fāyīn hái xūyào jìn yí bù móliàn.		Your pronunciation still needs some work.
(pronounce, this, MW, sound, when, tongue, should, place, at, where) Q）发这个音时，舌头应该放在哪儿？ Fā zhè ge yīn shí, shétou yīnggāi fàng zài nǎr?		When pronouncing this sound, what is the positioning of the tongue?
(tongue, should, place, at, mouth cavity, upper part) A）舌头应该放在口腔上部。 Shétou yīnggāi fàng zài kǒuqiāng shàngbù.		Your tongue should be placed on the roof of your mouth.
(pronounce, this, MW, sound, when, should, send, air) 发这个音时，应该送气。 Fā zhè ge yīn shí, yīnggāi sòngqì.		When you pronounce this sound, air should leave your mouth. (aspirated)

(raw, neglect)		
生疏	shēngshū	rusty
(I, just, return, China, my Chinese, still, has, a little, rusty) 我刚回中国，汉语还有一点儿生疏。	I just came back to China so my Chinese is a little rusty.	
Wǒ gāng huí Zhōngguó, Hànyǔ hái yǒu yìdiǎnr shēngshū.		

(fixed, arranged pairs)		
固定搭配	gùdìng dāpèi	set phrase, two words that always go together
("receive, superb, grades", in, "receive", and, "grades", is, set phrase) "取得优异成绩"中，"取得"和"成绩"是固定搭配。	In the phrase "qǔdé yōuyì chéngjì", "qǔdé" and "chéngjì" is a set phrase.	
"Qǔdé yōuyì chéngjì" zhōng "qǔdé" hé "chéngjì" shì gùdìng dāpèi.		

偏	piān	seldom used, rare
(this, MW, word, too, very, seldom, use) 这个词太偏了，很少用。	This word is very rare. It's not used often.	
Zhè ge cí tài piān le, hěn shǎo yòng.		

(unrefined, language)		
俚语	lǐyǔ	slang
(I, towards, slang, unusually, interested) 我对俚语非常感兴趣。	I have a deep interest in slang.	
Wǒ duì lǐyǔ fēicháng gǎn xìngqù.		

(mouth, language)

口语	kǒuyǔ	spoken language

(this, kind, way of speaking, in, spoken language, inside, often, use, QW) 这种说法在口语里常用吗？	Is this often used in spoken language?
Zhè zhǒng shuōfǎ zài kǒuyǔ li chángyòng ma?	

语气	yǔqì	tone

(this, MW, sentence, your, tone, not, enough, strong) 这句话你的语气不够强。	Your tone isn't strong enough.
Zhè jù huà nǐ de yǔqì bú gòu qiáng.	

声调	shēngdiào	tones

(this, MW, character, pronounce, what tone) 这个字发第几声？	What is this character's tone?
Zhè ge zì fā dì jǐ shēng?	
(you, able, tell, me, this, MW, character's, tone, QW) 你能告诉我这个字的声调吗？	Can you tell me this character's tone?
Nǐ néng gàosu wǒ zhè ge zì de shēngdiào ma?	
(this, MW, character, is, 4th, tone) 这个字是第四声。	This character's tone is the fourth tone.
Zhé ge zì shì dì sì shēng.	
(this, MW, character, is, many, pronunciation, character, in, here, pronounce, 2nd, tone) 这个字是多音字，在这里发第二声。	This is a character with more than one pronunciation. In this situation it is pronounced in the 2nd tone.
Zhè ge zì shì duōyīnzì, zài zhèli fā dì èr shēng.	

(this, MW, word, by itself, use, pronounce, 2nd, tone, but, here, pronounce, neutral tone)	When used by itself, this character is pronounced as the second tone, but when it is combined with another character it is pronounced as the neutral tone.
这个字单独用发第二声，但这里发轻声。	
Zhè ge zì dāndú yòng fā dì èr shēng, dàn zhèli fā qīngshēng.	

翻译	fānyì	translate
(this, MW, words, how, translate, into, English)		How do you translate this sentence into English?
这句话怎么翻成英语？		
Zhè jù huà zěnme fān chéng Yīngyǔ?		

(assist, lead)		
辅导	fǔdǎo	tutor
(I, today, have, tutor)		I am going to meet with my tutor today.
我今天有辅导。		
Wǒ jīntiān yǒu fǔdǎo.		

(word, gather together, amount)		
词汇量	cíhuìliàng	vocabulary
(I, must, enlarge, my, vocabulary)		I have to enlarge my vocabulary.
我得扩大我的词汇量。		
Wǒ děi kuòdà wǒ de cíhuìliàng.		
(his, vocabulary, very, big/small)		His vocabulary is very big/small.
他的词汇量很大/小。		
Tā de cíhuìliàng hěn dà/xiǎo.		

书面语	shūmiànyǔ	written language

(this, MW, sentence, only, used, in, written language, inside)	This word is only used in written language.
这句话只用在书面语中。	
Zhè jù huà zhǐ yòng zài shūmiànyǔ zhōng.	

(give, me, hold, MW, example, OK, QW)	Could you please give me an example?
给我举个例子，好吗？	
Gěi wǒ jǔ ge lìzi, hǎo ma?	

(his, Chinese, unusually, fluent)	He speaks Chinese fluently.
他汉语非常流利。	
Tā Hànyǔ fēicháng liúlì.	

(sorry, I, didn't, hear, clearly, you, can, repeat, one, time, QW)	I'm sorry. I didn't hear clearly. Could you please say it again?
对不起，我没听清楚，你能重复一遍吗？	
Dùibuqǐ, wǒ méi tīng qīngchu, nǐ néng chóngfù yí biàn ma?	

(this, MW, character's, original meaning, is, what)	What is the original meaning of this word?
这个字的原义是什么？	
Zhè ge zì de yuányì shì shénme?	

(this, MW, word, how, use, you, can, give, me, one, MW, language, environment, QW)	Can you please tell me the language environment in which this word is used?
这个词怎么用，你能给我一个语言环境吗？	
Zhè ge cí zěnme yòng, nǐ néng gěi wǒ yí ge yǔyán huánjìng ma?	

(this, MW, use, Chinese, how, say)	How do you say this in Chinese?
这个用汉语怎么说？	
Zhè ge yòng Hànyǔ zěnme shuō?	

(his, handwriting, very, neat/sloppy)	His handwriting is very neat/sloppy.
他的字迹很工整/潦草。	
Tā de zìjì hěn gōngzhěng/liáocǎo.	

(this, MW, word, I, use, appropriate, QW)	Did I use the word correctly?
这个词我用得恰当吗？	
Zhè ge cí wǒ yòng de qiàdàng ma?	
(you, just, speak, words, I, only, understand, half)	I understood about half of what you said.
你刚说的话我只懂一半儿。	
Nǐ gāng shuō de huà wǒ zhǐ dǒng yíbànr.	

(this, MW, sentence, has, quite a number of, layer, meaning)	This sentence has many different meanings.
这句话有好几层意思。	
Zhè jù huà yǒu hǎo jǐ céng yìsi.	

(this, MW, sentence, has, ambiguity)	This sentence is ambiguous.
这句话有歧义。	
Zhè jù huà yǒu qíyì.	

(listen, tape, is, improve, listening, good, approach)	Listening to tapes is a good way of improving your listening ability.
听磁带是提高听力的好办法。	
Tīng cídài shì tígāo tīnglì de hǎo bànfǎ.	

(this, MW, word, is, Mandarin, or, local dialect) 这个词是普通话还是方言？	Is this word Mandarin or local dialect?
Zhè ge cí shì pǔtōnghuà háishi fāngyán?	

(your, tongue, very, stiff, should, relax) 你的舌头很硬，应该放松。	Your tongue is too stiff. Please relax!
Nǐ de shétou hěn yìng, yīnggāi fàngsōng.	

(I, want, establish, MW, solid, Chinese, foundation) 我想打个扎实的汉语基础。	I want to establish a solid Chinese foundation.
Wǒ xiǎng dǎ ge zhāshi de Hànyǔ jīchǔ.	

(I, just now, speak, PT, words, tone, not accurate, so, you, not, listen, understand) 我刚才说的话声调不准，所以你没听明白。	I didn't say it clearly so you didn't understand.
Wǒ gāngcái shuō de huà shēngdiào bù zhǔn, suǒyǐ nǐ méi tīng míngbai.	

(this, MW, word, how to use) 这个词怎么用？	How is this word used?
Zhè ge cí zěnme yòng?	

(this, MW, word, in, daily life, inside, how to use)	How is this word used in everyday life?
这个词在日常生活中怎么用?	
Zhè ge cí zài rìcháng shēnghuó zhōng zěnme yòng?	

(this, MW, word, often, used, QW)	Is this word often used?
这个词常用吗?	
Zhè ge cí chángyòng ma?	

(sorry, just, say, words, not, express, my, meaning; my, language, feeling, not, right)	I'm sorry. What I just said was not what I meant to say. My understanding of Chinese is not right. (Maybe you said a word that makes sense in your mother tongue, but when translated into Chinese does not.)
对不起, 刚说的话没有表达我的意思。我的语感不对。	
Duìbuqǐ, gāng shuō de huà méiyǒu biǎodá wǒ de yìsi. Wǒ de yǔgǎn bú duì.	

(your, Chinese, speak, very, good)	You really speak Chinese well!
A) 你的汉语说得很棒!	
Nǐ de Hànyǔ shuō de hěn bàng!	
(you, too, compliment, me)	You are flattering me.
B) 你太抬举我了。	
Nǐ tài táijǔ wǒ le.	

(your, Chinese, very, good)	Your Chinese is very good.
A) 你的中文很好。	
Nǐ de Zhōngwén hěn hǎo.	

(no big deal, practice makes perfect, nothing more)	It is really not a big deal. Practice makes perfect, nothing more.
B) 没什么大不了的,**熟能生巧**而已。	
Méi shénme dàbuliǎo de, shú néng shēng qiǎo éryǐ.	

(your, Chinese, not bad)	Your Chinese is pretty good.
A) 你的**中文**不错。	
Nǐ de Zhōngwén búcuò.	
(you, over praise)	You are over-praising me.
B) 你过奖了。	
Nǐ guòjiǎng le.	

(your, Mandarin, speak, very, superb)	Your Mandarin is kicking!
A) 你的普通话说得很溜!	
Nǐ de pǔtōnghuà shuō de hěn liù!	
(I, only, study, PT, a little, nothing more, still, behind, far)	I have only scratched the surface. I still have a long way to go.
B) 我只学了点皮毛而已,还差得远呢。	
Wǒ zhǐ xuéle diǎn pímáo éryǐ, hái chà de yuǎn ne.	

(your, Chinese, indeed, with, Chinese, speak, same)	Your words are exactly like a Chinese person's.
A) 你的**汉语**简直**跟**中国人讲得一样。	
Nǐ de Hànyǔ jiǎnzhí gēn Zhōngguórén jiǎng de yíyàng.	
(not, dare, serve)	I am flattered.
B) 不敢当。	
Bù gǎndāng.	

(your, Chinese, level, soon, catch up to, Dashan) **A**) 你的**汉语水平快**赶上**大山**了。	Your Chinese level is approaching Dashan's.
Nǐ de Hànyǔ shuǐpíng kuài gǎn shàng Dàshān le.	
(I, how, can, with, Dashan, mutual, mention, together, discuss) **B**) 我怎么能跟大山相提并论？	How can I be mentioned in the same breath as Dashan?
Wǒ zěnme néng gēn Dàshān xiāng tí bìng lùn?	
(who, say, not, is) **B**) 谁说不是呢？	Who said it wasn't?
Shéi shuō bú shì ne?	
(that, still, need, say) **B**) 那还用说？	Is it necessary to say this? (Of course it is)
Nà hái yòng shuō?	

(he, speak, very, _____) 他说话很_____。	He speaks very _____.
Tā shuōhuà hěn _____.	

快	kuài	fast
(have, level)		
有水平	yǒu shuǐpíng	intelligent, refined
(big, sound)		
大声	dàshēng	loud
轻	qīng	light
慢	màn	slow
俗	sú	vulgar

If the name of a country ends in guó (法国 Fǎguó France, 德国 Déguó, Germany etc.), omitting the guó and adding yǔ will create the language that is spoken in that country (法语 Fǎyǔ French, 德语 Déyǔ German).

If the name of a country has been formed by its English counterpart (西班牙 Xībānyá, Spain, 丹麦 Dānmài Denmark), adding yǔ will form the name of the language spoken in that country (西班牙语 Xībānyáyǔ Spanish, 丹麦语 Dānmàiyǔ Dutch). Because Japanese already uses Chinese characters, 日语 Rìyǔ Japanese is an exception to this rule.

Please refer to list of countries in Section V *Category Dictionary: Countries*.

The History of Chinese Characters

In April of 2000, Chinese archaeologists unearthed a 4,800-year-old piece of pottery bearing Chinese characters. These pottery inscriptions, which were found in Juxian County, Shandong Province (Eastern China), trace the first usage of Chinese characters to a time when people recorded events by tying knots in ropes or strings.

Although there are a few different versions as to who invented Chinese characters, the most widely accepted is that court minister Ts'ang Chieh (仓颉, Cāngjié) invented characters to facilitate record keeping. It is believed that Ts'ang Chieh was inspired to create a system using lines, shapes and pictures to represent ideas after observing the footprints of birds and animals.

There are mainly four types of Chinese characters, *Borrowings* are borrowed from other characters but have different radicals that allow them to be differentiated. For example, 快 (kuài fast) and 块 (kuài piece). *Ideograms* are made by the association of two characters, such as 众 (zhòng crowd) which is made up of three 人 (rén persons). *Ideophonograms* are characters that are composed of two elements, one representing the meaning while the other representing the pronunciation. The character 湖 is comprised of 氵 (sāndiǎnshuǐ water) and 胡 which is pronounced Hú. *Pictographs* are characters that look like the actual thing that it is representing, such as 山 (shān mountain).

In Chinese, there are countless dialects including Mandarin, Hokkien, Fuzhou, Hakka, Min Nan, Cantonese, etc., but there are only two types of written characters, traditional and simplified. Traditional characters are still used in Hong Kong

(SAR) and Taiwan. Simplified characters, which were introduced in the late 1950s to create one standard Chinese language, are used in the mainland and Singapore. The largest Chinese dictionary contains mord than 50,000 characters. Fortunately, only 3,000 – 4,000 are needed for daily use.

Chapter VI

PERSONAGES

人物

Confucius (*551 BC—479 BC*), *Chinese Philosopher*

孔子 Kǒngzǐ

Confucius was probably the greatest moral philosopher in ancient China and has had by far the biggest impact on Chinese life. Born K'ung Ch'iu in the small feudal state of Lu (now Shandong Province) in 551 BC, Confucius led a rather uneventful life, that is, if compared to his impact following his death. His father died when he was only three and his mother took the role of educating him. He quickly developed a strong thirst for knowledge.

He had served in minor government posts before he married when he was 19. His knowledge of ritual, music, archery, charioteering, calligraphy and mathematics, coupled with his familiarity with classical traditions including poetry and history, allowed him to start teaching when he was in his 30s.

In his late 40s and 50s, Confucius served as a magistrate, as an assistant minister of public works, and as minister of justice in the state of Lu. Confucius's political career was short-lived as he did not get along well with some of the king's inner cabinet members. He felt that they were not interested in his objectives, especially those dealing with education. He later left the country in search of a state that was interested in his teachings. He was followed by hundreds of disciples and his name became synonymous with vision. Unsuccessful, he returned 12 years later to continue teaching. Confucius was known as a person with a righteous passion, who although faced great obstacles, still attempted to achieve his goals. He died in 479 BC at the age of 73.

Confucius was the first person in China who wanted to make education available to everyone. He held the belief that ordinary human beings could become awe-inspiring. He believed that human beings were teachable, could be improved, and perfected. He felt that the superior man was motivated by the desire to good deeds, and not by personal profit. Confucius considered himself the transmitter who consciously tried to re-animate the old in order to attain the new.

(three, people, together, walk, must, have, my, teacher)	
三人同行，必有我师。	If three of us are walking together, at least one of the other two is good enough to be my teacher; regardless of educational level, we can all teach each other something.
Sān rén tóng xíng, bì yǒu wǒ shī.	

(have, friend, from, far, place, come, not, also, happy, QW)	
有朋自远方来，不亦乐乎？	"Isn't it great that a friend from far away is coming?"
Yǒu péng zì yuǎn fāng lái, bú yì lè hū?	
(our, good, friend, Park, next week, will, come, China)	Our good friend Park will come to China next week.
A) 我们的好朋友朴下周要来中国。	
Wǒmen de hǎo péngyou Piáo xià zhōu yào lái Zhōngguó.	
(very, good, truly, is, "Isn't it great that a friend from far away is coming?")	Great! It truly is "A friend coming from a far place isn't a great thing?"
B) 太好了! 真是"有朋自远方来，不亦乐乎"。	
Tài hǎo le! Zhēn shì yǒu péng zì yuǎn fāng lái, bú yì lè hū.	

Sun Yat-sen, Chinese Revolutionary

孙中山　Sūn Zhōngshān

Born near southern China's Guangzhou on November 12th, 1866, Sun Yat-sen is considered the "Father of Modern China". In 1879, Sun traveled to the United States to be with his brother who emigrated earlier. There he became familiar with Western influences, but when his brother objected to his belief in Christianity, he decided to return home. In 1885 he married Lu Mu-chen, the girl selected for him

by his parents. The couple had two daughters and one boy.

Although Sun had earned his medical degree, he forsook his practice to help China break away from the years of humiliation at the hands of more technologically advanced Western powers. In 1894 Sun sent national leaders his ideas on how to make China a strong power, but all he received in return was the equivalent of a "thank you". In that same year, Sun founded the "Revive China Society", a secret organization whose membership was mainly drawn from the lower classes of society.

In 1911, the Qing Dynasty leaders nationalized the railway system, and in doing so encroached upon the interests of local leaders. This led to successful rebellions all over the country and Sun was named provisional president of the new Chinese republic. Influenced by Karl Marx, Sun's political theory was based upon the guiding principles of nationalism, democracy, and people's livelihood. Realizing that his regime was weak, Sun made a deal with Yuan Shikai, an imperial minister who had been entrusted with the court. Yuan Shikai became more and more dictatorial and Sun successfully revolted against him and became president of a self-proclaimed government in Guangzhou in 1921. He later became director of the Kuomintang Party (KMT).

In 1924, he joined forces with Chinese Communists and accepted aid from the USSR. He passed away in 1925 and is known today as a "pioneer of the revolution."

the Model Soldier

雷锋　Léi Fēng

Lei Feng was born into a poor peasant family on December 18, 1940 in Hunan Province. In his youth, his father was killed at the hands of the Japanese and his mother committed suicide. Lei Feng was saved by the communist party who fed and raised him. He joined the People's Liberation Army and was a model soldier. He sent his meager earnings to the parents of a fellow soldier who had been injured in a flood; he served tea and food to officers; and performed other deeds that showed his deep passion towards Chairman Mao and the Communist Party.

On August 15, 1962, while working at the Fushun Army Base, Lei Feng was struck and killed by a pole that was knocked down by a military truck. Lei Feng was rushed to a hospital but died soon afterwards. While alive Lei Feng was not an eminent soldier, but following his death, his diary was discovered and became the poster-boy of the Communist Party.

Chairman Mao called on the nation to envelop the spirit of Lei Feng. Mao asked all Chinese to dedicate themselves to the cause of others as well as the Party. Lei Feng's diary was reprinted, photographs of him were plastered everywhere, and movies were made about his life.

These posters, which read "Xiàng Léi Fēng Tóngzhì Xuéxí (Learn from Comrade Lei Feng)" are still hung today to encourage Chinese to become model citizens.

(my, life, is, finite, but, for, people, serve, is, infinite) 我的生命是有限的, 但是为人民服务是无限的。	My life is finite, but my dedication and service to the People (of China) is infinite.
Wǒ de shēngmìng shì yǒuxiàn de, dànshì wèi rénmín fúwù shì wúxiàn de.	

(study, should, develop, drill, and, squeeze, spirit) 学习要发扬钻和挤的精神。	Regardless of how busy you are, you should still find time to study.
Xuéxí yào fāyáng zuān hé jǐ de jīngshén.	

(you, are, MW, living, Lei Feng) 你是个活雷锋。	You are a living Lei Feng.
Nǐ shì ge huó Léi Fēng.	
If you see a person do a good deed, you can tell them that he/she is a living Lei Feng. If you see someone doing something mischievous, you can use this sentence in a sarcastic manner.	

(you, should, in the direction, Lei Feng, comrade, study)	You should be more like Lei Feng.
你要向雷锋同志学习。	
Nǐ yào xiàng Léi Fēng tóngzhì xuéxí.	
Propaganda, used to motivate and encourage the youth of China.	

Bruce Lee, Martial Arts Specialist & Actor

李小龙　Lǐ Xiǎolóng

Born Lee Jun Fan on November 27th, 1940, Bruce Lee is by far the most famous Chinese actor.

At three months, Bruce Lee made his first acting appearance as a baby girl in *Golden Gate Girl* and at age 6 made his first major childhood movie. In total, he appeared in 20 movies before the age of 18.

One day Bruce was beaten up by a Hong Kong street gang. This is the first and last fight that he lost. This incident brought him to take Kung-fu lessons under the tutelage of Master Yip Man. At age 18, Bruce entered the 1958 Boxing Championships and defeated the reigning three-year champion, attracting great attention.

Because of his involvement in many street fights, his mother sent him to the United States. As a way to earn money, Bruce taught martial arts in backyards and parks. In 1961, Bruce entered the University of Washington as a Philosophy major. In 1963, he opened the Jun Kung-Fu Institute and taught persons of all races, something that had never been done before. The Institute became successful and Bruce decided to open another school in Oakland. In 1964, Ed Parker, the Father of American Karate, invited Bruce to give a demonstration. At this demonstration, Bruce performed his famous two finger push-ups and his "one-inch punch". Hollywood producer William Dozier was in the audience that day and invited Bruce to give an audition.

In August of 1964, Bruce married Linda Emery and in 1965 their only son Brandon was born. In that same year Bruce was challenged by Wong Jack Man, a leading Kung Fu master, who disliked Bruce teaching non-Chinese. To his surprise, Bruce accepted the challenge and a stipulation was set that the loser must stop teaching. The fight only lasted a few seconds as Bruce pummeled Wong Jack Man. Although he won, Bruce felt that he was not in his best physical condition and decided to reevaluate his technique. He later created the concept of Jeet Kune Do, the art of intercepting the fist.

In 1966, Bruce starred on a television show called the *Green Hornet*. He was paid around $ 400 / episode but the show was a flop. During this time, Bruce Lee's exposure became greater and greater. He opened the third Jun Fan Kung-Fu Institute and gave private lessons to such stars as Kareem Abdul-Jabbar, James Garner and Roman Polanski.

In 1970, Bruce injured his sacral nerve and doctors said he would never kick again. Bruce documented his recovery and perfected his technique because of it. Bruce was offered the leading role in *The Big Boss*, released in the US as *Fists of Fury* and became famous overnight. His next film *Fist of Fury* released in the US as *The Chinese Connection* was even better received than his first movie and Bruce was on top to stay. In 1973, Bruce began to work on *Enter the Dragon*, the first-ever film jointly produced by Hong Kong and American film companies.

On July 20th, 1973, Bruce unexpectedly died of swelling of the brain. Doctors later declared that the cause of death was "death by misadventure". The premiere of the *Enter the Dragon* was delayed a few days but was a huge hit when it finally hit the screen.

Jackie Chan, Film Star

成龙 Chéng Lóng

Born Chan Kong-Sang on April 7th, 1954, his parents, Charles and Lee-lee, know that Jackie was going to be special when he was in his mother's stomach for 12 months.

In 1960, Jackie's father went to work in Australia
and his mother enrolled him in the Peking Opera
Boarding Shcool. There he met his mentor, Master
Yu Jim-Yuan, and studied Chinese traditional
singing, acting, performing, and martial arts. Jackie'
s mother joined her husband in Australia and Yu Jim-
Yuan became Jackie's godfather.

Jackie's acting career began in 1962 when he appeared in the Cantonese film *Big
and Little Wong Tin-Bar*. Before age 17, Jackie appeared in many films, both as
a stuntman and actor. In 1973, Jackie was an extra in two of Bruce Lee's films,
The Chinese Connection and *Enter the Dragon*.

In 1976, Jackie was renamed Sing Lung (which means become the dragon) and
had the leading role in *New Fist of Fury* which was a sequel to Bruce Lee's *The
Chinese Connection*. The film was not a huge success. Jackie later went to Australia
to join his parents. One of his father's friends, whose name was Jack, gave him a
job on a construction site. Jack knew that the other workers would not take to Sing
Lung so he gave him the name, Jack. Later Jack became Jackie and that is how
Jackie Chan was born.

In 1978, Jackie finally broke away from the Bruce Lee shadow when he acted in
Snake in the Eagle's Shadow, a film that showcases Jackie's martial arts and
comic abilities. Jackie later went to the United States where he had small parts in
the *Cannonball Run* movies. While in the US Jackie met some stuntmen and decided that this was a role in which he could excel. Jackie first became famous in the
US following his re-creation of Harold Lloyd's "hanging from the clock tower"
stunt where he fell three stories.

Jackie returned to Hong Kong where he starred in the box-office hits *Police Story*
and *Project A*. The film featured both martial arts and comedy and put Jackie on
top to stay. New Line Cinema's 1996 *Rumble in the Bronx* became the number
one movie in America and opened American eyes to adventure-comedy films. His
latest films include *Rush Hour* and *Shanghai Noon*.

Dr. Norman Bethune (1890 — 1939)

白求恩 Bái Qiú'ēn

One of the most famous foreigners in China is Dr. Norman Bethune, the Canadian Medical Hall of Fame surgeon who introduced the mobile blood bank to the battlefield. Born in Gravenhurst, Ontario in 1890, Dr. Bethune had a passion for medicine as a child. He studied medicine at the University of Toronto but his education was interrupted when he enlisted as a stretcher-bearer in World War I. In 1916 he finally received his M. D.

Dr. Bethune wrote extensively on the usage of surgical instruments that is still considered to be the hand guide for all surgeons today. Dr. Bethune also made contributions to the formation of Canada's national health care system. But Dr. Bethune is most saliently remembered for his work in China as a battlefield doctor where he shared his food, clothing and even blood with wounded soldiers while performing countless blood transfusions. A doctor to the end, in 1938 while in China, Dr. Bethune succumbed to the very disease to which he dedicated his life to curing, blood poisoning.

Upon hearing of his death, Chairman Mao wrote of Dr. Bethune, "Comrade Bethune and I met only once... I am deeply grieved of his death. Now we are all commemorating him, which shows how profoundly his spirit inspired everyone. We must all learn the spirit of absolute selflessness from him."Mao's essay later became required reading in China and Bethune's picture appeared on postage stamps and posters.

Like most non-doctors, before I came to China I rarely heard the name Norman Bethune. In China, however, where he is revered as a saint, you are bound to hear his name, especially from older generations.

Mark Roswell

大山　Dàshān

Canadian Mark Roswell, or Dàshān (Big Mountain) in Chinese, is by far the most well-known of all foreigners in China due to his remarkably fluent Chinese. Dàshān first started studying Chinese in Peking University's Chinese Department and became famous almost overnight after appearing on xiàngsheng, a traditional Chinese comic dialogue show.

Today, Dàshān performs comic skits and makes guest appearances on holiday programs. He also appears in a plethora of advertising campaigns. If studying Chinese in China, you will hear his name everyday, from the mouths of cab drivers to doctors.

Chapter VII

IDIOMS
成语

There are a few reasons why Chinese pay particular attention to idioms. For over 5,000 years, Chinese have been renowned for their keen interest in literature and the Chinese language is the channel in which these intellectuals utilize to convey their thoughts. Chinese believe that four-character idioms sound pleasant to the ear. Using just one or two words to express a thought is rather elementary, especially when there are more scholarly words that can express the same ieda. Indeed, idioms are one way of measuring the intelligence and educational level in a society in which great emphasis is placed on education.

It is worthwhile for the foreign student of Chinese to invest some time learning Chinese idioms as China's long history and language go hand in hand. It is consequential to become familiar with China's past in order to become proficient in modern Chinese. Behind every idiom there is a story, called a diǎngù which will allow the student to deepen their understanding of the Chinese culture while at the same time increasing their vocabulary. Lastly, properly using idioms will guarantee for you the praise of the Chinese on your way to becoming a Zhōngguótōng, an expert on China.

拔苗助长   Help Seedlings Grow by Pulling Them up

There once was an impatient farmer who lived during the Song Dynasty (960-1279 AD). Everyday the anxious farmer would measure the growth of the crops. To his dismay, his crops were growing much slower than he expected.

The farmer racked his brains trying to find better ways of planting in order to get quicker results. One day he finally came up with a solution. He started to physically pull the crops out of the ground, thus making them taller. The farmer worked very hard and at day's end he was physically exhausted but mentally happy as his plan had produced the desired results.

When the farmer went home, he told his son of his "brilliant" method. His son went to the field only to discover that all of his crops were dead.

(pull up, shoot, help, grow)		
拔苗助长	bá miáo zhù zhǎng	
The idiom is used today to refer to a situation where an impatient person does not fully consider the consequences of an action and therefore produces results that are contrary to the initial objective; spoil things by undue haste.		
教育孩子需要耐心,不能拔苗助长。	When educating children, one must be patient. You cannot pull the shoots up to help them grow.	
Jiàoyù háizi xūyào nàixīn, bù néng bá miáo zhù zhǎng.		

班门弄斧　　Show One's Mediocre Skill before a Master

There once was a master carpenter named Lu Ban who lived during the Spring and Autumn Period (770-476 BC). Lu Ban was very famous because he invented wood-working tools and built many bridges and palaces.

One day another carpenter, axe in hand, came to Lu Ban's doorway to display his average talents. When others heard of this act, they all laughed at the carpenter.

(name of the famous carpenter, door, demonstrate, axe)	
班门弄斧	Bān mén nòng fǔ
The idiom is used to describe a person who attempts to display their skills in front of the master.	
A) 我想给他看看我写的文章有多好。	I want to show him how well-written my article is.
Wǒ xiǎng gěi tā kànkan wǒ xiě de wénzhāng yǒu duō hǎo.	
B) 他是专家,最好别在他面前班门弄斧。	Don't forget that he is an expert, You'd better not to show off in front of him.
Tā shì zhuānjiā, zuìhǎo bié zài tā miànqián Bān mén nòng fǔ.	

半途而废   Leave Something Half-done

There once was a man named Yueyangtsi who lived during the Warring States Period (475—221 BC) who truly loved his wife.

One day, Yueyangtsi found a piece of gold on the ground and rushed home to give it to his dear wife. To his surprise, when he presented his wife with the gold, she was not excited. "How could you possibly give me something that someone is probably crazily looking for?" Yueyangtsi was moved by his wife's words and put the gold back where he found it .

The next year, Yueyangtsi left home to study classics with a famous teacher. One day while his wife was weaving a loom, Yueyangtsi entered the room. "Why are you home now?" she asked. He told her that while he was studying, he suddenly missed her so much that he decided to make the trip home.

"If something is done halfway, it might as well not have been started", she started to lecture. "Take for instance this loom, if I stop now, all the energy that I have exerted and all the time I invested will have been for naught. The same holds true for your studies. You have started, you need to finish." Yueyangtsi was moved by his wife's words and at once returned to his studies.

(half, road, but, give-up)		
半途而废	bàn tú ér fèi	leave something unfinished
The idiom is used to encourage a person to continue even the most daunting tasks.		
学习汉语绝对不能半途而废。		When studying Chinese, one must not "Leave Something Unfinished".
Xuéxí Hànyǔ juéduì bù néng bàn tú ér fèi.		

此地无银三百两 There Is No Silver Buried Here

Once upon a time there was a "clever" man named Zhang Sun who worked very hard. After a while he accumulated 300 silver coins and was nervous that a burglar would come to steal his fortune.

He thought about putting the money in a drawer but later decided against that as a burglar could easily find it. He also pondered hiding the loot in a locked chest but then realized that a thief could easily come in, take the chest and the silver. At last, Zhang Sun came up with the solution.

In the middle of the night, Zhang Sun quietly dug a hole in the ground and buried the silver. Although Zhang Sun originally thought this plan was full proof, he later once again became uneasy. "What if a person comes by and sees that the ground has been moved? They will suspect that something is buried there and will dig it up. When they do they will discover my silver!"

After thinking it over, Zhang Sun came up with another idea. He took a large piece of paper and wrote on it, "300 silver coins are not buried here". He posted the sign above the hole where the silver was buried and was finally at ease.

One of Zhang Sun's neighbors, Wang Er, heard the digging and became suspicious. The next day when he saw the note, he realized what Sun had done. During the next night, Wang Er dug up the silver. Wang Er was very excited but was also a little nervous. "What if someone discovers me?" he thought to himself. Suddenly, he came up with a great plan. He wrote on a piece of paper "Neighbor Wang Er never stole the silver" and placed it above the pit.

(this, place, no, silver, 300, a Chinese weight unit)		
此地无银三百两	cǐ dì wú yín sānbǎi liǎng	
The idiom is used to refer to someone who thinks they are clever by doing something to disguise an action, but in fact only makes themselves more obvious.		
A) 我没有吃你的冰淇淋。	I didn't eat your ice cream.	
Wǒ méiyǒu chī nǐ de bīngqílín.		
B) 此地无银三百两。我原本都不知道有人吃了我的冰淇淋, 现在知道是你。	There are not 300 *liang* of silver buried here. I hadn't noticed that someone had eaten my ice cream. By your telling me this, I know it was you!	
Cǐ dì wú yín sānbǎi liǎng. Wǒ yuánběn dōu bù zhīdào yǒu rén chīle wǒ de bīngqílín, xiànzài zhīdào shì nǐ.		

道听途说   Heard on the Streets, Told on the Streets

A long time ago there was a teacher named Ai Zi who was taking his students into town for an excursion and on the way bumped into his old friend Mao Kong.

Ai Zi asked Mao Kong, "I haven't been out in a while, anything interesting going on?"

MK: "You didn't hear? Someone's duck laid 100 eggs at one time!"

AZ: "I don't believe that. That's scientifically impossible."

MK: "Then it was two ducks."

AZ: "Still, two ducks, 100 eggs. I still don't buy it."

MK: "Yeah, you're right. It most likely was three ducks."

Mao Kong saw that his friend was not buying into his tale and kept changing the number of ducks to make the story more and more believable.

AZ: "Why do you change the number of ducks but not the number of eggs?"

MK: "I prefer to change the number of ducks because I have already committed to the number of eggs."

MK: "I still have another piece of news for you. Last month a huge piece of meat fell from the sky and almost killed three people. It had to be 100 feet long."

AZ: "How could that be?"

MK: "Then it was about 20 feet long."

AZ: "For argument's sake, let's concede that the piece of meat was 20 feet long. It is still impossible that it fell from the sky. Did you see it with your own eyes?"

MK: "No, I heard it from someone else."

Ai Zi turned to his students and said, "Our lesson for today is that you can never trust what is heard on the streets and told on the roads."

(road, hear, road, say)		
道听途说	dào tīng tú shuō	
The idiom is used to describe a rumor; hearsay		
他说的这件事只不过是道听途说。		What he was talking about was only a rumor.
Tā shuō de zhè jiàn shì zhǐ búguò shì dào tīng tú shuō.		

对牛弹琴   Playing a Zither to a Cow

A long time ago there was a famous composer and performer named Gongming Yi. On nice days Gongming would take his zither outside and play in the countryside. One day, Gongming went outside to play and happened to see an ox. Thinking that his harmonious music would entertain the bull, Gongming decided to set up his zither and play.

As Gongming played what he thought to be a perfect song, the bull continued to eat

his grass, unfazed by the music. Gongming thought, "Maybe this type of music does not suit the bull's taste." So Gongming decided to play a little more upbeat tune to brighten the bull's day. Mustering all of his skill, Gongming started playing his finest tune. To his dismay, however, the bull's only movement was to swat some flies away that were hovering over his head. Disheartened, Gongming picked up his zither and headed home.

(towards, cow, play, zither)	
对牛弹琴	duì niú tán qín
The idiom is used to describe a person who has no knowledge of a subject or wastes one's breath when trying to get your point across to an unreasonable person.	
他初中都没毕业，跟他谈相对论就像对牛弹琴。	He didn't graduate middle school. Talking with him about the Theory of Relativity is like playing a zither to a cow.
Tā chūzhōng dōu méi bìyè, gēn tā tán Xiāngduìlùn jiù xiàng duì niú tán qín.	

对症下药 The Remedy Should Suit the Illness

During the Han Dynasty (202 BC—220 AD), there was a famous doctor named Hua Tuo. One day two men named Li Yan and Ni Xun together visited Dr. Hua, complaining of headaches and fever. After his examination, Dr. Hua prescribed medication for the two men. Upon comparing the two prescriptions, the two men realized that although their symptoms were very similar, their medicines were very different. Puzzled, the two men asked Dr. Hua, "The two of us are suffering from the same illnesses, why are our medications different?"

Dr. Hua replied, "Treatment is prescribed according to the cause of the patient's symptoms. Your symptoms are similar, but their causes are different. Li Yan internally has nothing wrong but has contracted a cold from exposure to cold weather. Ni Xun has nothing wrong externally but has caught his cold from drinking too much. As the causes are different, of course the treatments will not be the same."

After listening to the doctor, the two men were relieved and a few weeks later their health returned.

(towards, illness, prescribe, medicine)	
对症下药	duì zhèng xià yào

The idiom is used to describe that although two problems on the surface might be identical, their causes might be different and therefore different measures should be adopted to solve them.

中国各地区发展情况不同,所以应该对症下药解决问题。	The developments of China's many regions are not the same, and so each case should be treated differently.

Zhōngguó gè dìqū fāzhǎn qíngkuàng bù tóng, suǒyǐ yīnggāi duì zhèng xià yào jiějué wèntí.

负荆请罪 Carry a Stick and Ask for Punishment

There once was a man named Lin Xiangru who was both intelligent and audacious. Unfortunately his country, the State of Zhao, was very feeble and consequently often bullied by the hegemonic State of Qin. One time, Lin Xiangru risked his life in a battle of words against the King of Qin and emerged victorious, thus saving his country. The King of Zhao was grateful of Lin Xiangru's success and rewarded him by granting him the highest ministerial position in the country.

The State of Zhao also had a very celebrated minister named General Lian Po who had also risked his life in order to save his country. Lian Po was a very macho man and once he heard that Lin Xiangru was elevated to the highest position in the land over him, became enraged with jealousy and anger.

Lian Po ridiculed Lin Xiangru, saying that his only ability was his mouth, and vowed to show who was the stronger of the two. Upon hearing this news, Lin Xiangru decided to avoid Lian Po, realizing that no benefit could come out of two high officials' quarrelling. If a ministerial meeting was held, Lin Xiangru would call out sick. After a while, Lin Xiangru's intentions became known and the other ministers started to think that he was a coward.

When asked the true reasons for his absence, Lin Xiangru said, "the King of Qin is an evil despot and I was willing to face him. I am not afraid of Lian Po, but I do feel that if the news got back to the State of Qin that there are battles going on within our state, they will feel that our state is susceptible to outside attacks. I am willing to sacrifice my personal shame for the better of the state."

When the other ministers heard this explanation, they all realized how patriotic Lin Xiangru was and never doubted him again. Lian Po heard the news, he felt so embarrassed that he went to Lin's residence, bent down on his knees with prickly stick on his back and begged for forgiveness.

(carry, prickly stick, ask for, punishment)		
负荆请罪	fù jīng qǐng zuì	
The idiom is used today for someone who acknowledges a wrongdoing and wishes to apologize for his/her mistakes.		
对不起,我昨天忘了去你家，我明天去你家负荆请罪。	Sorry, I forgot to go to your house yesterday. I will come over tomorrow to ask for punishment.	
Duìbuqǐ, wǒ zuótiān wàngle qù nǐ jiā, wǒ míngtiān qù nǐ jiā fù jīng qǐng zuì.		

画蛇添足 Add Feet to a Snake

There once was a family who used wine when performing worshipping rituals. One day when the service was completed, the family gave the remaining wine to their servants. Unfortunately, there was only a little bit of wine so the servants had to divvy it up.

One of the servants suggested that the servants have a snake-drawing contest. The servant who could draw the quickest, best snake would be the winner. This suggestion gave all men an equal chance and was accepted.

One servant drew a snake so fast that he started to mock the others. With one hand

on the wine and the other holding his paintbrush he said, "Look at you. Can't even draw a snake! By the time you are done, my snake will have feet." With that the man started to draw legs on the snake. Unfortunately, the man did not notice that one of the other servants was painting very fast and finished his snake before him, and in the process won the wine.

In the end, the cocky man could only angrily stand back and watch the man drink what should have been his wine.

(paint, snake, add, foot)	
画蛇添足	huà shé tiān zú
The idiom is used to describe someone who does something superfluously, and as a result ruins their originally good piece of work.	
你的文章写得很好。别再修改了，不然就是画蛇添足了。	Your thesis is well written. If you correct it again, that will be "Adding Feet to a Snake."
Nǐ de wénzhāng xiě de hěn hǎo. Bié zài xiūgǎi le, bùrán jiù shì huà shé tiān zú le.	

金玉其外，败絮其中 Gold and Jade on the Outside, Withered Cotton on the Inside

There once was a fruit peddler in Hangzhou who possessed great business acumen. Although his prices were high, his fruits were looked fresher and as a result well received.

One day a man went to the market and saw the vendor's ripe oranges and tanger-
ines. "I have never seen better-looking citrus fruits in my life", he thought to himself. "Although it is winter, these fruits seem to have just been picked off the tree.
I must have them." The man bought several pounds, the equivalent of one month'
s salary.

When the man returned home, he called his wife and children into the kitchen and
told them that he had a great surprise. However, to his dismay, upon cutting open
the fruits, he discovered the inside was as withered as cotton.

The outraged man returned to the market in search for the peddler. "Your oranges
look delectable from the outside but are withered on the inside. Simply inedible!"he
said in an infuriated voice.

Upon hearing the man's gripe, the peddler burst into laughter. "I have been selling
fruit around these parts since you were an infant. I have never had a dissatisfied
customer. Moreover, I am not the only one in this world that cheats people. What
about the officials? They sit in their beautiful chairs and fancy clothing and dictate
how we live our lives. If you are going to complain about anything, you should
complain about them."

With this, the man who bought the rotten oranges became speechless and walked
home.

(gold, jade, its, outside, withered, cotton, its, inside)

金玉其外，败絮其中	jīn yù qí wài, bài xù qí zhōng	

The idiom is used metaphorically to describe a person or thing that has a fine outer appearance but lacks real inner capabilities or strengths.

A）我挺喜欢小李的，他人长得帅，又有风度。	I really like Xiao Li. He is both handsome and mannerly.
Wǒ tǐng xǐhuan Xiǎo Lǐ de, tā rén zhǎng de shuài, yòu yǒu fēngdù.	

B）你可说错了。他人品其实很差，纯粹是"金玉其外，败絮其中"。	What you said is exactly wrong. His character is very poor, simply is a case of *Gold and Jade on the Outside, Withered Cotton on the Inside*.
Nǐ kě shuō cuò le. Tā rénpǐn qíshí hěn chà, chúncuì shì "jīn yù qí wài, bài xù qí zhōng".	

惊弓之鸟　The Goose That Starts at the Mere Twang of a Bow String

In the State of Wei there lived a very famous archer named Geng Lei. His ability was so well-known that even the king used him to shoot down geese.

One day Geng Lei was walking with the King's entourage looking for game.

Geng："Do you see that goose, Your Majesty? Without using a single arrow, I can make this goose your next meal!"

King："That is impossible. Do you have such ability?"

Geng："Please allow me the honor."

Geng Lei took the bow and drew his arrow back. There was a loud "Bang!" sound

and the goose beat its wings at an alarming rate, finally falling to the ground, dying instantaneously.

King: "Wow! That is the most amazing thing that I have ever witnessed! How did you do that?"

Geng: "I saw how weakly the goose was flying and realized that something was wrong with it. When I heard its feeble call, I knew that it had been struck before and had not totally healed. When I pulled back my bow, it became nervous as it did the first time that it was attacked and instantly had a heart attack and died."

(startle, bow, bird)	
惊弓之鸟	jīng gōng zhī niǎo

The idiom is used metaphorically to describe a person who, because of a past experience, is hesitant to do the same thing again.

他以前受过女人的伤害，现在成了惊弓之鸟，再也不敢谈恋爱了。	His heart was broken once. Now, he has turned into a "Starts at the Mere Twang of a Bow-string", not willing to get involved with another.

Tā yǐqián shòuguo nǚrén de shānghài, xiànzài chéngle jīng gōng zhī niǎo, zài yě bù gǎn tán liàn'ài le.

井中捞月   Fishing the Moon from the Bottom of a Well

There once was a genius named Huojia who went one night to fetch some water from the well. To his surprise, when he looked into the well, he discovered that the moon had somehow sunken to the bottom. The brave Huojia rushed home to get a hook to fish the moon out.

After a while, Huojia finally had a bite. He pulled with all his might causing the rope to snap, and in the process of propelling Huojia fell to the ground on his back. While on his back, he saw the fruits of his labor, the moon was returned to its rightful place in the sky. From that point, Huojia told everyone about his "heroic" adventure.

(well, inside, scoop, moon)	
井中捞月	jǐng zhōng lāo yuè
The idiom is used today to describe a person who does something of no use or impractical.	
管他借钱简直是井中捞月。	It's impossible for you to borrow some money from him.
Guǎn tā jiè qián jiǎnzhí shì jǐng zhōng lāo yuè.	

空中楼阁　A Castle in the Air

There once was a rich, stubborn man who visited a neighboring state to see how others built houses. He looked at many structures until finally finding the one that he set his eyes on, a three-storied piece of artwork. The man asked the owner if the architect would build him a house exactly like this? The owner directed the man to the architect and the two men talked about building the house in his home state.

"I am thrilled that you like the house and would be happy to build one for you," the architect said. The next day the architect rounded up a dozen workers and started to work on the project.

The workers labored day and night excavating the ground, laying the foundation, and assembling the building materials. Unfortunately, their speed was not fast enough for the impatient man. "You have been here for many days now and there is no progress," he said furiously.

The architect listened and replied, "Sir, don't you want a three-storied house? This is not a project that can be completed overnight."

Annoyed, the man replied, "Maybe there is a lack of understanding here. I don't want a three-storied house. I just want the top floor of a three-storied house."

The carpenter was at first taken aback by the man's stupidity but then realized that the man was dead serious. He patiently explained, "If you don't build the first story, you cannot build the second. If you don't build the second, you cannot build the third."

The silly man repiled, "If you work for me, you work on my conditions and this is how I want it to be done!"

"I am sorry, sir. Apparently I am not the right man for this job. You'll be better off trying to find someone else."

(sky, middle, castle)	
空中楼阁	kōng zhōng lóu gé
The idiom is used to describe a ludicrous theory or an idea that might sound attractive on paper but when put into practice does not achieve the desired result; no foundation.	
你光说不做，成功对于你就是空中楼阁。	You want to succeed without putting an effort forward. That is simply *A Castle in the Air*.
Nǐ guāng shuō bú zuò, chénggōng duìyú nǐ jiù shì kōng zhōng lóu gé.	

滥竽充数   Pass Oneself off as a Yu Player

During the Warring States Period (475—221 BC), there was a state called Qi, whose leader loved to listen to musical instruments. One day the king decided to assemble an ensemble of 300 players to play for him everyday while he drank his tea.

Mr. Nanguo was a citizen of the State of Qi but did not know the slightest thing about musical instruments. When he saw how well the king's ensemble was treated, he decided to become a member. After a few days of practicing the Yu, the king's favorite wood instrument, Mr. Nanguo realized that there was no chance of him ever being admitted based upon his playing ability. With no other options, Mr. Nanguo decided to try and fake it. "I can puff my cheeks and act as if I am playing. I will be amongst 300 of the State's finest, I'll blend right in."

Mr. Nanguo's plan was right on the nose. For a few years he enjoyed the special treatment of being a member of the king's ensemble while not being discovered.

Unfortunately, the king passed away and his son ascended to the throne. The new king kept the ensemble intact, but decided that the band as a whole was too loud. Everyday, he invited different members of the band to give him a solo performance. Mr. Nanguo decided that the time had come for him to quietly exit stage.

(abuse, musical instrument, make up, numbers)		
滥竽充数	làn yú chōng shù	Pass Oneself off as a Yu Player
The idiom is used to describe a person who passes himself / herself off as genuine, and gets away with it because he / she is amongst a large group.		
北大是中国最好的大学,但也有人在这里滥竽充数。		Peking University is China's best university, and yet there are still people there who pass themselves off as Yu players.
Běidà shì Zhōngguó zuì hǎo de dàxué, dàn yě yǒu rén zài zhèli làn yú chōng shù.		

乐不思蜀 So Happy as to Forget Home

During the period of the Three Kingdoms (3 AD), the Shu Kingdom was conquered by the Wei Kingdom. To show the other Kingdoms their strength and confidence, the Wei Kingdom leaders spared the life of the Shu Kingdom's King, Liu Chan. They did, however, force Liu Chan to relocate to Luoyang, the Wei Kingdom's capital.

In Luoyang, Sima Zhao, a Wei Kingdom General invited Liu Chan and his old staff to eat and listen to music from his former kingdom. The staff members were very sad as these tunes reminded them of their homeland which was now in the hands of the Wei Kingdom. Surprisingly, Liu Chan was not affected.

Seeing that Liu Chan was not sad, Sima Zhao asked him whether he was home-sick. Liu Chan replied, "I am very happy here and I do not miss my hometown at all."

(happy, not, miss, the state of Shu)	
乐不思蜀	lè bù sī Shǔ
The idiom is used to describe people who leave their homeland but find that they do not miss it at all.	
Q) 你喜欢中国吗?	Do you like China?
Nǐ xǐhuan Zhōngguó ma?	
A) 中国很好，我都乐不思蜀了。	China is great! I don't miss home at all.
Zhōngguó hěn hǎo, wǒ dōu lè bù sī Shǔ le.	

梁上君子 A Gentleman on the Beam

During the Eastern Han Dynasty (25—220 AD) there was an honest man named Chen Shi who went to great lengths to properly raise his children. One year, a horrible famine struck and robberies were rife. One evening, a burglar entered his house and decided to quietly wait on a ceiling beam until he could make his move. While waiting in the rafters, he was discovered by Chen Shi. Chen Shi decided to use this unique occasion to teach his children a lesson.

He called his children into the room where the thief was and began a serious lecture. "To be a productive member of society, one must place strict demands on himself so that he can develop and improve himself. One cannot become complacent, not even for the shortest length of time, otherwise, it is easy to succumb to evil. Evil persons are not inherently evil, but turn evil because of a lack of self-discipline and devoted studies. Those who commit crimes would not do so if they only had demanded more of themselves."

Pointing at the rafters, Chen continued, "Look at the poor gentleman that is sitting on the beam. He has turned to evil."

The burglar intently listened to Chen Shi's remarks and felt ashamed. Slowly climbing down from the rafters, the now trembling burglar started kowtowing at Chen Shi's feet. Chen Shi looked at the helpless burglar and said, "You do not seem like a bad man, just a person who has ran into difficulty. You should take this as a lesson and start over from here."

After concluding his speech, Chen Shi gave the thief some cloth and sent him on his way. Weeping, the thief thanked Chen Shi and promised to turn over a new leaf.

(beam, on, gentleman)	
梁上君子	liáng shàng jūnzǐ
The idiom is used to describe a thief or burglar.	
仅仅一个月，就有三个梁上君子先后光顾我们宿舍。	In only one month, already three thieves have honored our dorm with their presence.
Jǐnjǐn yí ge yuè, jiù yǒu sān ge liáng shàng jūnzǐ xiānhòu guānggù wǒmen sùshè.	

名落孙山　Name Falling behind Sun Shan's

In ancient times there was a scholar named Sun Shan. One summer he was riding to the provincial capital to take part in the imperial examination, when his neighbor approached him and asked if his son could accompany him as he was also taking the test. Sun Shan agreed and the two men headed for the capital.

The two men safely arrived in the capital and a few days later took the test. When the results were posted, many people crowded to see if their names were on the list, meaning that they had passed. Sun Shan squeezed to the front and discovered that his name was last on the list. He cried out, "I passed! I passed!"

He then decided to check if his neighbor's name was on the list. To his dismay, it was not. Sun Shan returned and comforted the young boy. That day Sun Shan set out for home with the good news. When he returned, everyone in the village came to congratulate him. Amongst the men was the father of the boy who inquired about his son's results. Sun Shan was a very respectful man and realized that if he told the man in front of the others that his son had failed the exam, it would make him feel uncomfortable.

Upon being pressed for answers, Sun Shan replied, "The last name on the list was Sun Shan and the young man's name came right after that." The old neighbor was a bit confused at first but then realized Sun Shan's meaning and morosely returned home.

(name, fall behind, Sun Shan)		
名落孙山	míng luò Sūn Shān	
The idiom is used metaphorically to express bad results in an examination or failure to be admitted into a university, company, etc.		

Q) 你考上北大了吗？	Did you test into Peking University?
Nǐ kǎo shàng Běidà le ma?	
A) 别提了，名落孙山。	Don't remind me. My name fell right behind Sun Shan's.
Bié tí le, míng luò Sūn Shān.	

杞人忧天　The Man from Qi Who Feared That the Sky Would Fall

A long time ago there was a man from Qi who often pondered strange things. One day he was sitting down and wondered what would happen if the sky fell down. The more he thought about it, the more scared he became.

He thought about moving to another place but then realized that the sky covers the entire world so avoiding it is impossible. He became so anxious that he could not sleep or eat. His condition became so bad that he decided to tell others about his theory.

Most people laughed and told him that he was crazy. There was one man who sympathized for the man and sat him down. "You are worrying yourself for no reason," he said in a caring voice. "How could the sky fall down? The sky is just a huge mass of air. It is everywhere and you come in contact with it everyday, so how could it possibly collapse?"

Obviously the neighbor's explanation was not very scientific, but was enough to set the man's mind at ease and cure his anxiety.

(ancient Chinese place, person, worry, sky)		
杞人忧天	Qǐ rén yōu tiān	
The idiom is used to depict a person who is worried about nothing.		
这件事问题不大，你不要杞人忧天。		This is not a big deal. Don't be "The Man from Qi Who Feared That the Sky Would Fall".
Zhè jiàn shì wèntí bú dà, nǐ búyào Qǐ rén yōu tiān.		

塞翁失马　　A Blessing in Disguise

There once was an old man living on the frontier who raised horses. One day, one of his horses escaped from his ranch, A few of his neighbors came to comfort him. To their surprise, however, the old man was not the least bit morose. "Although losing a horse is not a small thing, it also is not the end of the world either and just maybe, is a good thing."

In a few days, the horse found its way home and brought with it a few other horses that were even stronger and faster than his original horse. This time, his neighbors came to congratulate him. "This is not necessarily a good thing, and might even turn out to be a bad thing," the old man said.

After a few days, his words came true when his son fell off one of the new horses and suffered a broken leg. Once again his neighbors came to comfort him. Always looking at the glass half-full the old man replied, "This accident might very well bring my son happiness."

Later a war broke out and all eligible men were called upon to participate. In the war, the state was defeated badly and nine out of ten soldiers were killed, thus destroying many families. The old man's son, because his leg was broken, was not able to participate in the war and his life was spared.

(frontier, old man, lose, horse)		
塞翁失马	sài wēng shī mǎ	a blessing in disguise
The idiom is used to describe an event that initially is negative but later turns out to be positive.		
小王被炒了鱿鱼,但是之后找到了一份更好的工作。真是塞翁失马。		Xiao Wang was fired but later found a better job. It truly was "A Blessing in Disguise."
Xiǎo Wáng bèi chǎole yóuyú, dànshì zhīhòu zhǎo dàole yí fèn gèng hǎo de gōngzuò. Zhēn shì sài wēng shī mǎ.		

守株待兔   Wait for a Rabbit at a Stump

In ancient times there was a farmer who worked in the fields. One day he spotted a rabbit running around crazily and spun out of control and ran into a tree stump. The rabbit broke his neck and died instantaneously.

The farmer hurriedly ran over to see the dead rabbit. He thought to himself, "Without breaking a sweat or even lifting a finger, I have a delectable, fat rabbit to devour!"

When the farmer returned home, his wife saw the rabbit and was full of joy. "You are such a good provider. I am so lucky!" She proceeded to ask, "Where did you catch the rabbit?"

The farmer replied in a very self-satisfied voice, "I did not catch the rabbit, it was sent to us." The wife prepared the rabbit and the couple ate a delicious meal. After dinner the wife said, "If you can catch a rabbit everyday, I can always cook us tasty meals."

From then on, the farmer gave up the farming trade and sat by the same stump everyday and waited for more rabbits to collapse at his feet. To his dismay, there was no second rabbit and the fields became full of weeds.

(stand by, stump, wait, rabbit)		
守株待兔	shǒu zhū dài tù	
The idiom is used today to encourage people to aggressively go after the things that they want and not just wait for things to happen or trust them to luck.		
找工作的时候你应该积极一点儿，别守株待兔。	When looking for a job, one should be aggressive. Don't "Wait for a Rabbit at a Stump".	
Zhǎo gōngzuò de shíhou nǐ yīnggāi jījí yìdiǎnr, bié shǒu zhū dài tù.		

螳臂当车　A Mantis Trying to Stop a Chariot

During the Warring States Period, Qi Zhuanggong, the king of the State of Qi, was riding in a chariot to go on an outing. As the chariot was moving he noticed a mantis fighting furiously to stop the chariot.

King Qi was very curious by the mantis and wondered what would possess such a small creature into thinking that it could actually stop a chariot that outweighed it by 100,000 times. He asked the driver to stop the vehicle and asked, "What kind of bug is this?"

The driver replied, "It is a mantis, Your Majesty. It does not know its own limits and the word 'retreat' is not in its vocabulary."

"It is a shame the mantis is nothing more than an insect," the king said. "It has great courage and would make a great soldier. Let's go around him to spare his life."

(mantis, arm, block, vehicle)		
螳臂当车	táng bì dāng chē	
The idiom is used to describe a person or thing that does not have a good estimation of one's own abilities and subsequently does something that has no chance of accomplishing.		
让我防守麦克尔·乔丹, 那不是螳臂当车吗?		Asking me to defend Michael Jordan isn't like asking "A Mantis Trying to Stop a Chariot"?
Ràng wǒ fángshǒu Màikè'ěr Qiáodān, nà bú shì táng bì dǎng chē ma?		

完璧归赵   Return the Jade back to the State of Zhao

During the Warring States Period (475—221 BC) in the State of Zhao, a big piece of jade was unearthed by a farmer when he was doing his routine fieldwork. The farmer immediately turned over the precious stone to the Emperor. The Emperor of Zhao asked some craftsmen to carve the raw stone into a circular treasure.

After a short while, the Emperor of the Qin heard about the jade masterpiece and wanted to see it for himself. He dispatched some of his men to relay the message to the Emperor of Zhao that he wanted to get the jade at the expense of ten of his towns. The Emperor of Zhao was very troubled. If he refused, the much more powerful State of Qin might invade his State. On the other hand, if he allowed the Emperor of Qin to have a look at the jade, he feared that he would never see it again. One of the Emperor's cabinet members, Lin Xiangru, volunteered to go to the State of Qin with a few porters on behalf of the Emperor of Zhao. His mission was to allow the Emperor of Qin to look at the piece of jade and then return.

When the Emperor of Qin saw the piece of jade, he was in awe of its beauty. The Emperor showed it to everyone that he came in contact with. Lin Xiangru decided that he must take immediate action, otherwise, the Emperor of Qin would become attached to the jade and he would never be able to part with it.

In order to get the jade back, Lin made up a story that there was a flaw in the stone. The Emperor believed him and demanded that he point out the imperfection. When Lin got hold of the jade, he threatened to destroy the jade if the Emperor would not compensate the State of Zhao with land. The Emperor agreed, but Lin did not believe him. Lin then pushed the Emperor further, making him list the names of the towns, locations, etc. He suggested that both sides think it over for a day or two.

Meanwhile, Lin had secretly placed the jade in one of his porter's bags who escaped back to Zhao. The next day, when the Emperor of Qin demanded to see the jade, Lin told him that the jade was on its way back to Zhao and that if he was serious about the swap, he would do it in a public forum. Of course the Emperor of Qin did not make the deal and the jade was returned safely to the State of Zhao.

(intact, a round piece of jade, return, the state of Zhao)	
完璧归赵	wán bì guī Zhào
The idiom is used when returning something safely to its owner.	
谢谢你让我借用你的车，现在完璧归赵。	Thank you for letting me borrow your car. I am now "Returning the Jade back to the State of Zhao".
Xièxie nǐ ràng wǒ jièyòng nǐ de chē, xiànzài wán bì guī Zhào.	

亡羊补牢　Mend the Fence even after the Sheep are Gone

Once upon a time there was a shepherd who raised a lot of sheep. One night a wolf broke a hole in the sheep's pen and made off with a sheep. The next day when the shepherd counted his herd, he discovered that one sheep was missing. He then went to the pen where he discovered the hole made by the wolf. He did not immediately fix the pen, thinking that it did not matter when he got around to doing it.

Two nights later, the wolf returned and to his surprise, the hole had not been mended. He once again did not leave empty-handed, this time taking two sheep. The next day when the shepherd counted his sheep, he discovered that two more sheep were unaccounted for. He went to the pen only to discover that the hole in the fence was bigger than before. But once again, the stubborn shepherd refused to take immediate action. "This is just a great big coincidence," he thought to himself.

The next night, the wolf returned. Realizing this golden opportunity would not last forever, he decided to take three sheep. Just as before, when the shepherd counted his sheep the next morning, he discovered that he was once again shy of sheep. As the number of sheep slowly dwindled, the shepherd finally figured out that the hole in the fence probably had something to do with the missing sheep.

The shepherd finally decided to mend the fence. When the wolf returned a few nights later, the fence was fixed and he could no longer steal the sheep.

(lose, sheep, fix, enclosure)		
亡羊补牢	wáng yáng bǔ láo	
The idiom is used metaphorically to encourage a person who feels that they are too late or too old to start something.		
A) 我以前没有好好学数学, 现在很后悔。		I regret not studying math harder.
Wǒ yǐqián méiyǒu hǎohāo xué shùxué, xiànzài hěn hòuhuǐ.		
B) 现在还来得及。亡羊补牢, 为时不晚。		There is still time now. It is not too late to "Mend the Fence even after the Sheep Are Gone".
Xiànzài hái lái de jí. Wáng yáng bǔ láo, wéi shí bù wǎn.		

自相矛盾   Contradict Oneself

There once was a merchant who sold spears and shields. His selling pitch was quite interesting. "This spear is the sharpest in the world. There is none better. It can pierce any shield, regardless of the strength."

After realizing that no one was interested in his spear, he decided to push his

shield. "This shield is the best there is. There is no spear in the world that can pierce it."

The crowd listened to the man and started to laugh. Someone in the crowd asked, " Didn't you just say that your spear is the sharpest in the world and that there is no shield that it can't penetrate?"

The merchant proudly replied, "Yes, that is correct."

"And isn't your shield so solid that even the sharpest of spears could not penetrate it?"

"Yes, that is correct."

"Well, if that is the case, I just have one more question. If your shield is attacked by your spear, what will happen?"

The merchant became confused and started to stutter. With no recourse, the man picked up his spear and shield and returned home, losing face in the process.

(self, mutual, conflict)	
自相矛盾	zì xiāng máodùn
The idiom is used to describe something that is self-contradictory.	
你以前说过英语没劲, 现在又说英语特别有趣。你这不是自相矛盾吗?	You once said that English was uninteresting, now you are saying that it is fascinating. Aren't you contradicting yourself?
Nǐ yǐqián shuōguo Yīngyǔ méijìn, xiànzài yòu shuō Yīngyǔ tèbié yǒuqù. Nǐ zhè bú shì zì xiāng máodùn ma?	

Chapter VIII

SLANG

俚语

Slang, by definition, is very informal words sometimes containing vulgar or otherwise socially unacceptable language. Mirroring the changes in the socio-economic and political conditions of a society, slang allows outsiders to get a feel for the affects of these changes on the Average Joe's life. In a country that has experienced enormous changes over the past twenty years, Chinese slang is as rich as any other language in the world.

When there are 1.3 billion people living in one country, it is not possible to capture all of the slang. Phrases that are said in some parts of China may have never been heard in others. To ensure the highest rate of usage possible, we have conducted a familiarity test. Only if a majority of persons questioned knew the word was it selected.

Over the past decade, there have been a select few foreigners who have become household names because of their ability to speak slang. Learning how to properly use the words in this section will put the reader on the track of those elite Chinese-speaking foreigners.

八九不离十	bā jiǔ bù lí shí	pretty much; 80-90%
(heard, you, will, go, USA, right) **A)** 听说**你要去美国,是吧?** Tīngshuō nǐ yào qù Měiguó, shì ba?		I heard that you are going to the US, isn't that right?
(80-90%; if, no, the unexpected, I, next, MW, month, *stress*, leave) **B)** 八九不离十吧。**如果没有意外,我下个月就走。** Bā jiǔ bù lí shí ba. Rúguǒ méiyǒu yìwài, wǒ xià ge yuè jiù zǒu.		Pretty much. As long as there are no unforeseen changes, I will leave next month.

(*English*)		
拜拜	báibái	to break up with (boy/girlfriend)
(I, last, week, with, my, girlfriend, break up) 我上周跟我**女朋友**拜拜了。 Wǒ shàng zhōu gēn wǒ nǚpéngyou báibái le.		I broke up with my girlfriend last week.

摆谱	bǎipǔ	to show off
(this, fellow, always, love, at, friends, front, show off)	This guy loves showing off in front of his friends.	
这小子总爱在朋友面前摆谱。		
Zhè xiǎozi zǒng ài zài péngyou miànqián bǎipǔ.		

(half, 1 / 2kg, eight, 1 / 32 kg)		
半斤八两	bàn jīn bā liǎng	six of one and half a dozen of the other; the same
(his, study, grade, very, poor)	His grades really suck!	
A) 他的学习成绩很差。		
Tā de xuéxí chéngjì hěn chà.		
(you, don't, say, him, you, are, the same)	Don't talk about him. You two are pretty much the same.	
B) 你别说他，你们是半斤八两。		
Nǐ bié shuō tā, nǐmen shì bàn jīn bā liǎng.		

傍大款	bàng dàkuǎn	to date a wealthy man
(more and more, girl, like, date a wealthy man)	More and more girls like to date wealthy men.	
越来越多的女孩喜欢傍大款。		
Yuè lái yuè duō de nǚhái xǐhuan bàng dàkuǎn.		

包圆儿	bāoyuánr	to finish the remaining portion
(you, not, eat, QW; that's great, I, finish the remaining portion)	What, you guys are done eating? Great, I'll take care of the rest!	
你们不吃吗? 那好，我包圆儿了!		
Nǐmen bù chī ma? Nà hǎo, wǒ bāoyuánr le!		

倍儿 + 形容词	bèir + xíngróngcí	very + **adjective**
（your, Chinese, speak, very, great）		Your Chinese is really great!
你的汉语讲得**倍儿棒**。		
Nǐ de Hànyǔ jiǎng de **bèir bàng!**		

甭 + 动词	béng + dòngcí	there is no need, do not
（I, assure, nothing, do not, worry）		I am sure that there will not be a problem. Don't worry.
我肯定没事儿，**甭**着急。		
Wǒ kěndìng méishìr, béng zháojí.		
（we, are, good, friend, there is no need, to be polite）		We are good friends. There is no need to be so polite.
我们是好**朋友**，**甭客气**。		
Wǒmen shì hǎo péngyou, béng kèqi.		

甭 is one of the most interesting Chinese characters. It is comprised of a 不 bù, meaning no, and 用 yòng meaning need.

（knit, story）		
编**故事**	biān gùshi	to make up a story
（you, don't, trick, me, don't, make up a story）		Don't trick me. Don't make up a story.
你**别**骗**我**，别**编故事**。		
Nǐ bié piàn wǒ, bié biān gùshi.		

（don't, mention）		
别提了	bié tí le	Uhh, don't bring that up (it's really terrible)
（today, test, how is it）		How was your test today?
A）今天**考试**怎么样？		
Jīntiān kǎoshì zěnmeyàng?		

(don't bring that up, definitely, not, able, pass)	Oh, don't say that again. I definitely did not pass.
B) 别提了,**肯定不能**及格。	
Bié tí le, kěndìng bù néng jígé.	

(no, see, no, disperse)		
不见不散	bú jiàn bú sàn	Be there, or be square.
Not leave without seeing each other, it is definite that we meet, if one of us is late for any given reason, the other person will not leave.		
(we, 3 o'clock, at, the Imperial Palace, meet, definitely see you there)		Let's meet at 3 at the Imperial Palace. I'll definitely see you there.
我们 3 点在**故宫**见面,**不见不散**。		
Wǒmen sān diǎn zài Gùgōng jiànmiàn, bú jiàn bú sàn.		

(not, see, coffin, not, fall, tear)		
不见棺材不掉泪	bú jiàn guāncai bú diào lèi	refuse to be convinced until faced with grim reality
(I, think, you, are, refuse to be convinced until faced with grim reality, must, give, you, some, color, see, you, will, recognize, fault)		You refuse to be convinced until faced with grim reality. I'll have to give you a lesson to let you realize your fault.
我看你是不见棺材不掉泪,**非得给你**点儿颜色看看你才会认错。		
Wǒ kàn nǐ shì bú jiàn guāncai bú diào lèi, fēi děi gěi nǐ diǎnr yánsè kànkan nǐ cái huì rèncuò.		

不赖	bú lài	awesome, fat, not bad
(you, buy, new, car, truly, fat, definitely, spend, PT, not, small, money)		Your new car is beautiful. I'm sure it wasn't cheap.
你买的新车真**不赖**,肯定花了**不少**钱。		
Nǐ mǎi de xīn chē zhēn bú lài, kěndìng huāle bù shǎo qián.		

(not, like, words)		
不像话	bú xiànghuà	unreasonable

(you, this, way, do, too, unreasonable)	You are really being unreasonable.
你这样做太不像话了。	
Nǐ zhèyàng zuò tài bú xiànghuà le.	

(wipe, butt)		
擦屁股	cā pìgu	to finish things started by others, always undesirable

(he, every, time, open, party, all, leave, one, pile, trash, I, always, have to, for, him, do, this, kind, left behind, work)	Every time he throws a party, I get stuck cleaning up the mess like the mother who wipes the ass of her child.
他每次开 Party 都留下一堆垃圾，我总得给他干这种擦屁股的活儿。	
Tā měi cì kāi Party dōu liúxià yì duī lājī, wǒ zǒng děi gěi tā gàn zhè zhǒng cā pìgu de huór.	

蹭	cèng	scrounge, freeload
(he, always, go to, other, people's, house, in, freeload food, freeload drinks, very, annoy, people)	He always goes to other peoples' houses to scrounge meals. It really annoys people after a while.
他经常到别人家里蹭吃蹭喝，很讨人厌。	
Tā jīngcháng dào biéren jiā li cèng chī cèng hē, hěn tǎo rén yàn.	

(insert, mouth)		
插嘴	chāzuǐ	to butt in

(adults, speak, when, small, kids, not, should, butt in)	When adults are speaking, children should be seen and not heard.
大人说话的时候，小孩儿不要插嘴。	
Dàrén shuōhuà de shíhou, xiǎoháir búyào chāzuǐ.	

(fry, squid)		
炒鱿鱼	chǎo yóuyú	to fire a person from work
(he, again, no, good, work, I, then, fire, him) 他再不好好工作我就炒他鱿鱼。		If he continues to not work well, I will fire him!
Tā zài bù hǎohāo gōngzuò, wǒ jiù chǎo tā yóuyú.		

(pull, equal)		
扯平	chěpíng	to be even
(I, owe, you, one, MW, meal, this, MW, I, pay, we, two, then, even) 我欠你一顿饭,这顿我掏钱,咱俩就扯平了。		I owe you a meal. This time I'll pay so we are even.
Wǒ qiàn nǐ yí dùn fàn, zhè dùn wǒ tāo qián, zánmen jiù chěpíng le.		

成	chéng	OK, alright
(when, come, all, OK) 什么时候来都成。		You can come over whenever.
Shénme shíhou lái dōu chéng.		

(eat, full, PT, to the point of bursting)		
吃饱了撑的	chī bǎole chēng de	do something really stupid, foolish
(you, are, not, are, done something foolish, always, kick, that, MW, cat, doing, what) 你是不是吃饱了撑的,总踢那只猫干什么?		Have you done something stupid? Why do you always kick the cat?
Nǐ shì bu shì chī bǎole chēng de, zǒng tī nà zhī māo gàn shénme?		
This slang is not considered a curse word but is one of the strongest words in the Chinese language. If said in a serious manner, could very well lead to fist-a-cuffs. It can be said as a joke with close friends.		

(eat, wrong, medicine)		
吃错药了	chī cuò yào le	
This slang is a very negative word. Take the wrong medicine; crazy.		
(you, are, not, are, eat, wrong, medicine, release, such, big, temper, for what) 你是不是吃错药了，发这么大火干吗？ Nǐ shì bu shì chī cuò yào le, fā zhème dà huǒ gànma?		Did you eat the wrong medicine? Why the hell are you so upset over nothing?

(eat, soft, food)		
吃软饭	chī ruǎnfàn	
This slang describes a man who relies on his spouse or girlfriend for food and money.		
(he, very, no, prospects, depend, eat, soft, food, live, life) 他很没出息，靠吃软饭过活。 Tā hěn méi chūxi, kào chī ruǎnfàn guòhuó.		He is good for nothing, only depends on his wife.

吃香	chīxiāng	to get very popular
(these, few, years, software, engineer, more and more, popular) 这几年软件工程师越来越吃香。 Zhè jǐ nián ruǎnjiàn gōngchéngshī yuè lái yuè chīxiāng.		Over the past few years, software engineers are getting more and more popular

臭	chòu	very smelly; poor
(today, Laker, team, play, very, poor) 今天湖人队打得很臭。 Jīntiān Húrén Duì dǎ de hěn chòu.		The Lakers played horribly today.

(foul smelling, be pleased with oneself)

| 臭美 | chòuměi | to show off shamelessly (usually used as a joke) |

(I, am, not, am, very, beautiful)

A) 我是不是很漂亮? | Aren't I beautiful?

Wǒ shì bu shì hěn piàoliang?

(show off shamelessly)

B) 臭美。 | You are bragging shamelessly. Stop with that.

Chòuměi.

Conversation is among girls. Girl A is looking in the mirror talking to Girl B. *This slang can be used in response to a person who has made a self-compliment.*

(to leave, grid)

| 出格 | chūgé | exceed what is proper, overstep the bounds, inappropriate |

(he, in front of, girl students, face, tell, dirty joke, have, little, overstep, the bounds) | His saying a dirty joke in front of his female classmates was a little bit too much.

他当着女生的面讲黄色笑话，有点儿出格。

Tā dāngzhe nǚshēng de miàn jiǎng huángsè xiàohua, yǒudiǎnr chūgé.

| 串门儿 | chuàn ménr | drop in, to pay a friend a visit |

(you, have, time, when, come, drop in , MW) | When you have time, stop in.

你有空儿的时候，来串个门儿吧。

Nǐ yǒu kòngr de shíhou, lái chuàn ge ménr ba.

刺激	cìjī	stimulate, to make feel uncomfortable

(my, new, computer, use, very, awesome)	My new computer works really great!
A) 我的新电脑用起来很爽!	
Wǒ de xīn diànnǎo yòng qǐlai hěn shuǎng!	
(don't, make feel uncomfortable, me, I, still, no, computer)	Stop making me feel uncomfortable. I don't have a computer yet.
B) 别刺激我，我还没电脑呢。	
Bié cìjī wǒ, wǒ hái méi diànnǎo ne.	
(bungee jumping, very, stimulating)	Bungee jumping is very stimulating!
蹦极很刺激!	
Bèngjí hěn cìjī!	

(put together, suitable)		
凑合	còuhe	so-so, make do with

(you, recently, at, work unit, muddle along, how)	How has work been lately?
A) 你最近在单位混得怎么样?	
Nǐ zuìjìn zài dānwèi hùn de zěnmeyàng?	
(ah, so-so)	Ah, so-so.
B) 嗨，凑合吧。	
Hāi, còuhe ba.	
(your, that, MW, old, refrigerator, still, able, use)	Your old refrigerator still can be used?
X) 你那个老掉牙的冰箱还能用?	
Nǐ nà ge lǎodiàoyá de bīngxiāng hái néng yòng?	
(no, money, buy, new one, make do with, use)	I don't really have the money to buy a new one so it will have to do.
Y) 没钱买新的，凑合着用呗。	
Méi qián mǎi xīn de, còuhezhe yòng bei.	

(vinager, jar)		
醋坛子	cùtánzi	person easily jealous when his/her girl/boyfriend talks with another
(my, girlfriend, is, MW, jealous, once, see, me, with, other, girls, together, right away, unhappy) **我女朋友是个醋坛子，一看见我跟其他女孩在一起就撅嘴。**		My girlfriend is very easy to get jealous. The moment she sees me talking with other girls she is unhappy.
Wǒ nǚpéngyou shì ge cùtánzi, yí kànjiàn wǒ gēn qítā nǚhái zài yìqǐ jiù juē zuǐ.		

催	cuī	to rush
(wait, a moment, don't, rush, me) **等一会儿，别催我。**		Wait a minute. Don't rush me!
Děng yíhuìr, bié cuī wǒ.		

打的	dǎ dī	to take a cab
(you, take a cab, come over, I, for, you, reimburse) **你打的过来，我给你报销。**		Take a cab over. I will reimburse you.
Nǐ dā dī guòlai, wǒ gěi nǐ bàoxiāo.		

大大咧咧	dàdaliēliē	careless
(he, always, careless, often, lose, things) **他总是大大咧咧，经常丢东西。**		He is always careless, loses things left and right.
Tā zǒngshì dàdaliēliē, jīngcháng diū dōngxi.		

(big, wrist)		
大腕	dàwàn	celebrity, big shot
(Liu Huan, is, China, music circle, celebrity)		Liu Huan is a Chinese music industry celebrity.
刘欢是中国歌坛的大腕。		
Liú Huān shì Zhōngguó gētán de dàwàn.		

打住	dǎzhù	enough already
(enough already, I, don't have, time, any-more, with, you, mess around)		Enough already. I don't have time to mess around with you.
打住，我没有时间再跟你磨蹭了。		
Dǎzhù, wǒ méiyǒu shíjiān zài gēn nǐ móceng le.		

(player, confused, on-looker, clear)		
当局者迷，旁观者清。	Dāng jú zhě mí, páng guān zhě qīng.	The spectators see the game better than players.
(you, say, he, like, me; I, why, can't see)		You say he likes me. Why don't I see it?
A) 你说他喜欢我。我为什么看不出来？		
Nǐ shuō tā xǐhuan wǒ. Wǒ wèi shénme kàn bu chūlái?		
(player, confused, onlooker, clear)		The spectators see the game better than the players.
B) 当局者迷，旁观者清呗！		
Dāng jú zhě mí, páng guān zhě qīng bei.		

档次	dàngcì	taste, grade
(he, wear, clothing / speak, words, no, taste)		He has no taste in clothes. / He speaks with no class.
他穿衣服 / 说话没有档次。		
Tā chuān yīfu / shuōhuà méiyǒu dàngcì.		

倒霉	dǎoméi	unlucky
(I, very, unlucky, drink, cold, water, even, choke, teeth) 我很倒霉，喝凉水都塞牙。		I am so unlucky that I can't even drink a glass of cold water without spilling it all over myself.
Wǒ hěn dǎoméi, hē liáng shuǐ dōu sāi yá.		

(turn, one's, appetite)		
倒人的胃口	dǎo rén de wèikǒu	to make somebody sick
(your, words, too, disgusting, turn, my, appetite) 你的话太恶心了，倒我的胃口。		Your words are making me sick.
Nǐ de huà tài ěxin le, dǎo wǒ de wèikǒu.		

(suspend, appetite)		
吊胃口	diào wèikǒu	to tantalize
(you, know, I, today, bump into, PT, who) A）你知道我今天碰到了谁？		You'll never guess who I ran into today?
Nǐ zhīdào wǒ jīntiān pèng dàole shéi?		
(don't, tantalize, me, hurry, say) B）不要吊我的胃口，快说！		Stop tantalizing me. Tell me!
Búyào diào wǒ de wèikǒu, kuài shuō!		

顶事儿	dǐngshìr	of use, serve the purpose
(you, breakfast, eat, PT, what) A）你早饭吃了什么？		What did you have for breakfast?
Nǐ zǎofàn chīle shénme?		
(one, MW, chicken, egg) B）一个鸡蛋。		One egg.
Yí ge jīdàn.		
(that, at all, not, of use) A）那根本不顶事儿。		That's not enough at all.
Nà gēnběn bù dǐngshìr.		

(stand up to, mouth)		
顶嘴	dǐngzuǐ	to talk back
(this, MW, kid, love, with, his, parent, talk back) 这个小孩儿爱跟他父母顶嘴。		This kid loves to talk back to his parents.
Zhè ge xiǎoháir ài gēn tā fùmǔ dǐngzuǐ.		

(lose, face)		
丢份儿	diūfènr	embarrassing
(truly, embarrassing, grow, that, old, even, bike, not, able, ride) 真丢份儿，长这么大连自行车都不会骑。		How embarrassing! At this age you can't ride a bike.
Zhēn diūfènr, zhǎng zhème dà lián zìxíngchē dōu bú huì qí.		

逗	dòu	comical, amusing, tease
(this, MW, foreigner, pretty, comical) 这个老外挺逗的。		This foreigner is really funny.
Zhè ge lǎowài tǐng dòu de.		
(don't, be comical) 别逗了!		You cannot be serious! That is preposterous!
Bié dòu le!		
(tease, you, play) 逗你玩儿。		That is playing around with you.
Dòu nǐ wǎnr.		

(do a disservice to, audience)		
对不起观众	duìbuqǐ guānzhòng	heinously ugly
(she, look, let somebody down, audience) 她长得对不起观众。		She is heinously ugly.
Tā zhǎng de duìbuqǐ guānzhòng.		

讹	é	
It means to extort under false pretenses; claiming to be hurt in order to collect damages.		

(you, look, my, new, bike, by, you, hit, broken, compensate)	Look, you hit my bike and destroyed it. Pay up!
A）你看，我的新车被你撞坏了，赔吧。	
Nǐ kàn, wǒ de xīn chē bèi nǐ zhuàng huài le, péi ba.	
(your, bike, nothing wrong, don't, cheat, me)	There is nothing wrong with your bike. Don't try and extort me under false pretenses.
B）你的车没事儿，别讹我。	
Nǐ de chē méishìr, bié é wǒ.	

(two, hundred, five / 13, point)		
二百五 / 十三点	èrbǎiwǔ / shísāndiǎn	idiot, moron
(he, is, MW, idiot, don't, with, him, stoop to his level)	He is an idiot. Don't stoop to his level.	
他是个**二百五 / 十三点**，别跟他一般见识。		
Tā shì ge èrbǎiwǔ / shísāndiǎn, bié gēn tā yìbān jiànshi.		

(second, breast)		
二奶	èrnǎi	mistress; widely used in southern China
(now, have, very, many, Hong Kong, tycoons, go to, mainland, keep, mistresses)	There are a lot of Hong Kong tycoons that keep mistresses in the mainland.	
现在，有很多香港大款到大陆包**二奶**。		
Xiànzài, yǒu hěn duō Xiānggǎng dàkuǎn dào dàlù bāo èrnǎi.		

犯不着	fàn bu zháo	not worthwhile
(for, such, small, matter, with, her, fight, not worthwhile)	It is not worthwhile for you to get in a battle of words with her over such a small thing.	
为了**这么点儿小事儿**跟她**斗嘴**，**犯不着**。		
Wèile zhème diǎnr xiǎoshìr gen tā dòuzuǐ, fàn bu zháo.		

(convenient)		
方便	fāngbiàn	to relieve oneself
(excuse me, wash, hand, room, at, where; I, want, relieve myself, a little) 请问，洗手间在哪儿？我想方便一下。		Excuse me, where is the bathroom? I need to take a leak.
Qǐngwèn, xǐshǒujiān zài nǎr? Wǒ xiǎng fāngbiàn yíxià.		

(set free, dove)		
放鸽子	fàng gēzi	to stand somebody up
(tomorrow, 3 o'clock, meet; don't, stand me up) 明天三点见面。不要放我的鸽子。		We'll meet tomorrow at three. Don't stand me up. (usually said as a joke)
Míntiān sān diǎn jiànmiàn. Búyào fàng wǒ de gēzi.		
(he, yesterday, stand me up) 他昨天放了我的鸽子。		He stood me up yesterday.
Tā zuótiān fàngle wǒ de gēzi.		

(release, you, one, horse)		
放你一马	fàng nǐ yì mǎ	I'll let you go this time
(next, not, as precedence)		
下不为例	xià bù wéi lì	don't let it happen again
(teacher, I, today, forget, bring, homework; tomorrow, hand in, OK, QW) A) 老师，我今天忘带作业了。明天交可以吗？		Teacher, I forgot to bring my homework. Is tomorrow OK?
Lǎoshī, wǒ jīntiān wàng dài zuòyè le, míngtiān jiāo kěyǐ ma?		
(OK, today, I'll let you go; don't do it again) B) 好吧，今天我放你一马。下不为例。		I'll let you slide this time, but do not let it happen again.
Hǎo ba, jīntiān wǒ fàng nǐ yì mǎ. Xià bù wéi lì.		

(cost, blood)		
费血	fèixiě	cost an arm and a leg; exorbitant
(why, buy, such, good, car; too , exorbitant)		Why did you buy such a nice car? Way too expensive.
为什么买这么好的车？太费血了。		
Wèi shénme mǎi zhème hǎo de chē? Tài fèixiě le .		

风光	fēngguāng	on a roll
(he, this year, make a fortune, very, on a roll)		He made a fortune this year and is really on a roll now.
他今年发财了，非常风光。		
Tā jīnnián fācái le, fēicháng fēngguāng.		

盖帽	gàimào	superb, excellent
(his, English, superb)		His English is excellent.
他的英语盖了帽了。		
Tā de Yīngyǔ gàile mào le.		

(force, duck, on, perch)		
赶鸭子上架	gǎn yāzi shàng jià	ask someone to do something that they obviously can not do
(for, us, sing, MW, song)		Sing us a song!
A) 给我们唱个歌吧!		
Gěi wǒmen chàng ge gē ba!		
(you, this, not, forcing a duck onto a perch, QW)		Isn't this asking a duck to hop on a perch?
B) 你们这不是赶鸭子上架吗？		
Nǐmen zhè bú shì gǎn yāzi shàng jià ma?		

(make, certain)		
搞定	gǎodìng	get something done, ace
(I, will, IO, this, time, test, for, ace) 我要把这次考试给搞定。 Wǒ yào bǎ zhè cì kǎoshì gěi gǎodìng.		I am going to ace this test.
(your, airplane, ticket, get something done, QW) 你的飞机票搞定了吗？ Nǐ de fēijīpiào gǎodìng le ma?		Did you book your plane ticket yet?

(make, devil / cat, tricks)		
搞鬼 / 猫儿腻	gǎo guǐ / māornì	play tricks, up to no good
(you, two, now, make, what, devil / cat tricks) 你俩在搞什么鬼 / 猫儿腻？ Nǐ liǎ zài gǎo shénme guǐ / māornì?		What are you two up to?

(make, laugh)		
搞笑	gǎoxiào	funny
(this, MW, comedy, unusually, funny, very, worth, one, look) 这部喜剧非常搞笑，很值得一看。 Zhè bù xǐjù fēicháng gǎoxiào, hěn zhíde yí kàn.		This comedy is really funny, definitely worth seeing.

(older brother)		
哥们儿	gēmenr	
It was originally only used to describe a very close friend.		
(he, is, my, 20, year, close friend) 他是我二十年的哥们儿。 Tā shì wǒ èrshí nián de gēmenr.		He has been my close friend for twenty years.

(*name*, this, is, my, close friend, *name*)	Wang Gang, this is my close friend Li Ming.
王刚，这是我的哥们儿李明。	
Wáng Gāng, zhè shì wǒ de gēmenr Lǐ Míng.	

As time evolved, gēmenr became a greeting used with both intimate and average friends alike. In the above example, Li Ming is merely an acquaintance to the person speaking but is still introduced as a "close friend". This usage of gēmenr is used to make the person being introduced, in this case Li Ming, have a positive feeling.

(hello, buddy, go, Tian'anmen Square, how, go)	Hey, buddy, how do you get to Tian'anmen?
嘿，哥们儿，去天安门怎么走？	
Hēi, gēmenr, qù Tiān'ānmén zěnme zǒu?	

Today, the word gēmenr is used as a very common greeting between similar-aged males meeting for the first time.

哏儿	génr	interesting
(you, speak, words, very, interesting)	Your words are really interesting!
你说话挺哏儿的。	
Nǐ shuōhuà tǐng génr de.	

(enough, friend)		
够朋友	gòu péngyou	a true friend
(I, have, problem, moment, you, help, PT, me; you, truly, enough, friend)	When I had a problem, you were there for me. You are really a good friend.
我有困难时，你帮助了我。你真够朋友。	
Wǒ yǒu kùnnan shí, nǐ bāngzhùle wǒ. Nǐ zhēn gòu péngyou.	

够呛	gòuqiàng	probably not

(daddy, we, today, can, go, swimming, QW)	Daddy, can we go swimming today?
A）爸爸，**我们**今天**可以去游泳**吗？	
Bàba, wǒmen jīntiān kěyǐ qù yóuyǒng ma?	

(afraid, probably not, daddy's, work, still, not, done; tomorrow)	I'm afraid probably not. Daddy still has work to do. How about tomorrow?
B）恐怕**够呛**，爸爸的**工作**还**没做完**呢。**明天吧。**	
Kǒngpà gòuqiàng, bàba de gōngzuò hái méi zuò wán ne. Míngtiān ba.	

(appraise, estimate)		
估计	gūjì	to estimate, to have a hunch

(I, estimate, he, 20, years old)	I think he is around 20.
我估计他二十岁。	
Wǒ gūjì tā èrshí suì.	

(I, today, have, thing, look for, you; you, estimate, what time, able, get off work)	I have something that I need to talk with you about. What time do you think you will get off work?
A）我今天有事找你。你估计几点钟能下班儿？	
Wǒ jīntiān yǒu shì zhǎo nǐ. Nǐ gūjì jǐ diǎnzhōng néng xiàbānr?	

(probably, 8, o'clock)	Probably eight.
B）大概八点吧。	
Dàgài bā diǎn ba.	

鼓，腰包	gǔ, yāobāo	bulging, wallet
(heard, you, recently, earn, PT, one, big, amount, money)		I heard you made a lot of money lately.
A) 听说你最近挣了一大笔钱。		
Tīngshuō nǐ zuìjìn zhèngle yí dà bǐ qián.		
(your, wallet, compare, mine, bulging)		Your wallet is fatter than mine.
B) 你的腰包比我的鼓。		
Nǐ de yāobāo bǐ wǒ de gǔ.		

(concern, you, what, thing)		
关你什么事	guān nǐ shénme shì	it's none of your business (rude)
(you, last night, why, not, return, dorm, sleep)		Why didn't you sleep in the dorm last night?
A) 你昨晚怎么没有回宿舍睡觉？		
Nǐ zuówǎn zěnme méiyǒu huí sùshè shuìjiào?		
(it's none of your business)		It's none of your business!
B) 关你什么事。		
Guān nǐ shénme shì.		

拐弯儿抹角	guǎi wānr mò jiǎo	beat around the bush, talk in a round about way
(I, heard, you, bought, PT, I, favorite, that, kind, candy; I, have, a period, not, eaten; I, go, PT, very, many, places, buy, but, can't find)		I heard you bought my favorite candy. Come to think of it, I have not eaten it for quite some time now. I went to a bunch of stores to buy it, but no one had it...
A) 我听说你买了我最喜欢吃的那种糖。我有一阵儿没吃了。我去了很多地方买，但买不着……		
Wǒ tīngshuō nǐ mǎile wǒ zuì xǐhuan chī de nà zhǒng táng. Wǒ yǒu yízhènr méi chī le. Wǒ qùle hěn duō dìfang mǎi, dàn mǎi bu zháo…		
(don't, with, me, beat around the bush, directly, say, you, want, eat)		Stop beating around the bush. If you want a piece, just say so.
B) 别跟我拐弯儿抹角，直接说你想吃吧。		
Bié gēn wǒ guǎi wānr mò jiǎo, zhíjiē shuō nǐ xiǎng chī ba.		

规矩	guīju	behave oneself
(at, here, must, behave yourself, a little, otherwise, jailer, will, teach you a lesson) 在这儿得**规矩**点儿，**否则**看守会让你好瞧。 Zài zhèr děi guīju diǎnr, fǒuzé kānshǒu huì ràng nǐ hǎoqiáo.		You should behave yourself here, otherwise the jailer will teach you a lesson.

(devil, only, knows)		
鬼才知道	guǐ cái zhīdào	Only god knows!
(already, 12 o'clock, he, still, not, return; run to, where, go) A) 已经 **12** 点了，他还没回来。跑到**哪儿**去了？ 　　Yǐjing shí'èr diǎn le, tā hái méi huílai. Pǎo dào nǎr qù le?		It's already 12 and he still has not returned. Where the hell did he go?
(devil, only, knows) B) **鬼才**知道。 　　Guǐ cái zhīdào.		Only god knows!

(hurt, group, structural particle, horse)		
害群之马	hài qún zhī mǎ	the black sheep of a group of people, give a group a bad name
(cheat, foreigner, Chinese, are, Chinese, black sheep) **骗老外的**中国人是中国人的**害群之马**。 Piàn lǎowài de Zhōngguórén shì Zhōngguórén de hài qún zhī mǎ.		Those Chinese who cheat foreigners are the black sheep of the Chinese. (Most Chinese are very nice.)

(benefit, fee)

好处费	hǎochùfèi	pickings

To give hǎochùfèi is a way of thanking someone for helping you obtain an opportunity. Can be used with getting a person a good job, introducing someone, etc.

(if, you, help, me, find, job, I, can, give, you, money) 如果**你**帮**我**找到**工作**,我**可以**给**你**好处费。	If you help me find a job, I will give you some money.

Rúguǒ nǐ bāng wǒ zhǎo dào gōngzuò, wǒ kěyǐ gěi nǐ hǎochùfèi.

(fond of, feminine charms)

好色	hàosè	lover of girls

(he, this, MW, person, really, like girls) 他这个人真好色。	He is really fond of girls.

Tā zhè ge rén zhēn hàosè.

([not], work well)

(不)**好使**	(bù) hǎoshǐ	do (not) work well

The scope of the usage of this slang is very wide, ranging from a person's brain to any material thing.

(this, software, doesn't work well) 这**软件**不好使。	This software doesn't work well.

Zhè ruǎnjiàn bù hǎoshǐ.

(drink, west, north, wind)

喝**西北风**	hē xīběifēng	so poor that you are forced to drink wind

(you, must, work hard, otherwise, only, able, drink, west, north, wind) 你得好好工作,**不然**只**能**喝**西北风**。	You must work hard, otherwise you will be broken.

Nǐ děi hǎohāo gōngzuò, bùrán zhǐ néng hē xīběifēng.

(black)		
黑	hēi	to be cheated
(I, by, small, peddlar, cheat)		I got cheated by a peddlar.
我被小商贩黑了。		
Wǒ bèi xiǎoshāngfàn hēi le.		
(black, car)		
黑车	hēichē	illegal taxi
(we, take, MW, an illegal taxi)		Let's take an illegal taxi.
咱们打个黑车吧。		
Zánmen dǎ ge hēichē ba.		

轰 + 我们	hōng **wǒmen**	throwing us out, rushing us
(11 o'clock, close, classroom, quick, have, people, come, throw **us** out)		The classroom closes at 11, and people will come quickly to throw us out. (10:50)
十一点关教室,快有人来轰我们了。		
Shíyī diǎn guān jiàoshì, kuài yǒu rén lái hōng **wǒmen** le.		

(red, envelope)		
红包	hóngbāo	red envelope used when giving gifts or bribes
(now, doctors, not, allow, receive, red envelope)		Doctors are not permitted to accept "red envelopes".
现在医生不许收红包。		
Xiànzài yīshēng bùxǔ shōu hóngbāo.		

(red, eye, illness)		
红眼病	hóngyǎnbìng	jealousy

(looking, other, people, take, money, compare, him, more, he, then, suffer from, jealousy) 看着别人拿的钱比他多，他就害红眼病。	If others get paid more than him, he is very jealous.
Kànzhe biéren ná de qián bǐ tā duō, tà jiù hài hóngyǎnbìng.	

狐狸精	húlijīng	ho, a seductive-appearing woman

(she, truly, is, MW, seductive-appearing woman, you'd better not, know, her) 她真是个狐狸精，最好不要认识她。	She really is a ho. You're better off not getting involved with her.
Tā zhēn shì ge húlijīng, zuìhǎo búyào rènshi tā.	

花花肠子	huāhua chángzi	womanizer, player

(he, is, MW, player, girlfriend, change, truly, frequent) 他是个花花肠子，女朋友换得真勤。	He is a big player, swaps girlfriends very frequently.
Tā shì ge huāhua chángzi, nǚpéngyou huàn de zhēn qín.	

(paint, map)		
画地图	huà dìtú	wet one's bed

It literally means to draw a map, and in itself is not very comical. The meaning here is to wet your bed.

(you, little, when, piss, PT, your bed, QW)	Did you wet your bed when you were young?
你小的时候画过地图吗?	
Nǐ xiǎo de shíhou huàguo dìtú ma?	

会来事儿	huìláishìr	knows exactly what to say at the most appropriate time
(Lanna, because, know what to say, very, fast, become, PT, manager)	Lanna very quickly became manager because she knows what to say at the right time.	
兰娜因为会来事儿, 很快当上了经理。		
Lánnà yīnwèi huì láishìr, hěn kuài dāng shàngle jīnglǐ.		

(stupid, egg)		
混蛋	húndàn	bastard, bad apple
(you, this, MW, bastard)	You are a bad apple.	
你这个混蛋。		
Nǐ zhè ge húndàn.		

(fire)		
火	huǒ	hot, popular, prosperous
(English, in, China, very, popular)	Pizza Hut is really popular in China.	
必胜客在中国很火。		
Bìshèngkè zài Zhōngguó hěn huǒ.		

(muddle along, days)		
混日子	hùn rìzi	muddle along

(recently, live, how about)	How has life been recently?
A） 最近**过得怎么样**？	
Zuìjìn guò de zěnmeyàng?	
(I, currently, muddle along, days)	Life really sucks!（Can be used as a joke or exaggeration）
B） 我在混日子。	
Wǒ zài hùn rìzi.	

(chicken, feather, garlic, skin)		
鸡毛蒜皮	jī máo suàn pí	trifles, trivialities
(this, kind, trifle, insignificant matter, even, need, I, show up, QW)	Do I have to involve myself in such kind of trivialities?	
这种鸡毛蒜皮的**小事儿**还用**得着**我**出马**吗？		
Zhè zhǒng jī máo suàn pí de xiǎoshìr hái yòng de zháo wǒ chūmǎ ma?		

(mix, plug)		
加**塞儿**	jiāsāir	to butt in line
(wait, half, day)		
等**半天**	děng bàntiān	wait for a long time（exaggeration）
(I, wait, PT, long time, please, you, don't, butt in line)	I've waited for a long time. Please do not butt in line.（You inconsiderate fool）
我**等了半天了**，请你不要**加塞儿**。	
Wǒ děngle bàntiān le, qǐng nǐ búyào jiāsāir.	

(home, always, common, food)		
家常便饭	jiācháng biànfàn	a common occurrence, routine
(in, my, memory, he, and, his, girlfriend, argue, simply but, is, a common occurance) 在我的记忆里，他和他女朋友吵架简直是家常便饭。		If my memory serves me right, he was always fighting with his girlfriend.
Zài wǒ de jìyì li, tā hé tā nǚpéngyou chǎojià jiǎnzhí shì jiācháng biànfàn.		

(cunning, argue)		
狡辩	jiǎobiàn	to justify oneself (very negative)
(I, yesterday, go, have class; so, not, able, help, you) A) 我昨天去上课了，所以没能帮你。		I had class yesterday so I could not help you.
Wǒ zuótiān qù shàngkè le, suǒyǐ méi néng bāng nǐ.		
(you, yesterday, definitely, not, go to class, don't justify yourself) B) 你昨天明明没有上课，别再狡辩了。		I know for a fact that you did not go to class yesterday. Don't justify yourself.
Nǐ zuótiān míngmíng méiyǒu shàngkè, bié zài jiǎobiàn le.		

(foot, step on, two, MW, boat)		
脚踩两只船	jiǎo cǎi liǎng zhī chuán	to two-time a person, have two boy/girlfriends at the same time
(to fall, to tumble)		
栽	zāi	to blunder, to be unsuccessful

(you, not, able, two-time person, will, be unsuccessful) 你**不能脚踩两只船**, 会栽的。 Nǐ bù néng jiǎo cǎi liǎng zhī chuán, huì zāi de.		You cannot get away with having two companions at the same time.

较真儿	jiàozhēnr	nitpick, ask for specifics when it is not necessary
(here, should, read, "huār", not, is, "huā") **A**) 在这儿**应该**读"花儿", 不是"花"。 Zài zhèr yīnggāi dú "huār", bú shì "huā".		Here you should read huār, not huā.
(don't, with, me, nitpick) **B**) 不要跟我**较真儿**。 Búyào gēn wǒ jiàozhēnr.		Don't nitpick!

(release, boredom)		
解闷儿	jiě mènr	divert oneself from boredom
(I, very, bored, we, go, bar, divert from boredom) 我很无聊, 咱们去酒吧**解解闷儿**。 Wǒ hěn wúliáo, zánmen qù jiǔbā jiějiě mènr.		I am really bored. Let's go to the bar to liven things up a little.

(drive, night, vehicle)		
开**夜车**	kāi yèchē	pull an all-nighter

(I, tomorrow, must, hand in, thesis, tonight, must, pull an all-nighter)

我明天得交论文，今晚得开夜车。

Wǒ míngtiān děi jiāo lùnwén, jīnwǎn děi kāi yèchē.

I have to hand in my thesis tomorrow. Tonight I will definitely be pulling an all-nighter.

开涮	kāishuàn	to make fun of, to tease

(they, always, like, make fun of, Xiao Zhang, but, he, never, angry)

他们总喜欢拿小张开涮，可他从不生气。

Tāmen zǒng xǐhuan ná Xiǎo Zhāng kāishuàn, kě tā cóng bù shēngqì.

They always tease Xiao Zhang but he never gets upset about it.

侃	kǎn	to shoot the shit, to chat

(he, this, MW, person, nothing to do, then, love to chat)

他这个人没事儿就爱神侃。

Tā zhè ge rén méi shìr jiù ài shén kǎn.

When he doesn't have anything else to do, he likes to sit around and shoot the shit.

(see, go, eyes)

看走眼	kàn zǒuyǎn	to see wrong

(I, thought, this, MW, pen, is, mine)

A) 我以为这支笔是我的。

Wǒ yǐwéi zhè zhī bǐ shì wǒ de.

I thought this pen was mine.

(you, to see wrong, it, is, mine)

B) 你看走眼了，它是我的。

Nǐ kàn zǒuyǎn le, tā shì wǒ de.

You made a mistake. It is mine.

扛	káng	shoulder the responsibility; capable of doing something
(this, matter, not, easy, do, you, one, MW, person, shoulder, able, QW)		This is not an easy task. Can you handle it all by yourself?
这事儿不好办，你一个人扛得住吗？		
Zhè shìr bù hǎo bàn, nǐ yí ge rén káng de zhù ma?		

坑	kēng	to cheat
(I, from, airport, take a cab, to, hotel, by, cab, driver, cheat)		I was cheated by the cab driver from the airport to my hotel.
我从机场打的到饭店被出租车司机坑了。		
Wǒ cóng jīchǎng dǎ dī dào fàndiàn bèi chūzūchē sījī kēng le.		

抠门儿	kōuménr	very cheap, stingy
(you, too, cheap, one, time, even, not, treat, me, eat)		You are so cheap, haven't ever treated me.
你太抠门儿了，一次也没有请我吃饭。		
Nǐ tài kōuménr le, yí cì yě méiyǒu qǐng wǒ chīfàn.		

拉倒吧！	Lādǎo ba!	Get out of here with that! (junk)
(you, just, enter, company, half, year, right away, want, to be, manager, get out of here with that)		You just entered the company half a year ago and you want to be manager. Get out of here with that!
你刚进公司半年就想当经理，拉倒吧你。		
Nǐ gāng jìn gōngsī bàn nián jiù xiǎng dāng jīnglǐ, lādǎo ba nǐ.		

(sloppy/sloppy, devil)		
邋遢/邋遢鬼	lāta/lātaguǐ	very messy/a slob
(look, your, clothes, so, dirty, you, this, MW, slob)	Look at how dirty your clothes are. You slob!	
看你衣服那么脏，你这个**邋遢鬼**！		
Kàn nǐ yīfu nàme zāng, nǐ zhè ge lātaguǐ!		

(waste, mouth, tongue)		
浪费口舌	làngfèi kǒushé	waste your breath
(I, not, want, hear, any, excuse, don't, waste your breath)	I don't want to hear any excuses. Don't waste your breath.	
我**不想听**任何借口，不要**浪费口舌**。		
Wǒ bù xiǎng tīng rènhé jièkǒu, búyào làngfèi kǒushé.		

(earn, outside, money)		
捞外快	lāo wàikuài	earn extra money on the side
(he, daytime, work, nighttime, do part-time, earn extra money on the side)	He has a steady job during the day and does random things at night to earn some side money.	
他白天上班，**晚上兼职打工捞外快**。		
Tā báitiān shàngbān, wǎnshang jiānzhí dǎgōng lāo wàikuài.		

劳驾	láojià	excuse me (when asking for somebody's help)
(excuse me, let, me, go through)	Excuse me, please let me go by.	
劳驾，让我过去。		
Láojià, ràng wǒ guòqu.		

老百姓	lǎobǎixìng	middle class, average Joe
(I, am, MW, quiet, average Joe) 我是个默默无闻的老百姓。 Wǒ shì ge mòmò wú wén de lǎobǎixìng.		I am a very average person.

(old, falling out, tooth)		
老掉牙	lǎodiàoyá	outdated, obsolete
(this, MW, black-white television set, already, outdated, should, buy, MW, new one) 这台黑白电视机已经老掉牙了, 应该买台新的。 Zhè tái hēi-bái diànshìjī yǐjing lǎodiàoyá le, yīnggāi mǎi tái xīn de.		This black and white TV set is so old. You should buy a new one already.

(old, dirt)	
老土	lǎotǔ

This slang is usually used as a joke to insult a person. The scope of this word is very large. As long as you feel the person should be aware of, or know how to use a piece of equipment, but he does not, it can be used.

(computer, you, even, not, know, truly, is MW, person from the countryside) 电脑你都不知道, 真是个老土。 Diànnǎo nǐ dōu bù zhīdào, zhēn shì ge lǎotǔ.	You don't even know what a computer is. You really are a person who is behind the times.

(old, outside)	
老外	lǎowài	foreigner

This slang is the most common word used to describe foreigners. It first originated in the late 70s and early 80s following the Opening Up and Reform Policy.

(BLCU, foreigner, very, many)	There are many foreigners at Beijing Language and Culture University.
北京语言大学老外很多。	
Běijīng Yǔyán Dàxué lǎowài hěn duō.	

雷子	léizi	cop (Pig, derogative)
条子	tiáozi	
(you, crazy; here, so, many, cops, you, still, sell, porn)		You are crazy. This place is swarming with police and you still sell pornography?
你疯了？这儿那么多条子/雷子，你还卖毛片儿？		
Nǐ fēng le? Zhèr nàme duō tiáozi/léizi, nǐ hái mài máopiānr?		

(put down, pole)		
撂挑子	liào tiāozi	to quit a job
(as, student, cadre, you, shouldn't, during, work, most, critical, moment, to quit a job)		As class chairman, one cannot quit at the most critical point.
作为学生干部，你不能在工作最关键的时候撂挑子。		
Zuòwéi xuésheng gànbù, nǐ bù néng zài gōngzuò zuì guānjiàn de shíhou liào tiāozi.		

(two, kind, thing)		
两码事	liǎng mǎ shì	two different matters
(she, only, is, donkey shit ball, appearance smooth; you, why, with, her, together)		She is attractive but that is all. Why are you with her?
A) 她只是驴粪球表面光。你为什么跟她在一起？		
Tā zhǐ shì lǘfènqiú biǎomiàn guāng. Nǐ wèi shénme gēn tā zài yìqǐ?		

(don't, worry, make friends, and, marriage, are, two different matters)	Don't worry. Having a friend and getting married are two totally different things.
B) 别担心, 交朋友和结婚是两码事。	
Bié dānxīn, jiāo péngyou hē jiéhūn shì liǎng mǎ shì.	

哩咯儿楞	līgerlēng	tricks, games
(our, today's, class, by, cancel)	Today's class was canceled.	
A) 我们今天的课被取消了。		
Wǒmen jīntiān de kè bèi qǔxiāo le.		
(less, with, me, come, this, trick)	Stop messing around with me.	
B) 少跟我来这哩咯儿楞。		
Shǎo gēn wǒ lái zhè līgerlēng.		

This slang is almost always used in a joking manner between friends. Students **A** and **B** are classmates. **A** is joking around with **B** because he knows **B** does not want to go to class.

厉害	lìhai	fierce, strict, intense,
(his, cold, very, intense)	He has a really bad cold.	
他的感冒很厉害。		
Tā de gǎnmào hěn lìhai.		
(our, teacher, very, strict, if, late, right away, trouble)	Our teacher is really strict. If you are late one second, he is mad.	
我们的老师很厉害,如果迟到就麻烦了。		
Wǒmen de lǎoshī hěn lìhai, rúguǒ chídào jiù máfan le.		
(Iverson, basketball, play, very, intense)	Allen Iverson plays (basketball) very intensely.	
艾弗逊篮球打得很厉害。		
Àifúxùn lánqiú dǎ de hěn lìhai.		

(leave, music note)		
离谱	lípǔ	go beyond what is proper
(this, MW, clothing, quality, both, poor, and, ugly, ask, 300 yuan, too, go beyond what is proper) 这件衣服质量又差，又难看，要三百块钱，太离谱了。	This quality of this piece of clothing is both poor and ugly. Asking 300 RMB is absolutely crazy.	
Zhè jiàn yīfu zhìliàng yòu chà, yòu nánkàn, yào sānbǎi kuài qián, tài lípǔ le.		

(sharp, simply)		
利索	lìsuo	in an efficient manner
(he, work, too, efficiently) 他干活挺利索的。	He does things in a very efficient manner.	
Tā gànhuó tǐng lìsuo de.		

(stroll, corner)		
遛弯儿	liùwānr	to go for a stroll
(we, eat, over, dinner, go out, for a stroll, good, not, good) 咱们吃完晚饭，出去遛遛弯儿好不好？	After we finish eating dinner, what do you say we go for a stroll?	
Zánmen chī wán wǎnfàn, chūqu liùliùwānr hǎo bu hǎo?		

乱七八糟	luàn qī bā zāo	in an awful mess, at sixes and sevens
(his, room, in an awful mess) 他的房间乱七八糟。	His room is a pigsty.	
Tā de fángjiān luàn qī bā zāo.		

啰唆	luōsuo	annoying; taking 5 minutes to say something that should take 2
(get up, get up, even, already, 9 o'clock **A)** 起床起床,都已经九点了。 Qǐchuáng qǐchuáng, dōu yǐjing jiǔ diǎn le.		Get up! It's 9 o'clock already.
(you, how, this, annoying; I, again, lie, a while) **B)** 你怎么这么啰唆？我再躺会儿。 Nǐ zěnme zhème luōsuo? Wǒ zài tǎng huìr.		Why are you so annoying? I will be up in a minute.

路子野	lùzi yě	well-connected; know important people in high places
(you, know important people in high places, such, difficult, task, even, make it) 你路子够野的,那么难的事都办成了。 Nǐ lùzi gòu yě de, nàme nán de shì dōu bàn chéng le.		You really know important people in high places. Even the most difficult of tasks you still manage to get done.

(no, way of doing something) 没办法	méi bànfǎ	there is nothing that can be done
(so, late, you, still, study) **A)** 这么晚你还学习？ Zhème wǎn nǐ hái xuéxí?		It's so late. You are still studying, ah?
(no choice, tomorrow, will, have test) **B)** 没办法,明天要考试。 Méi bànfǎ, míngtiān yào kǎoshì.		I have no choice. I have a test tomorrow.

(nothing, say)		
没的说	méi de shuō	perfect, flawless
(his, girlfriend, both, pretty, and, smart, perfect)	His girlfriend is attractive and smart, flawless.	
他女朋友又漂亮又聪明, 没的说。		
Tā nǚpéngyou yòu piàoliang yòu cōngming, méi de shuō.		

(no, way)		
没法儿	méi fǎr	there is no way
(weather, too, cold, no way, swim)	It's too cold. There is no way to go swimming.	
天气太冷了, 没法儿游泳。		
Tiānqì tài lěng le, méi fǎr yóuyǒng.		
(I, have, thing, there is no way, go)	I have something to take care of. There is no way that I can go.	
我有事儿, 没法儿去。		
Wǒ yǒu shìr, méi fǎr qù.		

(without, interest)		
没劲	méi jìn	uninteresting, boring
(with, you, together, truly, uninteresting, I, leave)	Being with you is uninteresting. I gotta go.	
跟你在一起真没劲, 我走了。		
Gēn nǐ zài yìqǐ zhēn méi jìn, wǒ zǒu le.		

没门儿	méi ménr	no way
(you, able, IO, your, new, car, lend, me, QW) **A)** 你能把你的新车借我吗? Nǐ néng bǎ nǐ de xīn chē jiè wǒ ma?		Can I borrow your new car?
B) 没门儿! Méi ménr!		No way!

(no, music of the song)		
没谱儿	méi pǔr	not certain
(you, when, return, country) **A)** 你多会儿回国? Nǐ duǒ huìr huíguó?		When are you going home?
(this, thing, not certain, depend on, money, enough, not, enough) **B)** 这事没谱儿, 看钱够不够。 Zhè shì méi pǔr, kàn qián gòu bu gòu.		I am not sure. It depends on whether or not my money is enough.

(no, discussion)		
没商量	méi shāngliang	not open for discussion; closed case
(this, thing, not open for discussion, you, must, listen, mine, I, absolutely, not, wrong) 这事儿没商量, 你得听我的, 我绝对没错。 Zhè shìr méi shāngliang, nǐ děi tīng wǒ de, wǒ juéduì méi cuò.		This matter is not open for discussion; you have to listen to me on this one. I am absolutely positive.

(no, end, no, finish)		
没完没了	méi wán méi liǎo	no end
(they, once, drink, alcohol, then, no end) 他们一喝酒就没完没了。	Once they start drinking there is no end in sight.	
Tāmen yì hē jiǔ jiù méi wán méi liǎo.		
(he, raise, question, no end) 他提问题没完没了。	He asks a million questions. (very annoying)	
Tā tí wèntí méi wán méi liǎo.		
(If, you, again, laugh, me, I, then, with, you, no end) 如果你再笑我, 我就跟你没完。	If you continue laughing at me, you will not hear the end of it.	
Rúguǒ nǐ zài xiào wǒ, wǒ jiù gēn nǐ méi wán.		

没戏	méi xì	hopeless, no way
(I, able, test into, Peking University, QW) A) 我能考上北大吗?	Do you think I can test into Peking University? (China's best university)	
Wǒ néng kǎo shàng Běidà ma?		
(you, no hope; you, too, stupid) B) 你没戏。你 太 笨 了。	No way. You are too stupid!	
Nǐ méi xì. Nǐ tài bèn le.		

(no, shadow, thing)		
没影儿的事	méi yǐngr de shì	groundless, unfounded, preposterous

(I, heard, you, have, girlfriend)	I heard you have a girlfriend now.
A) 我**听**说你**有**女朋友了。	
Wǒ tīngshuō nǐ yǒu nǚpéngyou le.	
(that, is, groundless)	That is groundless. (He does not want others to know.)
B) 那是**没**影儿的事。	
Nà shì méi yǐngr de shì.	

(no, regret, medicine, can, eat)		
没有**后悔**药**可**吃	méiyǒu hòuhuǐ yào kě chī	there is nothing that can be done; there is no use being regretful
(I, truly, regret, not, with, that, MW, company, sign; result, now, even, work, don't have)	I really regret not taking that company's job offer. As a result, I have no job now.	
A) 我真**后悔没有**跟那家**公司**签约。结果**现在**连**工作**都没有。		
Wǒ zhēn hòuhuǐ méiyǒu gēn nà jiā gōngsī qiānyuē. Jiéguǒ xiànzài lián gōngzuò dōu méiyǒu.		
(now, regret, have, what, use; world, on, no, regret, medicine, can, eat)	What good does regretting it now do? In the world, there is no regret medicine that can cure your problem.	
B) **现在后悔有什么**用？**世界**上**没有后悔**药**可**吃。		
Xiànzài hòuhuǐ yǒu shénme yòng? Shìjiè shang méiyǒu hòuhuǐ yào kě chī.		

(no, track of a wheel)		
没辙	méi zhé	there is nothing that can be done

(you, why, so, early[earlier than expected], right away, go home)	Why are you going home so early?
A) 你**为什么**那么早**就**回家?	
Nǐ wèi shénme nàme zǎo jiù huí jiā?	
(my, wife, at, home, wait, me, no choice)	My old lady is waiting for me at home.
B) 我**老婆**在家**等我**, 没辙。	
Wǒ lǎopo zài jiā děng wǒ, méi zhé.	

(not, accurate)		
没准儿	méi zhǔnr	not definite, hard to say
(you, when, finish, this, work)	When are you going to finish this work?	
A) 你**什么时候**干完这活儿?		
Nǐ shénme shíhou gàn wán zhè huór?		
(that, *stress*, hard to say)	That is really hard to say. (I have no clue.)	
B) 那**可**没准儿。		
Nà kě méi zhǔnr.		

面子	miànzi		face, respect
Chinese are famous for their great concern over "face", the concept of respect.			
(give, face)			
给面子	gěi miànzi		to give respect
(he, in, colleague, front, say, PT, me, very, many, good, words, truly, is, very, give me respect)	His saying good things about me in front of my colleagues really gave me face.		
他在**同事面**前说了我很多好话, 真是很给我面子。			
Tà zài tóngshì miànqián shuōle wǒ hěn duō hǎo huà, zhēn shì hěn gěi wǒ miànzi.			

(have, face)		
有面子	yǒu miànzi	have respect, to be respected

(very, many, people, come, celebrate, his birthday, make, him, feel, very, have respect) 很多人来祝贺他的生日，让他觉得很有面子。	A lot of people came to celebrate his birthday so he felt very respected.
Hěn duō rén lái zhùhè tā de shēngri, ràng tā juéde hěn yǒu miànzi.	

(no, face)		
没面子	méi miànzi	no face, embarrassed

(you, in public, laugh, me, make, me, very, embarrassed) 你当众嘲笑我，让我很没面子。	Your laughing at me in public made me really embarrassed.
Nǐ dāngzhòng cháoxiào wǒ, ràng wǒ hěn méi miànzi.	

耐得/不住	nài de/bu zhù	can (not) tolerate

(she, can't tolerate, loneliness, not, again, study) 她耐不住寂寞，不再做学问了。	She can't stand being lonely, so she did not continue the life of research.
Tā nài bu zhù jìmò, bú zài zuò xuéwèn le.	

(take, person's, hand, short, eat, person's, mouth, soft)	
拿人的手短，吃人的嘴软	ná rén de shǒu duǎn, chī rén de zuǐ ruǎn

This slang is the principle that a favor must be returned by a favor; if someone does something for you, how can you refuse if they ask you for a favor?

(you, why, will, help, him) A) 你为什么要帮助他？	Why are you going to help him?
Nǐ wèi shénme yào bāngzhù tā?	

(no choice; he, treat, me, eat, PT, food, grab, person's, hand, short, eat, person's, mouth, soft)	I have no choice. He treated me to dinner so I must return the favor.
B) 没办法。**他请我吃过饭,拿人的手短,吃人的嘴软。**	
Méi bànfǎ. Tā qǐng wǒ chīguo fàn, ná rén de shǒu duǎn, chī rén de zuǐ ruǎn.	

哪儿知道	nǎr zhīdào	how is, are, am supposed to know? (used as a rhetorical question).
(he, when, come back) **A)** 他**什么时候**回来?		When is he coming back?
Tā shénme shíhou huílai?		
(I, where, know) **B)** 我**哪儿**知道?		How am I supposed to know?
Wǒ nǎr zhīdào?		

哪壶不开提哪壶	nǎ hú bù kāi tí nǎ hú	bringing up somebody's Achilles' Heel (said as joke)
(which, pot, not, boiled, raise, which, pot)		
(your, English, test, how) **A)** 你的英语考得**怎么样**?		How was your English test?
Nǐ de Yīngyǔ kǎo de zěnmeyàng?		
(don't, bring up somebody's Achilles' Heel) **B)** 不要**哪壶不开提哪壶**。		Let's not talk about that.
Búyào nǎ hú bù kāi tí nǎ hú.		

B has had difficulty with his English studies for quite some time so the mere fact that **A** is mentioning this topic makes him uneasy.

动词 + 腻了	dòngcí + nì le	to do something so much that you are sick of doing it
(McDonald's, I, already, eat, bored) 麦当劳,**我已经吃**腻了。		I have eaten so much McDonald's that I don't want to eat it anymore.
Màidāngláo, wǒ yǐjing chī nì le.		
(this, MW, game, I, already, play, sick of) 这个游戏**我已经玩儿**腻了。		I have played this game so much that I don't want to play it any longer.
Zhè ge yóuxì wǒ yǐjing wánr nì le.		

牛	niú	awesome, kick ass, great
(Philadelphia, 76ers, play, very, kick ass) 费城七六人队打得很牛。		The 76ers are really playing great.
Fèichéng Qī-liùrén Duì dǎ de hěn niú.		

(hit, board)		
拍板儿	pāi bǎnr	make the final decision
(this, MW, thing, boss, not, make the final decision, nobody, all, not, dare, move) 这件事儿老板没有**拍板儿**,谁都不敢动。		The boss has not made the final decision, so no one will dare do anything.
Zhè jiàn shìr lǎobǎn méiyǒu pāi bǎnr, shéi dōu bù gǎn dòng.		

(pat, horse, ass)		
拍马屁	pāi mǎpì	to kiss ass
(he, is, a, MW, love, kiss ass, small, person) 他是一个爱拍马屁的小人。		He is an ass-kisser.
Tā shì yí ge ài pāi mǎpì de xiǎorén.		

(fat, mound)		
胖墩儿	pàngdūnr	fat little kid
(look, you, this, MW, fat kid, heard, PT, diet, this, MW, word, QW) 看你这个胖墩儿，**听说**过**减肥**这个词吗？		Look at you, you fat bastard. Have you ever heard of the word diet?
Kàn nǐ zhè ge pàngdūnr, tīngshuōguo jiǎnféi zhè ge cí ma?		

(drop, anchor)		
抛锚	pāomáo	to breakdown (vehicle)
(my, car, at, half, road, on, break down) 我的**车**在**半路上**抛锚了。		My car broke down on the road.
Wǒ de chē zài bànlù shang pāomáo le.		

泡汤	pàotāng	did not come to fruition
(because, no, money, our, plan, finally, come to naught) 因为**没钱，我们的**计划**最后**泡汤了。		Due to lack of money, our plan did not come to fruition.
Yīnwèi méi qián, wǒmen de jìhuà zuìhòu pàotāng le.		

(trick, you, am, small, dog)		
骗**你**是**小狗**。	Piàn nǐ shì xiǎo gǒu.	If I am tricking you, I am a small dog. (I am telling the truth)
(I, not, believe, you, will, treat, me, eat, food) A) 我不相信你要请我吃饭。		I do not believe that you will take me out to eat.
Wǒ bù xiāngxìn nǐ yào qǐng wǒ chīfàn.		

| (I, will, if I am tricking you, I am a small dog)

B）我会的，如果骗你我是小狗。

Wǒ huì de, rúguǒ piàn nǐ wǒ shì xiǎo gǒu. | Of course I will. If I am tricking you I am a small dog. |

贫	pín	garrulous, always talking (very negative)
(you, this, person, very, garrulous) 你这人真贫。 Nǐ zhè rén zhēn pín.		You are a very talkative person. (Shut the hell up already!)
(do not, with, me, always talking) 别跟我贫！ Bié gēn wǒ pín!		Don't talk back to me! or Don't start talking trash with me. (I'm in no mood to hear it)

(money, not, is, 10,000, able, but, no, money, is, 10,000, 10,000, not, able)
钱不是万能的，但是没有钱是万万不能的。
Qián bú shì wànnéng de, dànshì méiyǒu qián shì wànwàn bù néng de.
Money is not everything, but no money means you can't do anything.

(lover, eye, inside, come from, one of the four famous beauties in ancient China)		
情人眼里出西施。	Qíngrén yǎn li chū Xīshī.	Beauty is in the eye of the beholder.
(his, girlfriend, not, good looking, but, he, very, like, her; truly, is, beauty is in the eye of the beholder) 他女朋友不好看，可他很喜欢她。真是情人眼里出西施。 Tā nǚpéngyou bù hǎokàn, kě tā hěn xǐhuan tā. Zhēn shì qíngrén yǎn li chū Xīshī.	His girlfriend is not pretty but he likes her anyway. It truly is a case that "Beauty is in the eye of the beholder".	

(poor, nothing left, egg)		
穷光蛋	qióngguāngdàn	poor egg, flat broke
(is, not, is, you, treat)	Aren't you going to take me out?	
A) 是不是你请客?		
Shì bu shì nǐ qǐngkè?		
(how, possible; I, am, one, MW, poor egg)	How can I take you out? I am flat broke.	
B) 怎么可能? 我是一个穷光蛋。		
Zěnme kěnéng? Wǒ shì yí ge qióngguāngdàn.		

人缘儿	rényuánr	ability to get along with others, popular
(his, ability to get along with others, very, good)	He is very popular.	
他人缘儿很好。		
Tā rényuánr hěn hǎo.		

(enter, town, follow, customs)		
入乡随俗	rù xiāng suí sú	when in Rome, do as Romans do
(arrive, PT, China, right away, should, use, chopsticks, "When in Rome, do as Romans do")	When you arrive in China, you should use chopsticks. "When in Rome do as Romans do."	
到了中国就应该用筷子，入乡随俗嘛。		
Dàole Zhōngguó jiù yīnggāi yòng kuàizi, rù xiāng suí sú ma.		

弱	ruò	pathetic, feeble
(you, too, pathetic; even, Word, not, able, use) 你太弱了吧！连 Word 都不会用！ Nǐ tài ruò le ba! Lián Word dōu bú huì yòng.		Are you that pathetic? You don't even know how to use Word!

(fill up, tooth, gap)		
塞牙缝	sāi yá fèng	not enough to fill up teeth gaps
(only, this, little, food, even, not, e-nough, fill up teeth gaps) 才这么点儿吃的，还不够塞牙缝的。 Cái zhème diǎnr chī de, hái bú gòu sāi yá fèng de.		This little amount of food can't even fill up teeth gaps.

(be born, not, bring, die, not, take away)		
生不带来，死不带去	shēng bú dàilái, sǐ bú dàiqù	
(don't, IO, money, look, too, heavy, be born, not, bring, die, not, take away) 别把钱看得太重，生不带来，死不带去。 Bié bǎ qián kàn de tài zhòng, shēng bú dàilái, sǐ bú dàiqù.		Don't place too much importance on money. It is not with you when you are born and you cannot take it with you when you die.

(teacher, instructor)		
师傅	shīfu	

The original meaning of shīfu is a model worker. Today it is used as a respectful way of addressing a male stranger, especially when you have a question to ask or need service in a store. It is similar to gēmenr, but a little bit more respectful.

(master, watermelon, how, sell)	Master, how much is the watermelon?
师傅,西瓜怎么卖?	
Shīfu, xīguā zěnme mài?	

甩	shuǎi	to dump boy/girlfriend
(he, IO, his, girlfriend, give, dump)	He dumped his girlfriend.	
他把他的女朋友给甩了。		
Tā bǎ tā de nǚpéngyou gěi shuǎi le.		

爽	shuǎng	awesome, comfortable, ecstasy
The usage of shuǎng is very wide. It can be used to describe a great feeling, the satisfactory usage of a product, and the happiness received from the participation in a given activity.		
主语 + 动词 + 起来 + 很爽	Subject + dòngcí + qǐlai + hěn shuǎng	
When the action is still in progress, use qǐlai.		
(this, MW, computer, use, very, comfortable)	This computer is really easy to use.	
这台电脑用起来很爽。		
Zhè tái diànnǎo yòng qǐlai hěn shuǎng.		
主语 + 动词 + 得 + 很爽	Subject + dòngcí + de + hěn shuǎng	
When the action has already been completed, use de.		
(we, today, eat, very, comfortable)	We ate really well today.	
我们今天吃得很爽。		
Wǒmen jīntiān chī de hěn shuǎng.		
(you, feel, how)	How do you feel?	
A) 你感觉怎么样?		
Nǐ gǎnjué zěnmeyàng?		

(very, comfortable)	I have a feeling of ecstasy!
B）很爽。	
Hěn shuǎng!	

说白了	shuō bái le	to be frank
(to be frank, I, not, want, go)	To be frank, I don't want to go.	
说白了，我不想去。		
Shuō bái le, wǒ bù xiǎng qù.		

(say, Cao Cao, Cao Cao, arrive)		
说曹操，曹操到。	Shuō Cáo Cāo, Cáo Cāo dào.	speaking of the devil
(speaking of the devil; we, just, discuss, you, you, then, come)	Speaking of the devil. We were just talking about you and here you are.	
说曹操，曹操到。我们刚议论你，你就来了。		
Shuō Cáo Cāo, Cáo Cāo dào. Wǒmen gāng yìlùn nǐ, nǐ jiù lái le.		

(speak, out, words, long)		
说来话长	shuō lái huà cháng	it's a long story
(Xiao Zhang, and, Xiao Wang, how, each other, not, speak, words)	Why don't Xiao Zhang and Xiao Wang talk anymore?	
A）小张和小王怎么互相不说话了？		
Xiǎo Zhāng hé Xiǎo Wáng zěnme hùxiāng bù shuōhuà le?		
(speak, out, words, long)	It's a long story!	
B）说来话长！		
Shuō lái huà cháng!		

(dead, definitely)		
死定了	sǐ dìng le	encounter a very unfavorable situation (usually used as a joke)
(you, dare, speak, true, words, you, right away, in bad situation)		If you tell the truth, it will not be pleasant.
你敢说实话, 你就死定了。		
Nǐ gǎn shuō shíhuà, nǐ jiù sǐ dìng le.		
(you, if, steal, eat, my, bread, you, then, in bad situation)		If you try and steal my bread, you will find yourself in a very unfavorable position. (joking)
你要是偷吃我的面包, 你就死定了。		
Nǐ yàoshi tōu chī wǒ de miànbāo, nǐ jiù sǐ dìng le.		

动词 + 死我了	dòngcí + sǐ wǒ le	verb + to a point of death
(you, scare, death, me)		You scared me to death!
你吓死我了。		
Nǐ xià sǐ wǒ le.		
(hungry, death, me)		I'm starving to death!
饿死我了。		
È sǐ wǒ le.		
(hold in, death, me)		I have to go to the bathroom very bad.
憋死我了。		
Biē sǐ wǒ le.		

套近乎	tàojìnhu	to get in good with someone, very derogative
(don't, try to get in with me, I, help, not, able, you, what, favor)		Stop trying to get in good with me. I can't do anything for you.
别跟我套近乎, 我帮不了你什么忙。		
Bié gēn wǒ tàojìnhu, wǒ bāng bu liǎo nǐ shénme máng.		

(jump, water trough)		
跳槽	tiàocáo	switch jobs
(other, company, give, him, even, higher, salary, so, he, switch jobs) 别的公司给他更高的薪水，所以他跳槽了。		Another company offered him a higher salary so he quit his job and went to work there.
Biéde gōngsī gěi tā gèng gāo de xīnshuǐ, suǒyǐ tā tiàocáo le.		

通融一下	tōngróng yíxià	make an exception
(female student, dorm, male student, not, able, enter) A) 女生宿舍男生不能进! Nǚshēng sùshè nánshēng bù néng jìn!		Men students are not permitted to enter the female students' dorm.
(he, is, my, brother, able, not, able, make an exception) B) 他是我哥哥，能不能通融一下? Tā shì wǒ gēge, néng bu néng tōngróng yíxià?		He is my brother. Can you make an exception?
* A is the security guard of B's dorm.		

(play, end)		
玩儿完	wánrwán	game over, come to the end, screw up
(this, MW, thing, you, must, very, careful, have, a little, mistake, our, plan, will, screw up) 这件事你必须非常小心，有一点儿闪失我们的计划就全玩儿完。		You have to carefully watch every step. Any mistake from you will screw up the entire plan.
Zhè jiàn shì nǐ bìxū fēicháng xiǎoxīn, yǒu yìdiǎnr shǎnshī wǒmen de jìhuà jiù quán wánrwán.		

(ask, this, ask, that)		
问这问那	wèn zhè wèn nà	ask a million questions
(you, don't, at, my, body, ask a million questions, annoy, death) 你**不要**在我身边**问这问那**,烦死了。		Don't always ask me a million questions. It annoys me to death.
Nǐ búyào zài wǒ shēnbiān wèn zhè wèn nà, fán sǐ le.		

窝囊废	wōnangfèi	good-for-nothing
(he, is, MW, utter, good-for-nothing, any, matter, all, do, not, able) 他是个十足的**窝囊废**,什么事儿都干不来。		He is totally good-for-nothing. He can't do anything.
Tā shì ge shízú de wōnangfèi, shénme shìr dōu gàn bu lái.		

无所谓	wúsuǒwèi	be indifferent, not matter
(you, want, eat, what) **A**)你想吃什么?		What do you want to eat?
Nǐ xiǎng chī shénme?		
(I, indifferent, listen, yours) **B**)我**无所谓**,听你的。		I'll eat whatever you want.
Wǒ wúsuǒwèi, tīng nǐ de.		

(fresh, flower, put, on, cow, shit)	
鲜花插在牛粪上	xiānhuā chā zài niú fèn shang
This slang is used to express a pretty girl with an ugly guy.	

(you, hear, our, school flower, and, class one's, Xiao Wang, hook up, QW)	Did you hear that the hottest girl in our school hooked up with Xiao Wang from class one?
A) 你听说咱们的**校花**和一班的小王谈上了吗？	
Nǐ tīngshuō zánmen de xiàohuā hé yī bān de Xiǎo Wáng tán shàng le ma?	
(no way, with, that, MW, fatty; truly, is, fresh flower placed inside cow's shit)	No way, with that fatty. That really is 'Fresh flower placed inside the shit of a cow'.
B) 不会吧，和那个**胖子**？真是鲜花插在牛粪上。	
Bú huì ba, hé nà ge pàngzi? Zhēn shì xiānhuā chā zài niú fèn shang.	

(first, down, hand, become, strong)		
先下手为强	xiān xià shǒu wéi qiáng	the early bird gets the worm; he who strikes first gets the advantage
(French fries, how, eat, nothing left)	How do you guys eat all the fries? (Some nerve of you!)	
A) 薯条怎么吃没了？		
Shǔtiáo zěnme chī méi le?		
(you, come, too, late, we, already, the early bird gets the worm)	You came too late. The early bird gets the worm.	
B) 你来得**太晚了**，我们已经先下手为强了。		
Nǐ lái de tài wǎn le, wǒmen yǐjing xiān xià shǒu wéi qiáng le.		

(small, dish, one, plate)		
小菜一碟	xiǎo cài yì dié	a piece of cake
(this, problem, too, easy, simply, be, piece of cake)	This problem is very easy, piece of cake.	
这问题太简单了，简直是小菜一碟。		
Zhè wèntí tài jiǎndān le, jiǎnzhí shì xiǎo cài yì dié.		

(little, secretary)		
小秘	xiǎomì	little secretary

A xiǎomì is the mistress of a married businessman. Obviously, he cannot say in public that his companion is his girlfriend, so she is introduced as his "secretary". Later this word evolved to describe any mistress or slutty girl. Very negative.

歇菜	xiēcài	stop, not being able to go on
(his, computer, level, very, pathetic, computer, once, appear, problem, he, then, be pissed off) 他**电脑**水平很差，**电脑**一旦**出**问题他就歇菜。		His computer skills are so pathetic that once something is wrong with his computer, he will be pissed off.
Tā diànnǎo shuǐpíng hěn chà, diànnǎo yídàn chū wèntí tā jiù xiēcāi.		

(heart, hurt)		
心疼	xīnténg	be stingy, cheap
(you, don't, be cheap with, your, vehicle) 你不要心疼你的车。		Don't be stingy with your car.
Nǐ búyào xīnténg nǐ de chē.		

修理	xiūli	to beat up someone

Xiūlǐ means to repair. When used as a slang means that you will beat someone up so as to fix them.

(I, will, fix, you) 我要修理你!		I will fix you!
Wǒ yào xiūli nǐ!		

(mute)

哑巴了？	Yǎba le?	What's wrong? Cat's got your tongue? Why aren't you speaking?

(you, how, not, speak, are you mute) 你怎么不说话了，哑巴了？		Why are you not speaking. What's wrong? Cat's got your tongue?

Nǐ zěnme bù shuōhuà le, yǎba le?

(press down, road)

轧马路	yà mǎlù	to take a stroll with boy / girlfriend

(they, two, everyday, all, go for a stroll) 他们俩每天都轧马路。		They go for a stroll together everyday.

Tāmenliǎ měi tiān dōu yà mǎlù.

Yà mǎlù is used to describe the action of a couple walking around their neighborhood.

(eye, not, see, heart, not, be annoyed)

眼不见，心不烦	yǎn bu jiàn, xīn bu fán	If you don't look at it, you won't be upset.

(heard, your, son, with, daughter-in-law, again, fight) A) 听说你儿子和儿媳妇又吵架了。		I heard your son and daughter-in-law are fighting again.

    Tīngshuō nǐ érzi hé érxífu yòu chǎojià le.

(I, don't get involved, anyway, they, not, live, in, house, inside, if I don't look at it, it won't upset me) B) 我才不管呢，反正他们不住在家里，我眼不见心不烦。		I don't get involved. They don't live here. As long as my eyes don't see it, it doesn't bother me.

    Wǒ cái bù guǎn ne, fǎnzhèng tāmen bú zhù zài jiā li, wǒ yǎn bu jiàn xīn bu fán.

(color)		
颜色	yánsè	facial expression (used to threaten sb.)
(I, will, give, you, a little, color, look, look) 我要给你一点儿颜色看看。		I am going to give you a good licking!
Wǒ yào gěi nǐ yìdiǎnr yánsè kànkan.		

(night, cat)		
夜猫子	yèmāozi	night owl; person who stays up late
(you, again, play, PT, all night, truly, are, MW, night owl) 你又玩儿了一通宵,真是个夜猫子。		You stayed up all night again! You really are a night owl.
Nǐ yòu wánrle yì tōngxiāo, zhēn shì ge yèmāozi.		

(same as, sensibleness)		
一般见识	yìbān jiànshi	to stoop to someone's level
To lower oneself to the level of somebody; to stoop to somebody's lower level; I am a better person than you are, therefore, there is no reason for me to argue with you.		
(I, not, want, with, you, stoop to your level) 我不想跟你一般见识。		I am not willing to stoop to your level.
Wǒ bù xiǎng gēn nǐ yìbān jiànshi.		

(one, piece, money, one, piece, goods)		
一分钱,一分货	yì fēn qián, yì fēn huò	you get what you pay for
(this, MW, TV set, quality, very, poor) A) 这台电视机的质量很差。		The quality of this television is very poor.
Zhè tái diànshìjī de zhìliàng hěn chà.		

(you, expect, what, you, only, spend, PT, $100; you get what you pay for.) **B）你指望**什么？**你才花了一百美金**。一分钱一分货。		You only spent US $100. What do you expect? You get what you pay for.
Nǐ zhǐwang shénme? Nǐ cái huāle yìbǎi měijīn. Yì fēn qián yì fēn huò.		

(one, mouthful, eat, not, able, MW, fat person)		
一口吃不了个胖子	yì kǒu chī bu liǎo ge pàngzi	things can't happen overnight (usually used to encourage or comfort a person)
(Chinese, too, difficult, study, I, want, quit) **A）汉语太难学了，我想放弃。**		Chinese is too difficult. I want to quit!
Hànyǔ tài nán xué le, wǒ xiǎng fàngqì.		
(there is no need, worry, things can't happen overnight, slow, slow, come) **B）甭着急，一口吃不了个胖子，慢慢来。**		Don't worry. It takes time. Don't rush yourself. It will come slowly but surely.
Béng zháojí, yì kǒu chī bu liǎo ge pàngzi, mànmān lái.		

幽默不起来	yōumò bù qǐlái	not funny
(he, always, want, funny, but, not funny) 他总是想幽默但是幽默不起来。		He always try to be funny but never succeed.
Tā zǒngshì xiǎng yōumò dànshì yōumò bù qǐlái.		

(have, money, able, make, devil, turn, millstone)		
有钱能使鬼推磨。	Yǒu qián néng shǐ guǐ tuī mò.	If you have money, you can do anything.

(OJ, how, not, be sentenced, death penalty)	How did OJ not get the death sentence?
A) OJ Simpson 怎么没有被判死刑?	
OJ Simpson zěnme méiyǒu bèi pàn sǐxíng?	

(have, money, able, make, devil, turn, millstone)	If you have money, you can do anything.
B) 有钱能使鬼推磨。	
Yǒu qián néng shǐ guǐ tuī mò.	

(have, interest)		
有趣儿	yǒuqùr	interesting
(this, MW, movie, very, interesting)	This movie is very interesting.	
这部电影很有趣儿。		
Zhè bù diànyǐng hěn yǒuqùr.		

有/没戏	yǒu/méi xì	have/don't have a chance
(you [polite], think, I, go to, Peking Univ., have, hope, QW)	Do you think I have a chance of getting into Peking University?	
您看我上北大有戏吗?		
Nín kàn wǒ shàng Běidà yǒu xì ma?		

缘分	yuánfen	destiny, fate
Yuánfen is the lot or luck by which people are brought together. It is a principle of Taoism and is believed by many Chinese.		
(you, two, how, know, PT)	How do you two know each other?	
A) 你们俩怎么认识的?		
Nǐmenliǎ zěnme rènshi de?		

(destiny)	It was destiny.
B) 缘分。	
Yuánfen.	

(far, look, beautiful, close, look, ugly)		
远看青山绿水，近看龇牙咧嘴	yuǎn kàn qīng shān lǜ shuǐ, jìn kàn zī yá liě zuǐ	good from far but far from good
(this, MW, girl, far, look, beautiful, close, look, ugly)		This girl looks good from far but is far from good.
这个女孩儿远看青山绿水，近看龇牙咧嘴。		
Zhè ge nǚháir yuǎn kàn qīng shān lǜ shuǐ, jìn kàn zī yá liě zuǐ.		

砸	zá	screw up, mess up, botch up
(whatever, thing, go to, his, hand, in, all, will, screw up)		He screws up everything that he does.
什么事情到他手里就会办砸。		
Shénme shìqing dào tā shǒu li jiù huì bàn zá.		

宰	zǎi	to cheat
(this, clothing, I, spend, PT, 50, pieces, money, is, not, is, cheap)		I spent 50 *yuan* on this piece of clothing, pretty cheap, huh?
A) 这衣服我花了 50 块钱，是不是便宜？		
Zhè yīfu wǒ huāle wǔshí kuài qián, shì bu shì piányi?		
(you, once again, been, cheat)		You once again got taken! (Very expensive)
B) 你又被宰了。		
Nǐ yòu bèi zǎi le.		

糟蹋	zāota	to waste
(we, don't, order, so, many, dishes, otherwise, waste) 咱们**别**点**那么**多菜，要不**糟蹋了**。		There is no need to order so much food, otherwise we will end up wasting a lot.
Zánmen bié diǎn nàme duō cài, yàobu zāota le.		

造	zào	to waste money on food
(we, tonight, eat, meal, waste, PT, 300, MW, money) 我们**今**晚吃饭**造**了三百块钱。		We spent 300 *yuan* on dinner tonight.
Wǒmen jīnwǎn chīfàn zàole sānbǎi kuài qián.		

(fight, ability)		
战斗力	zhàndòulì	eating ability
(your, fighting ability, very, strong) 你的**战斗力**很**强**！		You can eat a lot! I'm surprised how much you can eat. (said at the table)
Nǐ de zhàndòulì hěn qiáng!		

(occupying, toilet, not, shit)		
占着茅坑不拉屎	zhànzhe máokēng bù lā shǐ	occupying something but not using it
(you, on earth, use, not, use, computer, don't, take something while not using it) 你**到底**用不**用**电脑？别**占着茅坑不拉屎**。		Are you using the computer or not? Don't occupy something if you are not going to use it.
Nǐ dàodǐ yòng bu yòng diànnǎo? Bié zhànzhe máokēng bù lā shǐ.		

招人惹人了	zhāo **rén** rě **rén** le	to piss off a **person**
(you, why, curse, me, I, provoke, you provoke, you) 你为什么骂我，我招你惹你了？		Why did you curse me? Did I do something to piss you off?
Nǐ wèi shénme mà wǒ, wǒ zhāo nǐ rě nǐ le?		

(look for, beating)		
找瓩	zhǎo cèi	ask for a beating
(look for, thrashing)		
找揍	zhǎo zòu	ask for a beating
(your, mother, not, good looking) A）你妈妈不好看。 　Nǐ māma bù hǎokàn.		Your mom is ugly.
(you, looking for a beating) B）你找揍/瓩呢！ 　Nǐ zhǎo zòu/cèi ne!		You are really looking for a good beating!

(find, trouble)		
找茬儿	zhǎo chár	to deliberately find fault with someone or their behavior in order to initiate an argument or make them look bad.
(I, work, very well, but, he, always, find my fault) 我工作得很好，可他总是找我的茬儿。		I am very diligent but he always goes out of his way to find faults in my work.
Wǒ gōngzuò de hěn hǎo, kě tā zǒngshì zhǎo wǒ de chár.		

跩	zhuǎi	try to pass oneself as a master
(*zhi lu wei ma*, this, MW, idiom, is, how, derived, PT, you, know, QW)	Do you know the origin of the Chinese idiom zhǐ lù wéi mǎ?
A）指鹿为马这个成语是怎么来的，你知道吗？	
"Zhǐ lù wéi mǎ" zhè ge chéngyǔ shì zěnme lái de, nǐ zhīdào ma?	
(don't, with, me, pass oneself as expert, I, am, Chinese)	Don't try and pass yourself off as a master. I am Chinese. (Of course I know the origin, and I know it better than you do.)
B）别跟我跩，我是中国人。	
Bié gēn wǒ zhuǎi, wǒ shì Zhōngguórén.	
* A is a foreign student of Chinese and B is Chinese.	

装蒜	zhuāngsuàn	pretend not to know, feign ignorance
(I, not, know, who, eat, PT, your, candy)	I have no clue who ate your candy.
A）我不知道谁吃了你的糖。	
Wǒ bù zhīdào shéi chīle nǐ de táng.	
(don't, pretend not to know, precisely, is, you)	Don't pretend not to know. I know it was you.
B）别装蒜，就是你。	
Bié zhuāngsuàn, jiù shì nǐ.	

(leave, person)		
走人	zǒu rén	to leave, to roll

(if, you, continue, beat around the bush, I, right away, leave)	If you continue to beat around the bush, I'm outta here. (Tone is very strong)
如果**你**再**兜圈子**，我**立马**走人。	
Rúguǒ nǐ zài dōu quānzi, wǒ lìmǎ zǒurén.	

最起码	zuì qǐmǎ	at the very least
(he, at the very least, has, 30, age)	At the very least, he is 30.	
他**最起码**有三十岁。		
Tā zuì qǐmǎ yǒu sānshí suì.